TUSCANY
AND UMBRIA

Titles in this series include:

For further information about these and other Thomas Cook publications,
write to Thomas Cook Publishing, PO Box 227, Units 19–21, The Thomas Cook Business Park,
Coningsby Road, Peterborough PE3 8XX, United Kingdom.

Signpost
Guides

TUSCANY
AND UMBRIA

The best of Tuscany and Umbria,
including the artistic heritage of
Florence, Siena, Perugia and Assisi,
the hill-towns and landscapes of
the Italian heartland and the beaches
and seaside resorts, with suggested
driving tours

Brent Gregston

The
Globe
Pequot
Press

Thomas Cook
Publishing

Published by Thomas Cook Publishing
A division of Thomas Cook Holdings Ltd
PO Box 227, Units 19–21
The Thomas Cook Business Park
Coningsby Road
Peterborough PE3 8XX
United Kingdom

Telephone: +44 (0)1733 416477
Fax: +44 (0)1733 416688
E-mail: books@thomascook.com

For further information about
Thomas Cook Publishing, visit our website:
www.thomascook.com

ISBN 1-841573-37-X

Published in the USA by
The Globe Pequot Press
PO Box 480
Guilford, Connecticut 06437
USA

ISBN 0-7627-2652-0

Text: © 2003 Thomas Cook Publishing
Maps and diagrams: © 2003 Thomas Cook Publishing
Road maps supplied by Lovell Johns Ltd, OX8 8LH
Road maps generated from Bartholomew digital database © Bartholomew Ltd, 2000
City maps prepared by Polly Senior Cartography

Head of Publishing: Donald Greig

Written, researched and updated by: Brent Gregston
Series Editor: Edith Summerhayes
Project Editor for second edition: Caroline Ball

About the author

Brent Gregston studied International Relations at Pomona College in California and read for a degree in Modern European Languages in Germany and Italy. After a stint working for a charity in the Middle East, he turned to writing. He has written several guidebooks and contributes to *Wanderlust*, the travel section of the online magazine *Salon*. His *Signpost: Bavaria and the Austrian Tyrol*, was nominated by Thomas Cook for the British Travelex 'Best Guidebook of the Year' award. On assignment or for pleasure, Brent has been down almost every back road in Tuscany and Umbria, and still spends part of each year in the region.

Acknowledgements

I would like to say *mille grazie* to Alda and Claudio for firewood, wild mushrooms and other forms of hospitality, to Signpost series editor Christopher Catling for sharing his passion for Umbria with me, and to Laurie for our 10,000 kilometres together.

Contents

About Signpost Guides

Thomas Cook's Signpost Guides are designed to provide you with a comprehensive but flexible reference source to guide you as you tour a country or region by car. This guide divides Tuscany and Umbria into touring areas – one per chapter. Major cultural centres or cities form chapters in their own right. Each chapter contains enough attractions to provide at least a day's worth of activities – often more.

Star ratings
To make it easier for you to plan your time and decide what to see, every sight and attraction is given a star rating. A three-star rating indicates a major attraction, worth at least half a day of your time. A two-star attraction is worth an hour or so of your time, and a one-star attraction indicates a sight that is worth visiting, but often of specialist interest. To help you further, individual attractions within towns or theme parks are also graded, so that travellers with limited time can quickly find the most rewarding sights.

Chapter contents
Every chapter has an introduction summing up the main attractions of the area or town, and a ratings box, which will highlight its appeal – some places may be more attractive to families travelling with children, others to wine-lovers visiting vineyards, and others to people interested in finding castles, churches, nature reserves, or good beaches.

Each chapter is then divided into an alphabetical gazetteer, and a suggested tour or walk. You can select whether you just want to visit a particular sight or attraction, choosing from those described in the gazetteer, or whether you want to tour the area comprehensively. If the latter, you can construct your own itinerary, or follow the author's suggested tour, which comes at the end of every area chapter.

The gazetteer
The gazetteer section describes all the major attractions in the area – the villages, towns, historic sites, nature reserves, parks or museums that you are most likely to want to see. Maps of the area highlight all the places mentioned in the text. Using this comprehensive overview of the area, you may choose just to visit one or two sights.

One way to use the guide is to find individual sights that interest you, using the index, overview map or star ratings, and read what our author has to say about them. This will help you decide whether to visit the sight. If you do, you will find practical information, such as the address, telephone number for enquiries, website and opening times.

Symbol key

- ❶ Tourist Information Centre
- ⇄ Advice on arriving or departing
- ❷ Parking locations
- ◐ Advice on getting around
- ➲ Directions
- ❶ Sights and attractions
- ❶ Eating
- ◖ Accommodation
- ◕ Shopping
- ◉ Sport
- ◔ Entertainment

Practical information

The practical information in the page margins, or sidebars, will help you locate the services you need as an independent traveller – including the tourist information centre, car parks and public transport facilities. You will also find the opening times of sights, museums, churches and other attractions, as well as useful tips on shopping, market days, cultural events, entertainment, festivals and sports facilities.

Alternatively, you can choose a hotel, with the help of the accommodation recommendations contained in this guide. You can then turn to the overall map on pages 10–11 to help you work out which chapters in the book describe the cities and regions closest to your touring base.

Driving tours

The suggested tour is just that – a suggestion, with plenty of optional detours and one or two ideas for making your own discoveries, under the heading *Also worth exploring*. The routes are designed to link the attractions described in the gazetteer section, and to cover outstandingly scenic coastal, mountain and rural landscapes. The total distance is given for each tour, and the time it will take you to drive the complete route, but bear in mind that this indication is just for driving time: you will need to add on extra time for visiting attractions along the way.

Many of the routes are circular, so that you can join them at any point. Where the nature of the terrain dictates that the route has to be linear, the route can either be followed out and back, or you can use it as a link route, to get from one area in the book to another.

As you follow the route descriptions, you will find names picked out in bold capital letters – this means that the place is described fully in the gazetteer. Other names picked out in bold indicate additional villages or attractions worth a brief stop along the route.

Accommodation and food

In every chapter you will find lodging and eating recommendations for individual towns, or for the area as a whole. These are designed to cover a range of price brackets and concentrate on more characterful small or individualistic hotels and restaurants. In addition, you will find information in the *Travel facts* chapter on chain hotels, with an address to which you can write for a guide, map or directory.

The price indications used in the guide have the following meanings:

€   budget level
€€   typical/average prices
€€€   de luxe

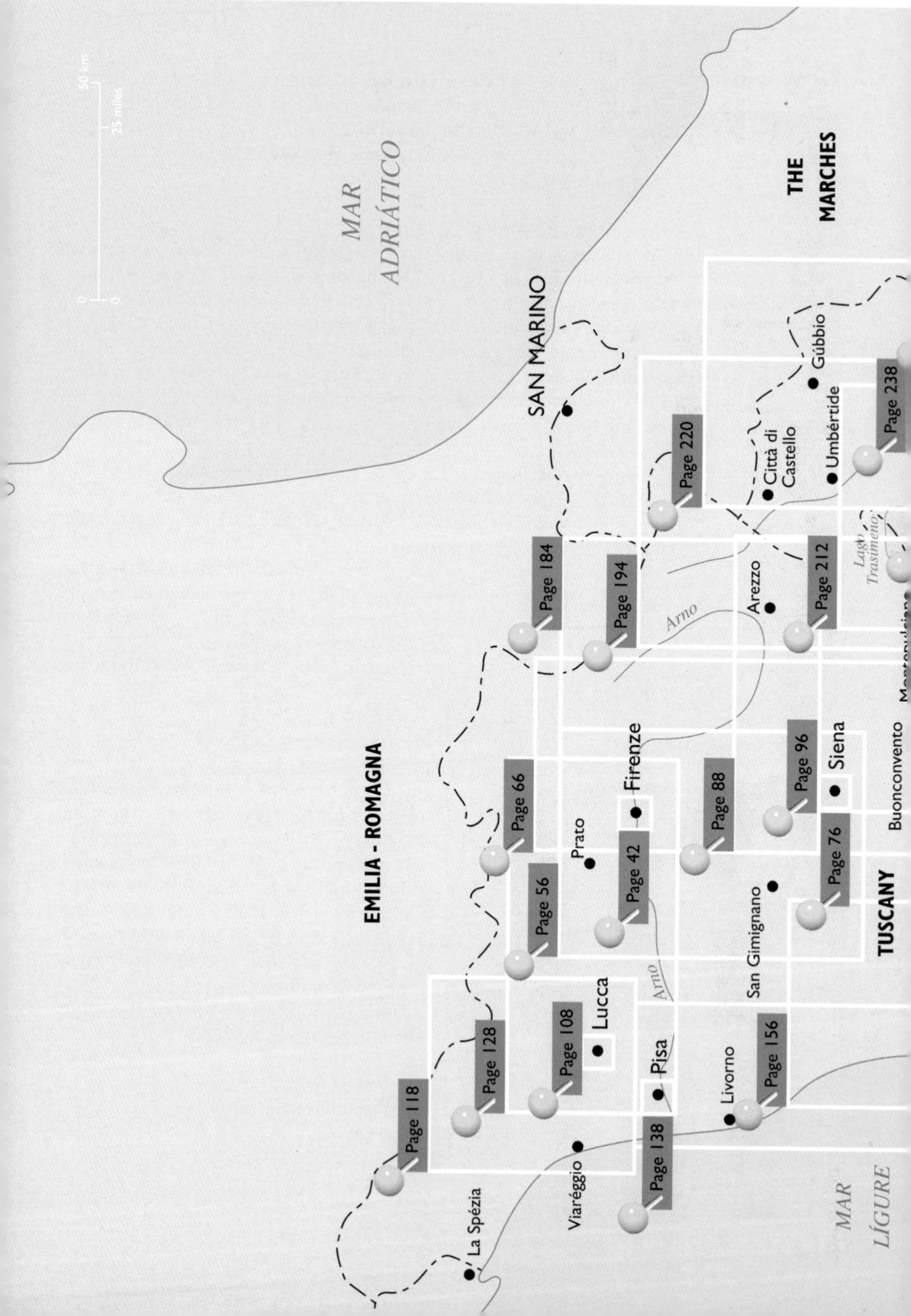

50 km

25 miles

MAR ADRIÁTICO

THE MARCHES

SAN MARINO

Gúbbio

Page 238

Città di Castello

Umbértide

Page 220

Page 184

Page 194

Arezzo

Page 212

Lago Trasimeno

Arno

EMILIA - ROMAGNA

Page 66

Firenze

Page 96

Siena

Prato

Page 88

Page 56

Page 42

Page 76

Buonconvento

Page 128

Lucca

San Gimignano

TUSCANY

Page 108

Page 118

Page 138

Pisa

Livorno

Page 156

Viaréggio

Arno

La Spézia

MAR LÍGURE

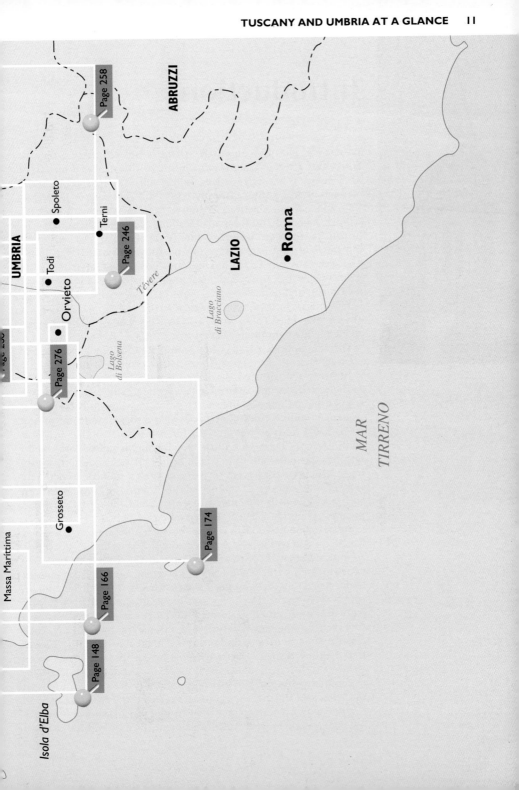

ABRUZZI

Spoleto

Terni

Page 258

Page 246

UMBRIA

Todi

Orvieto

Tévere

LAZIO

●Roma

Lago di Bracciano

Page 276

Lago di Bolsena

MAR TIRRENO

Grosseto

Page 174

Massa Marittima

Page 166

Page 148

Isola d'Elba

Introduction

Tuscany is paradise on earth in the minds of many northern Europeans: a region of hill-towns bristling with medieval towers, of lush vineyards and olive groves, rolling hills, Renaissance art and a Mediterranean coastline. Tuscany is also a theme park in Las Vegas, USA, and a line of American furniture. 'Tuscany' is in the title of best-selling cookbooks and the staple headline of lifestyle magazines. The British have put an imaginary county on the map – *Chiantishire* – inhabited, at least part of the year, by Tony Blair and David Bowie. The Germans have gone further and christened their left-wing politicos the 'Tuscan Faction' since they eschew beer and sauerkraut for Chianti and pasta. American New Agers are now seizing territory here – at least in their nous – because writer Frances Mayes bought a Tuscan villa, hired Polish workers to remodel it and wrote best-sellers about her 'life-transforming experience'.

There is, miraculously, a powerful antidote to all the hype: go there yourself. Outside of the coast, Florence and a couple of cities, Tuscany is not crowded with tourists. The region is, however, packed with medieval villages, monasteries, villas, castles, extinct volcanoes, hot springs, nature reserves and the crests of countless hills that reveal seemingly infinite vistas. Nature laps at the edge of most towns and even in the dreariest suburbs of Florence you sense that it is still within reach. Chianti, for all the good living, is full of dark woods, impenetrable bush and rutting wild boar. D H Lawrence, not an easy man to impress, observed: 'It is queer that a country so perfectly cultivated as Tuscany ... still has so much room for wild flowers'. In spring, the land is covered with entire fields of sunflowers, and poppies, Spanish broom, cornflowers and marigolds.

Tuscans founded modern city states – such as Pisa, Siena, Lucca and Florence – that recalled the achievements of Athens in the 5th century BC and anticipated those of New York in the 20th century. They experimented with Republican ideals when most of Europe lived under feudalism. They founded the first banks (with cheques and a prime rate) and suffered the first bankruptcies; built the largest cathedral and cathedral dome; and wrote the first Italian novel (Boccaccio), biography (Vasari) and autobiography (Cellini). They discovered linear perspective in painting and sculpted the first modern free-standing figures. Tuscans gave us love as broken-hearted bliss (Dante and Petrarch) and made the case for cynicism (Machiavelli). Florentines performed the first opera and a Pisan (Galileo) invented the telescope. Chianti wine producers created the first market label (Gallo Nero) and an explorer born in one of Chianti's hill-towns – Amerigo Vespucci – gave America its name. Anyone will feel tempted to assert a claim to a land so rich in experience and beauty, at least temporarily, as home.

Although Umbria seems to offer many of the same things as Tuscany, it is distinctly different. It has a deeply rural atmosphere, stretches of solitary wildernesses, and more medieval architecture. The green heart of Italy, as a poet once rightly called Umbria, is an area of small-scale agriculture, steep-sided hills cut by deep ravines, of farmsteads, monasteries and ancient cities separated from the countryside only by stone walls. If ever there was a region in Europe with deep mystic roots, it is here. The mountaintops were sacred places to pagan stargazers and later to St Benedict, the founder of Western monasticism. The ancient Umbrian seers codified the flight of birds to interpret the will of the gods. In the same land, 2000 years later, St Francis of Assisi taught Christians to see them as a manifestation of divinity.

Travel facts

Accommodation

Airports

Pisa's airport is easier to get in and out of and more convenient for reaching Tuscany than Rome's. It is also the destination of frequent charter flights. Both Pisa and Rome are about two hours' drive on the *autostrada* from Perugia, Umbria's capital. Florence's airport is used mostly by businesspeople. Tiny Sant'Egidio, 18km east of Perugia, now receives regularly scheduled flights from the UK as well as domestic flights from Milan and Bologna. Its facilities will be expanded at some point in the future. There are some international flights to Bologna, next to the *autostrada*, and charter flights to Rimini airport (Rimini to Perugia 223km), which is located between the toll-free Adriatic highway (S16) and A14 *autostrada*.

The charm of hotels in Tuscany and Umbria is that, with a few exceptions, they were built as anything but: Gothic townhouses, Renaissance palaces, monasteries, convents, 19th-century villas, barns and stables have all become hotels. Italian state authorities inspect these establishments regularly, apply all sorts of criteria, and give them stars (max 5).

Prices, based on these ratings, are regulated but may vary a lot depending on location and season; also many perfectly charming places such as *affitacamere* (rooms in private homes) are not rated at all. Two-star hotel rooms usually have a private bathroom, three-star rooms telephones and television. Four-star hotels, if they are not in the middle of the city, will probably have a swimming pool as well as more dubious extras like satellite television. Other forms of accommodation include campsites, youth hostels, holiday houses and apartments.

People on a driving holiday in Tuscany and Umbria have a well-known, and cheaper, alternative to hotels. Originally intended as a stimulus to the rural economy, *agriturismo* ('agricultural tourism') has succeeded beyond anyone's wildest dreams and paying guests have become the leading 'cash crop' in areas like Chianti; almost half of Tuscany's farmers participate in the programme. The consequences have not all been positive though, and it is important to choose an *agriturismo* situation carefully. During high season, most places have a minimum stay of one week; however, some allow for a minimum of two or three nights, particularly in the off-season. It is always advisable to book any form of accommodation ahead of time and to get a fax confirmation, especially for the month of August and during the Easter holidays.

Children

Travelling with a baby or young child is the easiest way to get attention in Italy, to say nothing of first-class service. Shopkeepers will spontaneously compare notes about parenthood; even jaded waiters will crack a smile. Discreet breastfeeding in public is no problem. Hotels and pensions are normally equipped to accommodate families. However, consider bringing safety seats for children with you as many car rental companies impose an extra daily charge for these, if they have them. Supermarkets in Tuscany/Umbria cater for the usual infant needs, but make a mental note of the opening times or they might be

Above
Medieval ironwork

Thomas Cook Foreign Exchange Facilities

Thomas Cook Travellers Cheques free you from the hazards of carrying large amounts of cash. The address of the Thomas Cook Foreign Exchange Bureau in Florence is given below. It provides full foreign exchange facilities and will change currency and travellers' cheques (free of commission in the case of Thomas Cook Travellers Cheques).

Thomas Cook Foreign Exchange Bureau

Thomas Cook Italia Ltd
Lungarno Acciaiolo,
Pontevecchio 6R
Florence
Tuscany 50123
Tel: +39 055 289781
Fax: +39 055 292084

Below
Romanesque lions in Assisi

closed just when you need them most. Ironically, a passion for children has not stopped Italy's dramatic falling birth rate, which is now the lowest in Europe.

Climate

The presence of the mountains and sea creates a wide range of climatic zones in Tuscany and Umbria. Spring begins early but is subject to bitter, cold winds called *tramontana*. May is the single most beautiful month of the year to visit when the wild flowers and vines are blooming and the green wheat is sprouting. Summers, particularly July and August, are invariably hot and dry. September is only slightly cooler and still high season on the coast. The end of September to late October is also a fine time of year to visit. The hillsides are changing colour and there are fewer tourists, but be prepared for some rain and mist. The Tuscan coast remains mild even in winter, while inland the cold can be intermittently harsh in the hill-towns and severe in the Apennines.

Currency and plastic

The unit of currency in Italy is the euro (€), available in 500, 200, 100, 50, 20, 10 and 5 euro notes, and 2 euro, 1 euro, 50 cent, 20 cent, 5 cent, 2 cent and 1 cent coins. There are 100 cents to the euro.

The best way to get cash in Italy is by using a cashcard at an ATM (*bancomat*). Tell your bank about your travel plans and make sure that your PIN number can be used abroad. A distant second – because of fees and potential interest charges – is to use your credit card for cash advances (again, check on the PIN). Use a Visa or Mastercard as a backup, at petrol stations, chain hotels and expensive restaurants. A few travellers' cheques are good for an emergency, though you will probably have to pay a small commission, about 1 per cent, when you buy them, and again when you cash them (in any bank). Some establishments also accept Eurocheques – ask beforehand. In an emergency, your bank or a friend can wire money through Western Union. American Express holders can take advantage of its Global Assist programme and arrange to have money wired within a couple of hours.

Customs regulations

There are no restrictions, taxes or duty on articles for personal use that you take into Italy (within reason: a truckload of whisky invites a few questions). Italy allows EU citizens to import or export duty-free: 800 cigarettes, 200 cigars, ten litres of spirits or 90 litres of wine or 110 litres of beer.

Disabled travellers

Italy still has far to go when it comes to addressing the needs of the disabled. Most museums, theatres, cinemas and public buildings do not yet have access ramps for wheelchairs. Major hotel chains are marginally more likely to offer special facilities to disabled travellers. Parking is free for disabled persons in the blue zones of cities and towns if you have an international disabled sticker for the car. In Britain, the Royal Society for Disability and Rehabilitation publishes a booklet called *Travel Abroad: A Guide for Disabled People* (*from RADAR, 12 City Forum, 250 City Road, London EC1V 8AF; tel: 020 7250 3222*).

Eating and drinking

Most hotels serve a meagre breakfast – Nescafé and yesterday's bread. It is better to go to a corner bar where you are sure of first-rate coffee and, probably, fresh pastries. Coffee with hot milk – *cappuccino* and *caffè latte* – is a breakfast drink in Italy. If you order a cup of coffee at any other time of day and don't insist on milk, you will automatically get an espresso. Tea is served as a cup of hot water with a tea bag on the side.

Once there were clear distinctions, and a gradation in prices and service, between a *pizzeria, osteria, trattoria* and a *ristorante*. Now many a *pizzeria* serves a wide range of dishes, while an *osteria* or *trattoria* may be as elegant as a *ristorante*. The elegance costs money, of course, and as a rough rule of thumb you can assume that the smarter the décor, the higher the prices are likely to be – without the food necessarily being any better. Tuscans and Umbrians traditionally eat three (or more) courses for the main meal (usually at lunch). However, if you decide to eat in a formal restaurant but only want to eat one course, this is perfectly acceptable: just say so before you take a table. In a simple *trattoria*, it is not at all unusual for two people to each eat a *primo* (first course) and then split a main course; or order one dessert and ask for two spoons. Many expensive restaurants (in Florence, for example), add a separate charge to the bill for *pane e coperto* (bread and tableware), usually about €2, sometimes more.

Tip: Italians usually arrive for the evening meal (*cena*) at about 2000 so show up before then if you don't have a reservation. If a *trattoria* or *ristorante* is good, their *vino della casa* should be good, too, and perfectly adequate to accompany a meal. Wine lists usually focus on local vintages and you should, too. Italians almost always order bottled water to go along with a meal. Occasionally, dessert wine or grappa is drunk after a meal.

Left
In a Tuscan kitchen

Electricity

The supply in Italy is 220 volts, 50 cycles AC. All UK appliances will work but will require an adaptor because plugs are of the European type with two round prongs. American appliances need a transformer and an adaptor.

Entry formalities

Citizens of the EU only have to show a valid passport to enter Italy for an unlimited stay. Citizens of the US, Australia, Canada and New Zealand can also enter Italy with a passport (valid for at least three months from the date of entry). No visa is required for a period of up to 90 days.

Insurance

No one should leave his or her home country without travel insurance. It can cover all sorts of emergencies (including the extra costs of private facilities), lost luggage, theft and cancelled tickets. Citizens of EU countries are entitled to free emergency medical care in a public hospital. Showing a passport might be enough but, ideally, you should carry a form E111 or a form E112 for those already undergoing treatment (British people can get one from main post offices). Non-EU citizens are covered only if they have travel insurance.

Maps

The Italian Touring Club and Kümmerly & Frey publish the best road maps.

Food

To quote a proverb, Tuscan and Umbrian cooking is 'peasant food fit for a king'. The recipes have been passed down through many generations and depend on freshness and simplicity of local ingredients and the careful way they are combined.

Tuscans eat beef from the Chiana valley as well as lamb, pork and goat. Umbrians eat more pork and pork sausages in all sorts of variations. Game, when in season, is popular everywhere except on the coast: wild boar, hare and pheasant are common themes. All kinds of wild mushrooms find their way into pasta sauces but the king of the *funghi* is the meaty *porcini*, best enjoyed on its own, fried in butter and garlic.

The main cheese is *pecorino*, made from sheep's milk and eaten fresh and aged. Vegetable and bean soups often take the place of pasta as a first course. Indeed, the Tuscans relish beans to the point of acquiring the nickname *mangiafagiole* ('bean eaters'). The Umbrians, for their part, grow lentils on a high mountain plain around the village of Castelluccio. Umbria is one of only two Italian provinces (the other is Piedmont) where the *tartufo* ('truffle') is abundant, particularly in late autumn and late winter. You will find them on the menu at all times of year in the main market centres, around Spoleto, the Valnerina, Nórcia and Scheggio. However, out of season, they will have been preserved by various means, with an inevitable loss of flavour.

Health

In general, standards of health care in Tuscany and Umbria are high
and health risks few. There are scorpions and jellyfish that sting but
they are not poisonous. *Vipere* ('vipers'), on the other hand, are very
poisonous. They have a triangular head that inflicts a triangular bite.
The chances of this happening are slight but if it does happen, go to
the nearest doctor. If you see a pharmacist on the way, stop there – he
might very well carry a serum antidote. *Zanzare* ('mosquitoes') are
common in low-lying coastal areas in spring and summer (don't
worry, there is no more malaria). Tap water is safe everywhere; sadly,
the same cannot be said of the river water. Even streams in the
mountains should be regarded as suspect. Boil the water ten minutes
before drinking it, or use iodine tablets like Potable Aqua. Ticks can be
a problem in some lower elevation forests and brush. If you find one
buried in your skin, do not pull it out. Coat it with oil or salt instead
and it should dislodge itself. The pharmacies (*farmacia*) take turns in
staying open for emergencies; the normal hours are Mon–Fri
0830–1230 and 1630–1900.

Information

Tuscany and Umbria have tourist offices in almost every town and in
some villages. They are usually located at or near the main railway
station and/or on the market square. APT (*Azienda di Promozione
Turistica*) offices are found in the main tourist areas; look also for EPT
(*Ente Provinciale per il Turismo*) and IAT (*Ufficio di Informazione e
Accoglienza Turistica*). In smaller places, there may only be a humble
little office with humble hours called a *Pro Loco*. Tourist offices are
particularly useful for finding rooms in smaller pensions or private
homes (sometimes charging a small fee). Usual hours are Mon–Sat
0900–1300 and 1600–1900; in winter the hours are shorter.

Italian Government tourist offices abroad

Canada *175 Bloor Street, Suite 907- South Tower, M4W3R8 Toronto
(Ontario); tel: 416 925 4882, fax: 416 925 4799; e-mail:
enit.canada@on.aibn.com; www.italiantourism.com.*

UK *1 Princes St, London W1B 2AY; tel: 207 399 3562, fax: 207 399 3564;
e-mail: italy@italiantouristboard.co.uk (brochure request line on 0891
600280).*

USA *630 Fifth Avenue, Suite 1565, New York, NY 10111; tel: 212 245
5618, fax: 212 586 9249; e-mail: enitny@italiantourism.com; www.
italiantourism.com.*

*500 North Michigan Avenue, Suite 2240, Chicago, IL 60611; tel: 312 644
0990, fax: 312 644 3109; e-mail: enitch@italiantourism.com;
www.italiantourism.com.*

Postal services

Post offices are normally open Mon–Fri 0830–1400 and Sat 0830–1200. The main post offices in larger towns are open until 1930. They have many services so make sure you go to the right counter for *francobolli* ('stamps'). You can also buy stamps sold in a *tabaccheria* ('tobacco shop'). Letters arrive much faster than postcards.

Public holidays

1 Jan	New Year's Day
6 Jan	Epiphany
Mar/Apr	Easter Monday
25 Apr	Liberation Day
1 May	Labour Day
May	Ascension Day
May/June	Whit Monday
June	Corpus Christi
15 Aug	Feast of the Assumption
1 Nov	All Saints' Day
25 Dec	Christmas Day
26 Dec	Boxing Day

Church opening hours

Church hours vary from place to place. In general, a church will be open daily, beginning at 0700 or 0800 and closing at 1900 or later in summer; in winter the hours are shorter. Churches are usually closed in the middle of the day from noon, 1300 or 1330 until 1530 or 1600. There are plenty of exceptions and some village churches are open only on Sundays and holidays. A visitor should have the sensitivity not to enter during church services, or – God forbid – weddings and funerals.

12400 Wilshire Boulevard, Suite 550, Los Angeles, CA 90025; tel: 310 820 1898; fax: 310 820 6357; e-mail: enitla@earthlink.net; www. italiantourism.com.

Australia *Level 26, 44 Market St, Sydney, NSW 2000; tel: 02 9262 1666; fax: 02 9262 1677; e-mail: enitour@ihug.com.au.*

New Zealand *Italian Embassy, 34–38 Grant Rd, Thorndon, Wellington; tel: 04 473 5339; www.italy-embassy.org.nz.*

Museums

Not only are Tuscan and Umbrian museums and art collections world-class but often they are 'museums within museums' since they are housed in ancient palaces, churches, aristocratic villas and converted monasteries. Most museums close on Mondays; most small town museums close for a long lunch, with shorter (or non-existent) winter hours; many of the larger city museums stay open until 2000 or 2100 at least one night a week (Tue, Wed or Thur).

Online services

There is a vast array of websites related to travel and tourism for Tuscany and Umbria. Here are a few of the more useful ones:
www.enit.it Italian Government tourist office.
www.museionline.it Italian museums online
www.camping.it Guide to Italian camping sites
www.provincia.fi.it The official website for the province of Firenze
www.regione.toscana.it The official website for Tuscany
www.castellitoscani.com Castles of Tuscany
www.provincia.perugia.it The official website for Umbria
www.regione.umbria.it/turismo/ Umbria's regional tourist office.

Opening times

In general, opening times are confusing and 'lunch break' can mean anything from two to five hours beginning at 1200 or 1300. Larger shops are normally open Mon–Sat 0900–1300 and 1600–2000. Most other shops are closed on Monday mornings. Food stores are usually closed on Wednesday afternoons. Only major supermarkets like Coop near large cities, and petrol stations on the *autostrade* stay open during the middle of the day. In tourist places or during the summer, shops may remain open longer in the evenings and on Sundays. However, many businesses, even restaurants, take a holiday in August. Weekly markets (selling fresh produce, meat and often shoes and clothing) are generally held in the mornings between 0800 and 1200. Banks are generally open Mon–Fri 0830–1300 and 1430–1600 (later on Thursday). Restaurants will normally open at 1130 and close around 2300; almost all of them close in the afternoon.

Safety and security

Florence has a real drug and crime problem so watch your wallet or handbag. If a robbery or break-in does occur, report it immediately to the police, if for no other reason than to back up insurance claims. By law, a person is always required to carry identification such as a passport.

Packing

Take light clothes but also a raincoat and umbrella. Warm clothes and waterproofs are essential for the mountains – regardless of the time of year. Definitely bring suntan lotion or block and something presentable to wear. Italians dress up a little more often than in Anglo-Saxon countries with an emphasis on quality rather than flashiness. Also recommended are: adaptor plugs and/or transformers for electrical devices; English-language books; aspirin, which you can buy only in a pharmacy; mosquito repellent; a flashlight, most useful in Etruscan tombs or the recesses of a dimly lit church; and binoculars or good-quality opera glasses to appreciate fully the details on Renaissance frescos and stained-glass windows.

Reading

(Most titles are available in Penguin editions)

Barzini, Luigi, *The Italians*: worldly wise musings on the Italian psyche by one of Italy's most respected journalists.

Boccaccio, Giovanni, *The Decameron*: the first and never surpassed Italian novel.

Cellini, Benvenuto, *Autobiography*: blow by blow (literally) life of a querulous, egomaniacal, hypochondriac, sexually omnivorous – and perhaps typical? – Renaissance artist.

Below
Gúbbio's narrow streets

Forster, E M, *A Room with a View*, and *Where Angels Fear to Tread*: blissfully predictable.

Lawrence, D H, *Etruscan Places*: communing at the end of his life with a mysterious people.

McCarthy, Mary, *The Stones of Florence*: the perfect literary antidote to all the nonsense written about this amazing and 'terrible' city.

Origo, Iris, *The Merchant of Prato*: life of a medieval merchant as told in his letters.

Romer, Elisabeth, *The Tuscan Year: Life and Food in an Italian Valley*: reverent peek into grandma's kitchen on a farm near the Tuscan-Umbrian border.

Unsworth, Barry, *After Hannibal*: a must-read for would-be ex-pats.

Vasari, Giorgio, *Lives of the Artists*: utterly fascinating, sometimes spiteful and at least partly true.

Telephones

Telephone kiosks are found on most main streets and squares. Telephone cards (*carta telefonica*) are more practical than coins for long-distance calls; they cost €3, 4, 7 and 10 from tobacco shops and some newsagents. The perforated corner of the card must be torn off before you insert it into the machine. In big cities and railway stations you may find telephone centres where you can make a call and pay afterwards, using a credit card if you prefer. Hotel telephone rates range from exorbitant to outrageous. Mobile phones in Italy use the GSM European standard.

To make an international call dial the access code 00, then the country code (UK = 44, Ireland = 353, US and Canada = 1, Australia = 61, New Zealand = 64) followed by the local number, omitting the first digit. Calling from the UK or any other country, the code for Italy is 00 39.

Direct dial numbers:

UK: BT 172 0044; Cable & Wireless 172 054

Ireland: 172 0353

US: AT&T 172 1011; MCI 172 1022; Sprint 172 1877

Canada: 172 1001

Australia: Telstra 172 1061; Optus 172 1161

New Zealand: 172 1064

Shopping

Popular souvenirs that you can take away from Tuscany and Umbria include shoes, leather goods, linen and clothes. The local markets, held outdoors, offer local colour as well as handicrafts and the makings of a picnic. Flea markets are a good bet to visit on Saturdays to find some unusual gifts. Other items to consider are *pecorino* (mountain cheese) and smoked ham (note: you are not allowed to import cheese to the USA unless it is 'commercially sealed'). Italy has a Value Added Tax (IVA) added to most goods and services. In theory, visitors from outside the European Union are entitled to a refund of this tax on purchases exceeding €155 from any one store. In practice, it is a hassle to obtain the refund. Look for the Tax Free Shopping in the shop window and ask the clerk for the necessary paperwork. The papers must be stamped by a customs official upon leaving Italy.

Time

Italy is one hour ahead of GMT in winter and two hours ahead in summer (from the end of March to the end of September).

Tipping

Service is normally included in the price (*servizio compreso*) with the exception of some fancy restaurants, where it is added separately (the practice should be written clearly on the menu). No one expects a tip though you can leave something extra if you feel so inclined, but do not tip with a credit card.

Toilets

There are toilets in any petrol station on the *autostrade* and in bus and train stations (*Uomini* for men and *Donne* for women). Otherwise, public toilets are rare. It is usually acceptable to duck into a café simply to use the restroom.

Left
Perugian pasta shop

Right
Umbrian wines

Sports

The Apennines and Apuan Alps, and Monte Amiata have hundreds of kilometres of well-marked trails and vast cave systems for spelunking. Extended hikes often involve staying overnight in mountain huts. Abetone, Monte Amiata and Nórcia are the most popular skiing regions. Most lakes in Tuscany and Umbria are clean enough to swim in. There are spectacular routes for mountain bikers but trails are not always clearly designated. There is rafting in the mountain rapids in the Apennines. Cycling is popular as a sport rather than a means of getting around and Day-Glo cyclists are a fixture on many roads during the weekend; local drivers seem more considerate towards cyclists than pedestrians. If cycling, it helps to be truly fit because Tuscany and Umbria are full of steep hills. It is possible to hire bicycles locally, but serious cyclists will want to bring their own. Both Alitalia and British Airways will check bicycles on board as luggage on Gatwick–Pisa flights.

Wine

Tuscany has the greatest winemaking tradition in Italy; however, it is now busy turning tradition on its head and becoming one of Europe's most innovative wine regions. Producers are experimenting with French grape varieties and ageing reds and whites in oak. The very boundaries of DOC regions (*Denominazione di origine controllata*) are being revised to make the designation more meaningful. In addition to Chianti, hill-towns Montalcino and Montepulciano produce two of Italy's headiest reds, Brunello and Vino Nobile respectively, as well as some of the most interesting new blends. There are amazing wine bargains to be had, as well as some wildly overhyped and overpriced vintages sold mostly to foreigners. Although Umbria is not in the same wine league as Tuscany there are still some excellent wines that are good value for money. There are richer, traditional versions – called *Orvieto Abbocato* – of neutral-tasting, dry white Orvieto. Grecchetto is a breezy white wine that competes locally with Orvieto. The best and most expensive reds are produced by winemakers like Lungarotti and Adanti. However, they are now being challenged by Sagrantino, a wine made in Montefalco from an unusual grape supposedly imported by a medieval Saracen. Vin Santo, Tuscany's delectable dessert wine, tastes like Madeira or medium-dry sherry (named 'holy wine' because of its popularity with priests). Sagrantino Passito is made with late-harvested and semi-dried grapes. It is a naturally sweet red wine that tastes something like port.

Driver's guide

Accidents

If you have a serious accident in Italy, you must wait for the police to arrive. Emergency services are usually efficient. On the other hand, if it is a minor accident with no injuries, the police might not be willing to investigate at all. In that case, look for a witness and have them write down what they saw and sign it. Of course, you will also want to exchange insurance details with the other driver(s).

Breakdowns

The first thing to do if you have a breakdown is to pull over on the road, if possible; then place a warning triangle 100m behind the vehicle (or a passenger with waving arms). Call 116 for assistance. The tow truck driver will probably not speak English but will be equipped with a multilingual auto parts manual. You will have to pay for towing and parts. However, if you are a member of an automobile club in your own country, you should be able to arrange for Italian cover. Enquire at your local automobile club about a letter of introduction.

Below
Monte Subásio rises above the morning mist

Caravans and camper vans

The speed limit for caravans (over 3.5 tonnes) and camper vans is 100kph on *autostrade*, 80kph on the highway and country roads, and 50kph in towns.

Car hire

To hire a car in Italy, drivers must be over 21 and in possession of a driving licence from their home country or state and a credit card. Car rental rates in Italy have become more competitive over the last few years. The major international and European rental companies are represented in Tuscany/Umbria.

Make plans for a rental car in advance. The rates vary a lot so shop around and/or ask your travel agent for help. The major rental companies have offices in Rome and Pisa for pick up and delivery. Auto Europe

City driving

It is possible to overcome and even to get used to the white-knuckled terror of driving on the Italian *autostrade*. Navigating Italian cities and hill-towns is another matter. Every city and every hill-town is a new puzzle. Where possible, avoid the temptation to drive to the very top or the very heart of a hill-town that was built to be unassailable and probably still is to a foreign driver. Chances are you won't find legal parking there anyway. Florence and Perugia have expensive public parking but it is still preferable to getting lost. And beware of narrow streets that narrow even further.

Fuel

Unleaded gasoline (*senza piombo*) is sold everywhere. Diesel is available at most petrol stations. Leaded petrol is also still available at many stations.

Information

Automobíle Club d'Italia (ACI) *Via Marsala 8, 00185 Rome; tel: 06 491115; www.aci.it.*

(*www.autoeurope.com*) offers some of the most competitive rates. *Toll-free numbers: from Australia 1800 12 6409; from New Zealand 0800 44 0722; from the UK 0800 169 6414; from North America 888-223-5555.*

The question of insurance should be resolved ahead of time, too – and you will have to get what is called a Collision Damage Waiver from the rental company. If you and your passengers already have travel insurance, you might not need personal accident insurance.

Documents

You are allowed to drive in Italy with a British or American driving licence. Though neither the police nor rental agencies seem to bother about the international driving permit, it is still worth getting it, just in case, from a local automobile association.

Drinking and driving

Italy, like most of Europe, has strict limits on the amount of alcohol a driver can have in his or her blood – 0.08 per cent. A driver who exceeds this limit faces stiff penalties. A driver involved in an accident with a high blood-alcohol level also runs the risk of being automatically considered at fault.

Driving conditions

Tuscany and Umbria have an excellent and well-maintained system of roads. The green signposted *autostrade* are toll roads. There are always alternatives such as the four-lane highways connecting Florence with Siena or Livorno, the road down the Tuscan coast and the roads joining Arezzo to Perugia and Perugia to Spoleto. However, the most scenic routes, such as the ones described in this book, are country roads and not the quickest way from A to B.

Emergency telephone numbers

Military police (*carabinieri*). *Tel: 112.*
Police emergencies (*polizia*). *Tel: 113.*
Fire emergency (*vigili del fuoco*). *Tel: 115.*
Medical emergency (*pronto soccorso*). *Tel: 118.*
ACI Breakdown Service (Italian Automobile Association, for road assistance). *Tel: 803.*

Parking

Italy has the highest number of cars per capita in Europe. The cities and villages in Tuscany and Umbria, most of them at least as old as the Middle Ages, cannot cope with the traffic. Each town has its own

Seat belts

The driver and all passengers in the car, front and back, are legally required to wear seat belts.

strategy and they are all failing. In general, the *Centro Storico* (historic town centre) is partly closed to motor traffic or surrounded by a labyrinth of one-way streets; in smaller towns, the centre is sometimes reserved for residents (*riservato ai residenti*) during certain hours. Parking is normally signposted in blue.

It is often free to park on the street in smaller towns, but sometimes subject to a time limit. In the case of paid street parking, a central machine (one per street) accepts money and issues a printed ticket which should be placed, clearly visible, inside the windscreen. Generally, parking garages have a cashier. You receive a time-stamped ticket when you enter the car park or garage. You are not required to leave the ticket in the car. Before leaving, step up to the *cassa* and pay for the ticket; then retrieve your vehicle, drive to the exit and insert the ticket to open the gate.

Police

Polizia urbana deal with traffic and parking offences in towns and the *polizia stradale* deal with most traffic violations on the motorway (equivalent to the state highway patrol in the US). To report a theft, you should go to the nearest *questura* ('police station') and ask for a *denuncia*, a stamped form that is essential for filing insurance claims. The *carabinieri* handle more serious crime.

Security

Italy has high rates of car theft and break-ins. Although the risks are considerably lower in rural Tuscany and Umbria than in urban Italy, remember that anything left in a car could be stolen (and 97 per cent of thefts in Italy go unsolved).

Speed limits

The speed limit on the *autostrade* is 130 kp/h. It is important to realise that the faster you go, the faster you will have to slow down at the next traffic jam. Lower speed limits are posted when the road is dangerous or passes through an urban area (usually 100kph, but they vary between 80kph and 110kph) or when construction is underway (usually 60kph) – and you are required by law to slow down.

In towns, the limit is 50kph. Some residential areas now post speed limits of 30kph. The maximum speed limit on country roads is 90kph. It can be truly dangerous to speed on country roads. Often, they have no shoulder and there is simply no margin of error if you drift even slightly off the road. They pass directly through towns and villages where a blind turn can come between you, the driver, and villagers using the same road for strolling, gossiping, flirting, as extra parking, or for a weekly shoe market.

Tolls

Most of the *autostrada* system in Italy is based on tolls, which are sometimes paid at ridiculously frequent intervals. However, the rates are low compared to many other countries – France for example. The normal procedure is to take a ticket at the beginning and pay at the end either with cash or a bank or credit card.

Six highly dangerous habits of (some) drivers on Italian roads

Tailgating

Driving on Italian roads is up close and personal. Some drivers will come within inches of your bumper at any speed.

Straddling the dividing line

One unmistakable custom on Italian roads is to straddle the dividing line. Fortunately, the drivers in question are probably not drunk or falling asleep. Rather, it seems to be a peculiar reluctance on the part of some drivers to accept the existence of two (or more) lanes.

Not using signals

Never assume that anyone will signal before turning or passing. By law, cars in Italy are equipped with signal lights but some drivers use them only as an afterthought.

Passing in the oncoming lane

In theory, you have the right of way in your own lane. Nevertheless, don't be surprised to find that some drivers in an oncoming lane make use of your lane as if you were not there.

Driving with one hand

Some drivers constantly gesticulate with one hand and/or talk on a cellphone while driving. Though they would never admit it, this can affect their ability to steer the car.

Running red lights

A red light is only truly red after a few seconds have elapsed. In other words, some drivers will acknowledge the change in colour only after they have had time to think about it – and to drive through an intersection or complete a left turn.

Right
San Miniato al Monte,
near Florence

Getting to Tuscany and Umbria

Airlines – UK

Alitalia *Tel: 0870 544 8259; www.alitalia.com*

British Airways *Tel: 0845 77 333 77; www.britishairways.com*

Go! *Tel: 0870 60 76543; website: www.go-fly.com*

KLM UK *Tel: 08705 074074; website: www.klm.com*

Meridiana *Tel: 020 7839 2222; www.meridiana.it.*

Ryanair *Tel: in Ireland, 0818 30 30 30; tel: in UK, 0871 246 0000; www.ryanair.com*

Virgin Express *Tel: 020 7744 0004; website: www.virgin-express.com*

Discount air tickets

STA Travel *86 Old Brompton Rd, London SW7 3LQ; tel: 0870 1 600 599; www.statravel.co.uk*

Trailfinders *194 Kensington High St, London W8 7RG; tel: 020 7938 3836; www.trailfinders.co.uk*

The best travel deals require planning ahead – or waiting until the last minute. An APEX ('advance purchase excursion') fare is 30–40 per cent cheaper than the full economy fare for a transatlantic or cross-channel flight but subject to restrictions: purchase 21 days ahead of time, a stay of at least two weeks, return in 90–120 days. APEX fares are not fully refundable so cancellation insurance is advisable. The Internet is an excellent source of information for last-minute flights (try *www.cheapflights.co.uk*, *www.lastminute.com*, *www.travelselect.com* or *www.flightline.co.uk*).

From the UK

Obviously, it is much easier to fly from the UK than to drive to Tuscany and Umbria. The advantages of bringing your own car have to be weighed against the high price and added time it takes. Stopping overnight, it takes about three days (about 36 hours if you drive non-stop) to reach Tuscany/Umbria from the UK, using the main north–south motorways. Add together the price of crossing the Channel, tolls, petrol and overnight stays en route and it quickly becomes expensive. Aside from the considerable stress of driving, it also means deducting up to six days from your holiday. However, it might well be worth considering for people travelling as a group of four or more.

London, as the European capital of discount flights, offers many different options. British Airways and Alitalia have flights several times a day to Rome, Milan and Pisa and there are also cheap charter flights to these cities as well as to Bologna and Rimini. Florence's small Peretola airport (car hire available) is handy for Perugia and northern Umbria, too. Driving time to Perugia is about two hours.

Of course, hiring a car requires an extra layer of planning but there are many fly/drive packages on offer from London, Manchester and Birmingham.

Trains

The train has no advantages – in terms of price or time – for travellers to Italy from the UK unless they want to visit destinations on the way. Contact Eurostar (*Tel: 0870 5 186 186 ; www.eurostar.com*) for trains to Paris (with overnight connections to Florence for Perugia, Spoleto and

Fly-drive

Search on www.virgin.com

Established tour operators offering fly-drive holidays:

Citalia Tel: 020 8686 5533; www.citalia.co.uk

Italiatour Tel: 01883 621 900; www.italiatour.co.uk

Sunvil Holidays Tel: 020 8232 9788; www.sunvil.co.uk

Channel ferries

Some cross channel operators now offer an 'Apex'-type discount for advance bookings.

Eurotunnel Tel: 08705 35 35 35; www.eurotunnel.com

Hoverspeed Tel: 0870 240 8070; www.hoverspeed.com

P&O European Ferries Tel: 0870 242 4777; www.poferries.com

P&O Stena Line Tel: 087 0600 0600; www.posl.com

SeaFrance Tel: 0870 571 1711; www.seafrance.com

Discount air tickets

In USA, **Council Travel** Tel: 1 800 226 8624; www.counciltravel.com

In USA, **STA Travel** Tel: 1 800 781 4040; www.sta-travel.com

In Canada, **Travel CUTS** 187 College St, Toronto, Ontario M5T 1P7; tel: 416 979 2406; www.travelcuts.com

Orvieto); Citalia (*see sidebar*) for Italian rail tickets and passes; or Rail Europe (*tel: 08705 848 848; www.raileurope.co.uk*).

From North America

Although there are no direct flights to Tuscany or Umbria, many airlines fly daily to Rome and Milan with possible connecting flights to Pisa or Perugia.

Airlines

Air Canada Tel: 1 888 247 2262; www.aircanada.com

Alitalia Tel: in US, 1 800 223 5730; in Canada, 1 800 361 8336; www.alitalia.com

Delta Tel: in US and Canada, 1 800 241 4141; www.delta.com

KLM Tel: in US and Canada, 1 800 447 4747; www.klm.com

Lufthansa Tel: in US, 1 800 645 3880; in Canada, 1 800 563 5954; website: www.lufthansa.com

TWA Tel: in US, 1 800 221 2000; www.twa.com

United Airlines Tel: in US, 1 800 241 6522; website: www.ual.com

Above
San Gimignano

Above
The Piano Grande near Nórcia

Setting the scene

Geography

The Apennines and the Apuan Alps border Tuscany to the north and northeast. The Apennines – *lo dosso d'Italia* or 'spine of Italy' – continue down through Umbria and form its border with the neighbouring Marche province.

Tuscany's 329-km coastline is mostly flat and developed though the population density is much greater to the north than in the south. The peninsula of Monte Argentario was actually an island, until silting joined it to the mainland in the 19th century, while the coastal plain of Maremma consists of reclaimed swampland. South of Siena are the strange clay hills known as the Crete, which look like a grey desert in places. They roll into the verdant hills around the extinct volcano of Monte Amiata and westwards towards the Metallifere mountains, an almost uninhabited area with vast reserves of geothermal energy that provide much of Tuscany's electricity.

Seventy per cent of Tuscany is hilly, with the population concentrated in the lowlands in river valleys like those of the Arno and Tiber. The upper and middle valley of the River Tiber dominates Umbria, bracketed on the east side by the Apennines. It has a number of wide basins that were once lakes, such as the Vale di Umbra, and one that still is, Lago di Trasimeno, as well as plains around Gúbbio and Terni, and the spectacular mountain plain, the Piano Grande.

Timeline

800–400 BC Etruscan settlements between the Tiber and Arno rivers – Populonia, Vetulonia, Roselle, Chiusi, Cortona, Arezzo, Fiesole, Volterra, Perugia and Orvieto; Umbrians settle on the left bank of the Tiber and found the cities of Narni, Amelia, Terni, Spoleto, Assisi and Gúbbio.

400–350 BC The Golden Age of Etruscan civilisation.

350–250 BC Rome conquers the Etruscans and Umbrians, step by step. As part of their expansion, Romans build *coloniae* – retirement settlements for army veterans – along the strategic *Via Flaminia*, the road built to provide a swift route between Rome and its northern frontiers. Rome adopts Umbrian and Etruscan practices such as foretelling the future by studying birds in flight, forks of lightning or the organs of sacrificial animals.

AD 13–14 The Romans create the provinces of Umbria and Tuscia, left and right of the Tiber.

493–552 After the fall of the Roman empire, Tuscany and Umbria are invaded and ruthlessly plundered by Goths.

568–71 The Longobards (Lombards) conquer the region and found their own dukedoms in Lucca and Spoleto. The area between Perugia and Amelia remains in Byzantine hands. The Longobards are converted to Christianity.

756 Peppin seizes Byzantine Umbria and gives it to the Pope. This is the beginning of the Papal State, destined to have a profound influence on Italian politics for the next 1 000 years.

774 Charlemagne and the Franks conquer the region. Charlemagne is crowned Holy Roman Emperor. Tuscany and Umbria become provinces of his empire.

1050 Power struggle between the Holy Roman Emperor and the Pope contributes to the growth of autonomous city states in Pisa, Florence, Lucca, Siena, Arezzo, Prato, Perugia and Spoleto. The rise of guilds and the cloth industry; creation of Europe's first banks.

1063 Pisa beats off the Saracens and develops one of the most important harbours on the Mediterranean.

1125 Florence destroys Fiesole and begins to expand its territory. The Florentines fight wars with the Ghibelline cities of Pisa and Siena.

1210 Rise of Franciscans and Dominicans.

1260 Siena defeats Florence in the bloody battle of Montaperti.

1269 Florence defeats Siena near Colle Val d'Elsa.

1284 Pisa loses out to Genoa in struggle for control of the sea. Building boom of town halls: Prato (1284), Siena (1288), Pistoia (1294) and Florence (1299).

1342 Edward III of England defaults on his loans and ruins the major banking houses of Florence and Siena, setting off an economic crisis.

1348 The plague strikes Tuscany and Umbria, killing almost half of the population. Cities like Siena and San Gimignano never fully recover their importance.

1378 Revolt of the *ciompi* ('weavers') in Siena, Lucca, Florence and other cities. The Medici – a wealthy Florentine family – become bankers to the Pope.

1406 Florence conquers Pisa, builds a new harbour in Livorno and wages war with Naples, Milan and Lucca. During a period of unrest in Florence, Cosimo de'Medici sides with the people's party and is driven into exile.

1434 Cosimo Il Vecchio returns to Florence in triumph and remains in power until his death (1464).

Guelphs and Ghibellines and the Middle Ages

'Guelph' and 'Ghibelline' were used to denote the factions of this age, supporters of the Pope and the Holy Roman Emperor respectively. At another level the terms can be seen as political labels: the Guelph party was essentially made up of the rising middle class of merchants, bankers and members of the trades guilds, whose wealth was growing and with it a desire for greater control over public affairs. They supported the Pope because, temporarily at least, the papal cause seemed to offer the only hope of release from the imperial yoke. By contrast, the Ghibellines represented the old feudal aristocracy, which was interested in independence from external control but not in a broad-based city democracy. For them, allegiance to the Emperor was a small price to pay for maintaining a virtual autocracy within the sphere of their own city state. As a consequence, there was tension at every level in medieval Tuscany and Umbria: between the superpowers of Church and Empire; between factions who nominally supported one or the

1478 War between Florence and the Pope. The Medici prince, Lorenzo the Magnificent, survives an assassination attempt by the Pazzi conspirators.

1501 Michelangelo's *David* graces the square before the town hall in Florence.

1530 The end of Florence as a Republic. The Medici rule as tyrants with the help of Spanish troops.

1540 Perugia falls to Pope Paul III. The Papal State now controls most of Umbria. Its administration is so corrupt and its taxes so high that the Umbrian countryside suffers depopulation.

1555 Florence besieges Siena, starves out its population and puts an end to the last Republic in Italy.

1569 Cosimo I, proclaimed Duke of Tuscany, controls the entire region except for Lucca, Massa-Carrara and the islands.

1590–1790 The dullest period in Italian history with general economic and cultural stagnation.

1798–9 Napoleon occupies Tuscany and Umbria. His sister Elisa rules the Duchy of Lucca from 1805 to 1814.

1814 After the Congress of Vienna, Napoleon is banished to Elba. Tuscany is ruled by the Habsburgs, Umbria by the Papal State.

1848 Risorgimento. Italians rebel against the rule of foreigners and the Papal State but the Austrians and Pope regain control.

1860 Unification of Italy. After popular referenda, Tuscany and Umbria join the new state. The name Umbria, which had not been used for centuries, is reintroduced.

1936 Hitler–Mussolini pact.

1940–5 Italy enters the Second World War as Germany's ally. Heavy fighting between Germans and Italian partisans in the Apennine mountains. Livorno, Pisa and San Gimignano suffer heavily. The industrial city of Terni is almost destroyed by Allied bombing. Following Italy's armistice with the Allies, in July 1944 the Germans blow up all the bridges in Florence, except for the Ponte Vecchio.

1966 Catastrophic flood sweeps through Florence.

1993 Bomb attack on the Uffizi Gallery in Florence kills four people and causes major damage to the museum and its collection.

1997 A strong earthquake hits Umbria, leaving 30,000 people homeless. Part of the ceiling frescos in the upper basilica of the cathedral in Assisi collapse.

2002 An ambitious engineering project saves the leaning tower of Pisa from the threat of collapse; it is reopened to visitors.

**Guelphs and
Ghibellines and the
Middle Ages** (cont)

other cause; between
merchants and
aristocracy; between
rival families, many of
whom maintained
private armies which
they deployed against
each other in the
struggle for city control;
and between individual
city states, each seeking
to extend its sphere of
influence and control.

Art and architecture

Almost everything we know about the Etruscans comes from their tombs and the art and furniture they placed inside them. Although scholars insist that there is nothing 'mysterious' about the Etruscans, lots of writers, artists and New Agers seem to know better. The solitary, semi-wild location of many tombs adds to the effect; it is sometimes difficult to know whether Etruscans, medieval warlords or extra terrestrials deposited a particular pile of red volcanic stone. Almost nothing is known of the Umbrians' culture. They left behind a few portions of city wall built of massive blocks in places like Amelia, and seven bronze tablets found near Gúbbio that give lessons in divination and the ritual sacrifice of birds and unwanted neighbours.

Many people in Tuscany and Umbria still live in houses built in the Middle Ages. Their home might have benefited from Renaissance or baroque additions and they might park their car in an Etruscan tomb downstairs; or perhaps they live in one of the traditional 18th-century stone farmhouses in which animals and farmers shared each other's body heat. In the region's churches and cathedrals, the centuries are just steps apart. Recycled Roman stones support the roof above many an altar painted in the Renaissance. Architectural styles that are chronological in a guidebook might have to be parsed in reverse order.

Romanesque

Florence is celebrated as the cradle of the Renaissance. However, the profile of most historic cities in Tuscany and Umbria was created by Romanesque and Gothic. The Romanesque style (10th–12th centuries) unites geometry – rectangles, cubes, semicircular arches – with unprecedented ambition to build upwards. Although not directly of Roman origin, many Romanesque *pievi* (parish churches) were built in the countryside on top of sites sacred to Etruscans. and Romans. The Pisan Romanesque style was strongly influenced by Byzantine and Islamic architecture. Some of the best early churches are:
* Abbadia San Salvatore (1036) in the Crete
* Sant'Ántimo (1100) in the Crete
* San Pietro, Spoleto (façade *c.* 1150–1210)
* Duomo, Sovana (1150)
* Pieve di Romena (1150) near Castello di Romena.
Some of the best Pisan Romanesque churches are:
* Baptistry (1152), Duomo (1063–1180) and Campanile (1173–1350) in Pisa
* San Frediano (1112) and San Michele in Foro (1143) in Lucca
* Duomo (1108–1311) and Sant'Andrea (1180) in Pistóia
* Duomo (1211) in Prato.
Among the best Florentine Romanesque churches are:
* Baptistry (1059–1128) and San Miniato al Monte (1050) in Florence.

Gothic

There are few purely Gothic structures in Tuscany and Umbria. Most Gothic buildings contain Romanesque elements or were built upon or around previous Romanesque buildings. Gothic architecture took a distinctly different form south of the Alps, retaining the dome, using less vertical thrust and giving frescos, rather than stained-glass windows, centre stage. The best examples of this style are:

- Basilica di San Francesco, Assisi (1228–53)
- San Galgano, in central Tuscany (1224–30)
- Duomo, Siena (1225)
- Duomo, Orvieto (1290–1330)
- Duomo, Florence (1294)
- Santa Maria della Spina, Pisa (1323).

Renaissance

The 15th century was a revolutionary period that profoundly changed many aspects of European life – housing, language, warfare, diet, cities, technology and education for example. Certainly, the Florentines themselves saw this age as a rebirth of classical learning and artistic ideals and called it a *Rinascità* ('Rebirth'). However, the idea of the Renaissance as a sudden Florentine watershed between the medieval and the modern is essentially a 19th-century theory that has been subject to heavy revision. In fact, the late Middle Ages paved the way for many 'modern' changes to such an extent that a piece of the late medieval period has been appropriated as 'Proto-Renaissance'. Its dominant artistic figure is Giotto (1266–1337), generally considered to be the first artist since antiquity to create realistic representations of people, space and things.

Art historians have picked 1420 to be the magic moment when the Early Renaissance began, the year when Brunelleschi won the contract to put a dome on top of the cathedral in Florence (it was not finished until 1467, after his death). Brunelleschi had already rediscovered linear perspective (the ancients were familiar with it) and his approach to architecture was radically new though his buildings have Gothic and Romanesque elements, too. Painters Paolo Uccello, Piero della Francesca and Masaccio would make full use of perspective to pioneer the illusion of space and the dimensions of nature on a flat surface. Donatello and Ghiberti incorporated the new principles into sculpture.

The most important figures of the High Renaissance were Michelangelo, Leonardo da Vinci and Raphael. This period spanned little more than a generation, roughly 1490–1520. Admittedly, Leonardo was so busy privately inventing things like the helicopter, bicycle and flame-thrower that he painted little. Raphael, by contrast, was prolific but died young, in 1520. His work possesses in perfect balance the grace and harmony that Renaissance artists aspired to. Michelangelo carried on until 1564 and the incredible age of 89 but by then he had himself broken the Renaissance mould and opened the door to new styles. The best Renaissance buildings are:

- Spedale degli Innocenti (1419–24); Sagrestia Vecchia in San Lorenzo (1419); Cappella dei Pazzi in Santa Croce (1442); San Lorenzo (begun in 1425), all in Florence and by Brunelleschi
- San Marco in Florence, Michelozzo (1437–52)
- Piazza del Duomo in Pienza, Rossellino (1459–62)
- San Biagio in Montepulciano, Sangallo (1513–43)
- Sagrestia Nuova, San Lorenzo in Florence, Michelangelo (1520).

Mannerism

The term 'Mannerism', even by the standards of art history jargon, is woolly. It was originally a put-down by Tuscan artist Giorgio Vasari referring to artists who came after Michelangelo and who worked *alla maniera di Michelangelo* (the most hyperactive 'wannabe' was Vasari himself). Michelangelo had given impetus to it: his Medici Chapel (in San Lorenzo) was, in Vasari's words, 'more varied and novel than that of any other master', putting artists 'under a great and eternal obligation to Michelangelo, seeing that he broke the fetters and chains that had earlier confined them to the creation of traditional forms'. The most prominent figures in this school are the painters Pontormo, Bronzino and Rosso Fiorentino and sculptors Benvenuto Cellini and Giambologna. It is ironic that the Tuscan Renaissance bang ended in a Mannerist whimper – a self-conscious, angst-ridden style alien to the classical spirit but with some striking parallels to modern art.

Festivals

The calendar of Tuscany and Umbria is full of festivals. Most are purely local events that celebrate a region's food (mushrooms, *pecorino*, chestnuts, truffles, wild boar, grilled thrush); they offer the perfect chance to eat, drink and make merry with Tuscans and Umbrians. The more famous 'medieval' pageants are a mysterious mix of tourist hype and authentic local tradition – none more so than the most hyped (and insanely crowded) of all festivals, the *Palio di Contrade* in Siena, which nevertheless has deep roots in the city's history and psyche. Some of the seasonal festivals in the region, though adapted to Christianity, have their origins in pagan ritual. One event that stands out is this respect is the *Corsa dei Ceri* in Gúbbio. Music, theatre and art festivals fall into a third category. The one with the most cachet is the Festival of Two Worlds in Spoleto but there are many others. The local tourist office is always a good source of information about festivals. Some are mentioned in individual chapters of this book.

Below
Madonna and Child in Todi's San Fortunato church

April/May

- *Maggio Musicale* in Florence (Apr–June).
- *Calcio Storico* in Florence.
- *Coloriamo i cieli* ('Let's paint the skies') in Castiglione del Lago. Every even-numbered year a Kite Festival is held on the banks of Lake Trasimeno (second Sun in May).
- *Corso all'Anello* ('Ring Race') in Narni. Young men dressed in medieval costume attempt to thrust the tip of a lance through a ring which is suspended on a string between the houses along the Via Maggiore (first Tue in May).
- *Calendimaggio* in Assisi. A three-day celebration in commemoration of St Francis with singing, theatre performances, dance, processions, archery and banner-waving, not to mention knights and maidens in full regalia (early May).
- *Corsa dei Ceri* ('Candle Race') in Gúbbio. Three gigantic wooden 'candles', each weighing about 50 kilos and mounted with statues of saints, are carried by young candle-bearers to the Basilica di Sant'Ubaldo, situated on top of Monte Ingino.
- *Balestro del Girifalco* in Massa Maríttima.

June

- *Festival dei Due Mondi* in Spoleto. International prose, theatre, dance and musical performances by leading artists from Europe and the Americas. This is one of the high points of the Italian social and artistic calendar, and you will have to book well in advance if you want to attend any events, or even find a hotel room in the city (June and July).
- *Palio della Balestra* in Gúbbio. Contests with medieval bows and arrows between Gúbbio and Sansepolcro.

Right
Festive Siena

- *Calcio Storico* in Florence.
- *Gioco del Ponte* in Pisa.
- *Rockin' Umbria* in Perugia. This rock festival has taken place each year since 1986 not just in Perugia, but also in Umbértide and Città di Castello. Although you won't find the rock world's big stars here, you will find promising up-and-coming musical performers (last 10 days in June–first 10 days in July).

July
- *Palio di Contrade* in Siena.
- *Umbria Jazz* in Perugia and other Umbrian cities. One of the most important jazz festivals in Europe (last two weeks in July–first week in Aug).

August
- *Balestro del Girifalco* in Massa Maríttima.
- *Bravio delle Botti* in Montepulciano.
- *Giostra del Saracino* in Arezzo.
- *Torneo/Sagra* in Montalcino.
- *Palio di Contrade* in Siena.
- *International Ceramics Competition and Exhibition* in Gualdo Tadino. It dates back to 1959 and is attended by well-known ceramicists and exhibitors of widely differing artistic trends (mid-Aug–30 Sept).

September
- *Luminaria di Santa Croce* in Lucca.
- *Gioco delle Bandiere* in Volterra.
- *Giostra del Saracino* in Arezzo.
- *Todi Festival* in Todi. A wide variety of works in the fields of music, ballet and film produced by young, up-and-coming artists hailing from Italy and abroad.
- *Sagra Musicale Umbra* in Perugia. This is a highly regarded event in the European music world at which 20th-century religious music is performed.

October
- *Torneo/Sagra* in Montalcino.

November
- *Rassegna Antiquaria* in Perugia. An exhibition of antiques.

December
- *Celebrazioni di Santo Natale* in Assisi and Amélia. During this time, Christmas concerts are held in many churches and the Nativity scene is portrayed by live animals and actors.
- *Mostra Mercato del Tartufo* in Città di Castello. The entire city is transformed into a heaven for fans of truffles (24 Dec–6 Jan).

January/February/March
- *Holy Week* in Assisi.
- *Carnevale* in Viareggio. A spectacular Shrove Tuesday parade with floats poking fun at local and national politicians.

Highlights

The best of Tuscany and Umbria:

- Archaeology museums: *Chiusi, Florence, Orvieto, Volterra.*
- Art museums: *Uffizi, Bargello* (Florence), *Perugia, Siena, Montefalco.*
- Baptistries: *Florence, Pisa, Pistóia.*
- Beaches: *Castiglione della Pescáia, Vada, Marina di Alberese, Baratti.*
- Castles: *Castiglione d'Órcia, Poppi, Radicófani.*
- Cathedrals: *Assisi, Barga, Florence, Orvieto, Pisa, Siena, Spoleto.*
- Cities: *Florence, Lucca, Siena, Perugia.*
- Etruscan arches: *Perugia, Volterra.*
- Etruscan cemeteries: *Golfo di Baratti, Orvieto, Perugia.*
- Festivals (art and music): *Festival of Two Worlds in Spoleto, Umbria Jazz Festival.*
- Festivals (traditional): *Palio di Contrade in Siena, Corsa dei Ceri in Gúbbio.*
- Frescos: *Monte Oliveto (Signorelli, Sodoma), Basilica di Assisi (Cimabue, Giotto), Cappella Brancacci in Florence (Masaccio, Masolino, Filippino Lippi), Chiesa di San Francesco in Montefalco (Benozzo Gozzoli), Collegio di Cambio in Perugia (Perugino), Duomo San Francesco in Arezzo (Piero della Francesca), Palazzo Pubblico in Siena (Ambrogio Lorenzetti).*

Below
Near Lake Trasimeno

- Geology: *Le Balze near Volterra, Larderello.*
- Historic squares: *Bevagna, Castiglione d'Órcia, Lucca, Massa Maríttima, Pienza, Perugia, Siena, Volterra.*
- Historic towns: *Montepulciano, San Gimignano, Spoleto, Volterra.*
- Hot springs: *Bagno Vignoni, Calidario in Venturina, Cascate del Mulino in Saturnia, Fosso Biano in Bagni San Filippo.*
- Islands: *Isola Maggiore and Isola Polvese in Lago di Trasimeno.*
- Lakes: *Lago di Trasimeno.*
- Markets: *Arezzo (antiques), Florence (Mercato Centrale).*
- Monasteries: *Monte Oliveto, Sant'Ántimo.*
- National Parks: *Parco Naturale della Maremma, Parco Naturale di Monti Sibillini.*
- Palaces: *Palazzo Vecchio, Palazzo Medici-Riccardi (Florence), Palazzo dei Priori (Perugia).*
- Roman ruins: *Cársulae, Ponte d'Augusto in Narni.*
- Wine: *Fonterútoli, Montalcino, Montefalco, Montepulciano, Torrigiano, Volpaia.*

Florence

Ratings

Architecture	●●●●●
Art	●●●●●
Food and drink,	●●●●●
Museums	●●●●●
Shopping	●●●●●
Children	●●○○○
Scenery	●●○○○
Nature	●○○○○

Above
Baptistry

Florentines discovered three-dimensional perspective, football, opera and ice cream – not bad for a city of moneylenders and cloth-makers. Having invented the Renaissance, Florence still monopolises much of it in the space of a few hundred square metres and the resulting density of tourists rivals Disneyworld. Its architecture has been repeated all over the world in private and public buildings – a sense of *dejà vu* is inevitable. Michelangelo may be the presiding genius but virtually every Italian Renaissance artist of any rank made his mark here. Despite claustrophobia, noise and summer heat, the city still offers sanctuary to the art lover, beginning in its cathedral. Many of the galleries, churches and museums are far from the madding crowd, as are the cloisters of San Lorenzo, Santa Croce and Santa Maria Novella.

Sights

ⓘ APT office *Via Cavour 1, tel: 055 290832/3, fax 055 2760383; www.firenze.net & www.firenze.turismo.toscana.it. Open Mon–Sat 0830–1830; Sun 0830–1330.*

ⓘ Battistero € *Piazza del Duomo/San Giovanni; tel: 055 2302885. Open Mon–Sat 1200–1900, Sun 0830–1400.*

Battistero❖❖❖

The Battistero (Baptistry) is the oldest building in the city. Its origins are mysterious, but the foundations are probably from the 4th to 8th centuries while the current building – described by art historians as 'proto-Renaissance' – dates from 1059–1128. Medieval Florentines, including Dante (baptised here in 1245), thought it was built by the Romans and it does, in fact, stand at the former intersection of the town's two main Roman roads, and the four bronze doors are aligned with them. The south door (1330–6) by Andrea Pisano depicts scenes from the life of John the Baptist, the patron saint of Florence. Lorenzo Ghiberti worked for almost half a century on the other two doors. He decorated the north door (1403–24) with 28 scenes from the lives of Jesus and the four evangelists. The east door, however, is his crowning achievement and one of the finest things created during the

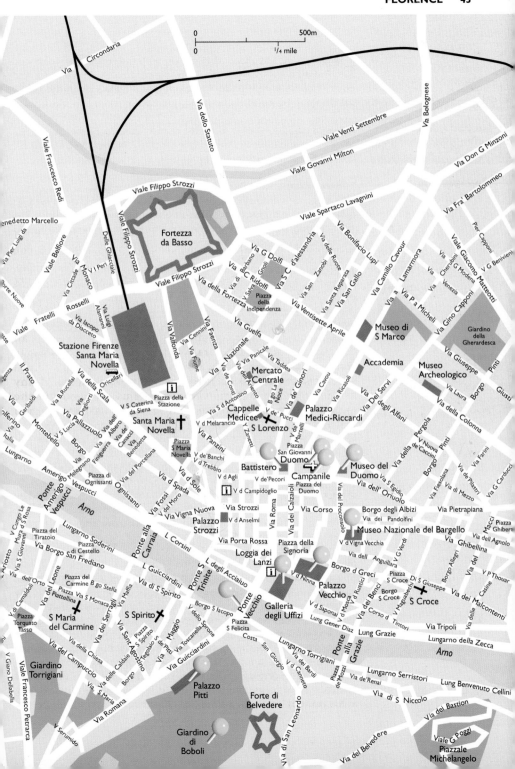

Museo Nazionale del Bargello €€ *Via del Proconsolo 4; tel: 055 2388606. Open Tue–Sat 0815–1350; also 1st, 3rd and 5th Mon 0815–1350; and 2nd and 4th Sun of every month 0815–1700.*

Campanile €€ *Piazza del Duomo; tel: 055 2302885. Open daily 0830–1930.*

Renaissance. Its ten gilded panels begin with the creation of Adam and Eve, followed by Cain and Abel, the Flood, Noah's drunkenness and other episodes from the Old Testament (the originals are in the Museo del Duomo). Ghiberti's self-portrait is in the fourth panel – the head at the top. Michelangelo, normally a merciless critic, called them the 'doors of paradise'. Inside, the 13th-century mosaics in the apse were a source of inspiration to Dante while writing *L'Inferno* ('hell'). Look for the Devil with a mouthful of the sinners.

Museo Nazionale del Bargello✦✦✦

The Bargello is strangely neglected in favour of the Uffizi though its collection of sculpture rivals that of any museum in the world. The 13th-century palace, built for sessions of the city council, symbolised the triumph of elected government in Florence. Three centuries later, it stood for the opposite, after Medici tyrants turned it into a prison. The charming courtyard wall was the last thing condemned prisoners saw before their execution. The Bargello's repertoire of nude bodies in stone – twisting, raging, lusting and musing atop their pedestals – expresses a revolution in taste, ie, the Renaissance – and an obsession with the human body. It puts today's cult of the supermodel and Schwarzeneggers to shame for sheer lack of imagination.

The ground floor displays the only bust Michelangelo ever carved, of *Brutus*. The work had distinct Republican overtones because it could be seen as a reference to the assassination of the Medici tyrant, Alessandro I. His *Drunken Bacchus* carries a somewhat different message. The same room contains his *Tondo Pitti* and *David-Apollo* as well as Benvenuto Cellini's bust of *Cosimo I* and Giambologna's *Flying Mercury*. Upstairs is Donatello's homoerotic, under-age *David* – the first nude statue of the Renaissance, and one of the most remarkable works of art in Florence. Other high points include Ammannati's *Leda and the Swan* and Ghiberti's powerful *The Sacrifice of Isaac*. It's easy to overlook, but on the wall of the first floor are two panels submitted by Brunelleschi and Ghiberti in a competition for the commission to do the Baptistry doors. If you have any attention span left, there are still 30,000 odd coins and medallions to look at.

Campanile✦✦

Giotto was appointed architect of the cathedral in 1334 but he never got beyond building this tower and then only a third of it. He decorated it with octagonal pilasters and a colour scheme that would later be applied to the cathedral – white marble (Carrara), green marble (Prato) and red marble (Maremma). The reliefs were added over the next century by Andrea Pisano, Luca della Robbia and Donatello. They portray nothing less than the history of humanity, beginning with Adam, and illustrating human progress through crafts, the planets that influence human nature, the seven liberal arts that perfect it and the seven sacraments (originals are in the Museo del Duomo).

Opposite
Giotto's Campanile and the Duomo

Duomo Santa Maria del Fiore €

Piazza del Duomo; tel: 055 2302885. Open Mon–Wed and Fri 1000–1700, Thu 1000–1530, Sat 1000–1645 (1st Sat of every month 1000–1530), Sun 1330–1645.

Cupola del Duomo
Piazza del Duomo; tel: 055 2302885. Open Mon–Fri 0830–1900, Sat 0830–1740 (1st Sat of every month 0830–1600).

Giardino di Boboli €
Palazzo Pitti. Open daily Jun–Aug 0815–1930; Apr, May, Sept, Oct 0815–1830; Mar 0815–1730; Nov–Feb 0815–1630. Closed first/last Mon of month.

Museo dell'Opera del Duomo €€ Piazza Duomo 9; tel: 055 2302885. Open Mon–Sat 0900–1930, Sun 0900–1340. If you want to see the workshop that is now used to repair the Duomo, walk around the corner to Via dello Studio 23r.

Duomo Santa Maria del Fiore✦✦✦

When it was built, the Duomo was the largest church in the world – 53m long and 38m wide. Today, it is still the fourth largest cathedral in Europe. The overachieving medieval builder, Arnolfo di Cambio, began the Duomo in 1296 at the same time that he was busy with the Palazzo Vecchio and Santa Croce. Filippo Brunelleschi designed the dome (1420–34), the first of its size since the Pantheon in Rome. Climbing to the top of it is one of the most unforgettable experiences of a trip to Florence for its simultaneous views of the city's red-tiled rooftops and a plunging look into the marble canyon of the church interior.

Giardino di Boboli✦

Instead of a theme park or virtual reality, the 16th-century Medici rulers had this vast fantasy-filled garden to kill time in. The Florentine public didn't get its first peek until 200 years later. Avenues lined with cypresses intersect ensembles of Roman and Renaissance statues and stately cedars of Lebanon shade strange grottoes. Performances of Europe's first operas took place in its amphitheatre. Fountains are ubiquitous, from the fabulous Mannerist Oceanus to secluded, leering fauns that spit water into Roman sarcophagi.

The originals of Michelangelo's *Slaves* once decorated the Grotta del Buontalenti (left of the entrance) until the early 1900s. Copies have replaced them. Deeper inside, beneath the stalactites, is Giambologna's alarmingly endowed *Venus*. The steep climb up from the Pitti Palace to the top of the Boboli Gardens is rewarded with a cinematic view of Florence and the surrounding Tuscan countryside.

Museo dell'Opera Duomo✦✦✦

Without seeing this museum, you haven't really seen the monuments of Florence – many of the most impressive pieces of the Battistero, Duomo and Campanile are kept here to preserve them from pollution and vandalism. The 13th-century building behind the cathedral served as its workshop for centuries. This is where Michelangelo sculpted *David* during 1501–4.

Sculptures from the unfinished cathedral façade that was torn down in 1587 line the walls of the ground floor. Central among them is a Madonna (with the glass eyes) by Arnolfo di Cambio, the cathedral's architect. The 80-year-old Michelangelo sculpted the *Pietà* (1548–55) for his own tomb in Rome portraying himself in the figure of St Nicodemus – the old man in a cowl. Dissatisfied late one night, he fell into a rage and tried to smash it. This is the first recorded incident in history of an artist destroying his own work. Christ is scarred by the hammer blows and missing his left leg. Donatello is represented by the early, powerful sculptures of prophets Jeremiah and Habakkuk (1420) and a late Maria Magdalena in wood (1455). There are also pulpits by him and Luca della Robbia, the latter famous for its rows of

Galleria Palatina €€
*Palazzo Pitti, Piazza
Pitti; tel: 055 2388614.
Open Tue–Sun 0815–1850.*

*Other museums in Palazzo
Pitti open Tue–Sat
0815–1850, also 1st, 3rd
and 5th Sun, and 2nd and
4th Mon of every month
(same hours).*

Palazzo Vecchio €€
*Piazza della Signoria; tel:
055 2768465. Open daily
0900-1900 (closes Thu
1400).*

dancing children. The panels of the recently restored Doors of Paradise are on the ground floor.

Palazzo Pitti✦✦
The vast Pitti Palace was built at the edge of Florence by Luca Pitti and greatly expanded by Medici tyrant Cosimo I in his determination to put a little space between himself and liberty-loving Florentines who might try to get up close and personal. He ordered his court architect, Giorgio Vasari, to join the Palazzo to the Uffizi by way of a corridor over the Arno so he could sneak in and out of the Palazzo Vecchio (his former residence) and quickly escape across the river. His paranoid son, Ferdinand I, went a step further and built the Forte di Belvedere above the gardens of the palace – its cannons were aimed at Florence.

The palace contains no less than eight museums (mercifully, two are closed indefinitely), devoted to fashion, silver, coaches, and so on. The **Galleria Palatina✦✦** is one of Europe's great art museums. It has a brace of Caravaggios, 11 paintings by Raphael, 13 Titians and works by Rubens, Tintoretto and Giorgione, to say nothing of the gifted and possibly mad Rosso Fiorentino. Two signature works alone would more than justify a visit: Rubens's *The Consequences of War* and Raphael's *Portrait of a Lady*.

Palazzo Vecchio✦✦
The palace is still the City Hall of Florence. It was the work of Arnolfo di Cambio (1299–1314) but Michelozzo created the early Renaissance courtyard in 1453. Two centuries after its completion, Vasari decorated the walls with frescos, now badly faded, of Austrian cities to celebrate a wedding between the house of Medici and an Austrian princess. The clock, added in 1667, still ticks.

War damage

The Germans
dynamited all of
Florence's bridges
except the Ponte
Vecchio in 1944 (they
blew up houses at each
end instead).

Ponte Vecchio✦✦
One of Europe's most photographed structures, the 'old bridge' occupies a place used in Roman times as a crossing over the Arno for the *Via Cassia*. Today's bridge was built in 1345. Originally, there were butcher shops and tanners (who dumped their bloody scraps in the river). Ferdinand I wanted the bridge to be more upmarket, reserving its shops for jewellers and goldsmiths, and so it has remained.

Culture shock

Something strange happened to French novelist Stendahl one day in 1817 during a visit to the Uffizi. His heart raced and he began to sweat and tremble. Shortly afterwards, he broke down in tears. After 12-hour days of absorbing art and architecture, anyone could be susceptible to his affliction, now diagnosed as Stendahl Syndrome. In essence, it is a type of nervous breakdown brought on by an overdose of Renaissance culture. Florentine doctors and psychologists treat dozens of cases of *sindrome di Stendahl* each year.

Uffizi €€€ *Piazzale degli Uffizi 6; tel: 055 2388651. Open Tue–Sun 0815–1850; reservations Mon–Fri 0830–1830, tel: 055 294883, fax: 055 264406; www.uffizi.firenze.it.* Booking a ticket means you don't have to wait in line but it costs a little more. The present, extended, opening hours are experimental and subject to change.

Above
The Arno river façade of the Uffizi

Uffizi✦✦✦

Giorgio Vasari designed the Uffizi ('offices') for Medici ruler Cosimo I and his bureaucracy in the 16th century. Today, it is Italy's most popular museum (around 1.5 million visitors a year and growing) with 1000 works of art from the 13th to the 17th centuries displayed in 45 rooms. Its most famous icon, Botticelli's *Birth of Venus* (or 'Venus on the half shell') challenges the *Mona Lisa* for the status of world's most recognised painting.

Of all Italy's museums, the embarrassment of riches here is the most embarrassing. It inspired Mark Twain's stoic boast that he had wandered 'weary miles of picture galleries' in Florence. If your focus is the Renaissance, plan to spend the day in the first 15 rooms without forgetting, however, that the Uffizi is also one of Europe's great international collections, with major works by northern Europeans such as Dürer, Cranach, Brueghel and Rembrandt.

Accommodation and food

Many hoteliers will assure you that 'low season' does not exist in Florence. However, high season climbs even higher in April to June, September and October. Sometimes rates drop 25–50 per cent in winter but it all depends on the hotel. Regardless of the time of year, the city is always packed and people without reservations might have to choose between a night in the train station or the suburbs.

Hotel J and J €€€ *Via di Mezzo 20; tel: 055 2345005; fax: 055 240282; e-mail: jandjhotel@hotmail.com.* Few hotels even in Florence have such a beautiful setting: 19 rooms are located off the courtyard of a 16th-century convent and decorated with frescos, wrought-iron beds and fine hardwood furniture. The Duomo is just 500m away. Parking at a nearby garage.

Royal €€ *Via delle Ruote 52; tel: 055 483287; fax: 055 490976.* One of the more accessible hotels by car which is still central with traditional touches and comfortable rooms. You can drive here directly from the peripheral road between Fortezza da Basso and Piazza della Libertà. It has parking in its courtyard.

Hotel Orto dei Medici €€ *Via San Gallo 30; tel: 055 483427; fax: 055 461276; www.ortodeimedici.it.* Recently renovated family-run villa with balconies, a frescoed breakfast room and loggia. Breakfast is on a terrace looking out on the church of San Marco. Parking is available in garage around the corner.

Hotel Crocini € *Corso Italia 28; tel: 055 212905; fax: 055 210171; www.hotelcrocini.com.* Long established, the Crocini prides itself on being one of the last 'authentic' English-style pensions. It is solidly furnished and located in a quiet residential area. The rooms are spacious for Florence and there is a back garden and parking lot. A 10-minute walk from the centre of town.

Hotel Aprile €€ *Via della Scala 6; tel: 055 216237; fax: 055 280947; www.hotelaprile.it.* Eager management and well-appointed rooms in what was the 15th-century Palazzo dal Borgo. It is located near Piazza Santa Maria Novella, 300m away from the train station. The 28 rooms either overlook a garden or have double-glazed windows (ask for the former). Parking in nearby garage.

Villa La Massa €€€ *Candeli, on the Arno river 7km east of Florence; tel: 055 62611; fax: 055 633102; www.villalamassa.com.* Absolute luxury in a magnificent 17th-century Florentine villa, now flanked by tennis courts and a swimming pool, that used to be the residence of the noble Pecori Giraldi family. It lies in the Tuscan hills in an expansive park on the banks of the Arno. Ambitious new owners renovated it in 1998. It also has the ever-so-refined Il Verrocchio restaurant. A courtesy bus whisks guests in and out of Florence.

La Torricella € *Via Vecchia di Pozzolatico 25; tel: 055 2321808; fax: 055 2047402; e-mail: latorricella@tiscalinet.it.* Two-night minimum stay. A bed and breakfast in a villa on the outskirts of Florence, run by the attentive and friendly Manetti family. It is an easy drive from the Certosa exit of the A1 *autostrada*. There is public transportation to the city centre.

Below
Copy of Michelangelo's *David* in Piazza della Signoria

Cucina alla Fiorentina

Florentine cuisine is simplicity itself. *Crostini* are slices of toasted Tuscan bread with chicken-liver pâté, tomatoes or mushrooms, or just dipped in unspeakably good olive oil. Soup often takes preference over pasta: *ribollita* in winter and *pappa di pomodori* in summer. Florentines also like to eat hare, wild boar and pheasant. *Bistecca alla fiorentina* is simply a steak – of local Tuscan beef, from the Valdichiana – marinated in herbs, garlic and the finest olive oil, and cooked to perfection over wood coals. *Tortino di carciofi*, an artichoke omelette, and *funghi alla griglia* ('grilled mushrooms') are among the few things for a vegetarian. The more expensive restaurants sometimes have bargain lunch menus. In Florence, in particular, restaurants are likely to charge for *pane e coperto* ('cover') and sometimes for *servizio* (10 per cent). It will always be stated clearly on the menu.

Enoteca Pinchiorri €€€ *Via Ghibellina 51r; tel: 055 242777; www.enotecapinchiorri.com. Closed Sun, Mon and Tue.* Tuscan cuisine with a heavy French accent (explaining perhaps its two Michelin stars). The wine cellar ranks with any in Europe and inspires near-religious awe among connoisseurs.

La Pentola dell'Oro € *Via di Mezzo 24r; tel: 055 241808. Open evenings only, closed Sun and Aug.* Chef Giuseppe Alessi goes tradition one better by serving Renaissance-style dishes – *Piatti Rinascimentale* – and vegetarian meals.

Da Sergio € *Piazza San Lorenzo 8r; tel: 055 281941. Closed Sun and Aug.* Right off the Mercato Centrale. The menu is limited but impeccable. In addition to *bollito misto* ('stewed meats') there are lots of things *in umido* ('in broth'), such as cod, tripe and rabbit.

Mario € *Via Rosina 2r; tel: 055 218550. Closed Sun.* Lunch-only no-nonsense *trattoria* with generous quality and quantity price ratio, also near the Mercato Centrale. Come early, before it fills up with students.

Below
Eating out in Piazza della Signoria

Il Cibreo €€ *Via de'Macci 118r; tel: 055 2341100 (no reservations). Closed Sun and Mon, last week of Jul and Aug.* This *trattoria* is an annex to a more expensive restaurant next door. The food is truly outstanding at modest prices. However, it doesn't accept reservations and is always packed. The best tactic is to arrive early, say at 1930. *Anatra ripiena al forno* ('stuffed roast duck') is a speciality. One oddity – they don't do pasta.

Cantinetta del Verrazzano € *Via dei Tavolini 18r; tel: 055 268590. Closed Sun.* Very near the Duomo and an ideal place for a break. Excellent for a small meal – a *focaccia* or a sandwich made from *prosciutto di cinghiale* ('wild boar') or roasted *porcini* mushrooms washed down with a glass of wine or an espresso. Raspberry and honey *tortini* are luscious.

Suggested tour

P There are large car parks near the main train station (Fortezza da Basso) and the cheaper Piazza della Libertà (Parterre). The best chance of finding a space is in the Oltrarno – on the left side of the Arno. Study the signs carefully, making sure they are not for residents only (*ecetto residenti autorizatti*) and that street cleaners are not about to bear down on the spot. Don't park in or near the notorious (for break-ins) Piazzale Michelangelo. For more information, see www.firenzeparcheggi.it.

Below
The Ponte Vecchio

If Dante were alive today, he would surely add driving in Florence to the punishments of hell. You do not cruise in and out of this city; rather, you bite your lip and run the risk of killing someone (and later, as a pedestrian, of being killed). Most of the *Centro Storico* is *Zona Blu* ('blue zone'), meaning that only residents are allowed to park on the streets; cars parked illegally in this zone are towed away (and held for ransom; *tel: 055 308249*). Hotel guests have the dubious privilege of squeezing through an army of *vespas* and tourist hordes to unload their luggage in the centre; if the hotel has no parking, they must drive right back out again. One could debate the wisdom of spending one's holiday in search of a free parking place in Florence. A cheap and easy alternative for a day trip to Florence is to book a hotel in an outlying town and take the train.

Total distance: 2km.

Time: To see everything on this route would require at least three days; to do it in any less time might trigger the medical condition known as Stendahl Syndrome (*see Culture shock, page 47*). If you have only a day, skip the detours, climb the stairs of the **DUOMO**, walk the walk and, on the way, choose between the **UFFIZI** or **BARGELLO**.

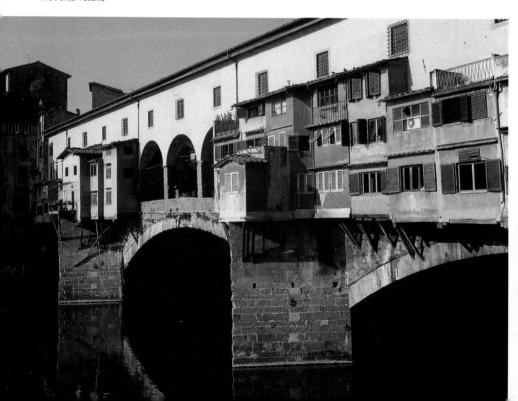

Florence profits from its past but remains a working city engaged in an astonishing range of crafts and trades, particularly shoes, handbags, textiles, nightgowns, bookbinding and art restoration. Most of the work is done in the Oltrarno (left bank of the Arno) in small shops, some the size of a cupboard.

Route: The Piazza del Duomo is the ancient, clotted heart of Florence, where the Roman roads once met. John Ruskin was already comparing it to a crowded bus station a century ago. Begin with a look at the **BATTISTERO** ❶ then visit the **DUOMO SANTA MARIA DEL FIORE** ❷ – to appreciate it fully, climb up the steps to the top of the dome. A second, even more dizzying view is possible over the edge of the **CAMPANILE** ❸.

Detour: On the north side of the Duomo, take the Via de'Martelli. After one short block, have a look at the **Palazzo Medici-Riccardi** ❺ and walk into its arcaded courtyard, one of the finest in Florence. This was the family home of the Medici until they moved to the Palazzo Vecchio in 1659. The Palazzo was designed in 1444 by Michelozzo and later much copied by upwardly mobile Florentine merchants. The marble medallions are copies of cameos from the legendary Medici collection.

San Lorenzo ❻ is just a stone's throw away down the Via de'Pucci. The unfinished façade hides one of the most perfectly proportioned buildings of the Renaissance: Filippo Brunelleschi rationalised every inch of the space divided between nave and chapels. The bronze reliefs on the pulpit are late masterpieces by Donatello who also decorated the Sagrestia Vecchia. The altar has an annunciation by Filippo Lippi. The entrance to the **Cappelle Medicee** ❼ is behind the church. Michelangelo designed the Sagrestia Nuova as a monumental tomb for the Medici family, achieving a sense of harmony between sculpture and architecture unknown in Western art since classical Greece.

Just a few paces further on is Florence's gastronomic paradise, the elegant 19th-century iron and glass **Mercato Centrale** ❽ (*Via dell'Ariento. Mon–Sat 0730–1300; Sat also 1600–2000*) – inspired by the market at Les Halles in Paris which no longer exists. It is the town's main market and one of the best places in Italy to buy food or eat lunch – try **Da Nerbone** in the market or **ZaZa** on the Piazza. Both will serve a roast suckling pig sandwich and a glass of Chianti. *Coniglio* or *verdure fritte* (fried rabbit or vegetables) are also classics; braver stomachs will want to try *trippa alla fiorentina* (tripe in tomato sauce) and the tender, almost eggy *lampredotto* (stewed cow's stomach) served in broth (*umido*) or as a sandwich (*panino*).

Walk around the cathedral past the newly restored **MUSEO DELL'OPERA DEL DUOMO** ❹ where you can see Ghiberti's original Doors of Paradise. Now enter **Via del Proconsolo**, still a pedestrian zone, though you will have to practise the art of dodging taxis and mopeds while craning your neck to see city towers. The **Palazzo Nonfinito** ❾ contains the Museo Nazionale di Antropologia e Ethnologia, the first anthropological museum in Italy and the only one in Florence (founded in 1869, *free admission*). The Romanesque cloister of **Badia Fiorentina** ❿ is a small oasis of peace in the middle of Florence. It was here, in the church, that Dante wistfully spied on Beatrice at Mass. The lanes around it are known as the 'Dante quarter'. Opposite the Badia is the grim façade and muscular tower of the **BARGELLO** ⑪. Cross the Piazza San Firenze, a stone canyon of rustication.

Detour: The narrow street of Borgo dei Greci leads into Piazza Santa Croce. You are now entering a neighbourhood where residents actually outnumber tourists and there is a feeling of community in its narrow streets. The largest Franciscan church in Italy, **Santa Croce** ⑫, was the work of Arnolfo di Cambio (but the façade is 19th century). It has been called the Westminster Abbey of Florence. Inside are masterpieces by artists from Giotto to Donatello, and tomb-spotters will quickly alight on Michelangelo, Machiavelli, Galileo and Rossini. Dante's exile finally ended after 500 years when a pompous memorial was built for him in 1863. Few people pay the price of admission to see the **Cappella dei Pazzi** (1430–46) next door, which is now part of a museum – the **Museo dell'Opera di Santa Croce**. It is arguably the most perfect of all the designs created by Filippo Brunelleschi, built according to the golden mean (the principle behind the acropolis in Athens). Brunelleschi was also responsible for the cloister.

Walk right into the imposing Piazza della Signoria and along to the **PALAZZO VECCHIO** ⑬. This was the scene of the Bonfire of the Vanities, when Savonarola convinced Florentines to burn their carnival costumes and licentious paintings only a few short months before they subjected him to the same treatment (after he was declared a heretic). Beneath the three graceful arches of the **Loggia dei Lanzi** ⑭ is a most remarkable open-air ensemble – Roman, Renaissance, Mannerist and 19th-century sculpture. Most of the figures are engaged in fighting, rape or decapitation. The name 'dei Lanzi' refers to the Swiss mercenaries of Cosimo I who stood on guard here. The **UFFIZI** ⑮ stands at the south end of the square. Follow its length (and the waiting line of tourists) to the **PONTE VECCHIO** ⑯. The bridge is officially monopolised by goldsmiths though most people are taking pictures or snogging or both. Across the bridge, it is just one block further to the **PALAZZO PITTI** ⑰. The **GIARDINO DI BOBOLI** ⑱ is behind the palace. From here, buses 36 and 37 return to the central train station.

Also worth exploring

There are sweeping views of Florence and the Arno valley from **Fiésole**, 8km outside the city. It is a refreshing break from congested streets and crowded museums. Fiésole was an Etruscan town and later a medieval rival to Florence until the Florentines destroyed it (on a flimsy pretext) in 1125. The Duomo San Romolo remains, as well as ruined Etruscan walls and an evocative Roman theatre.

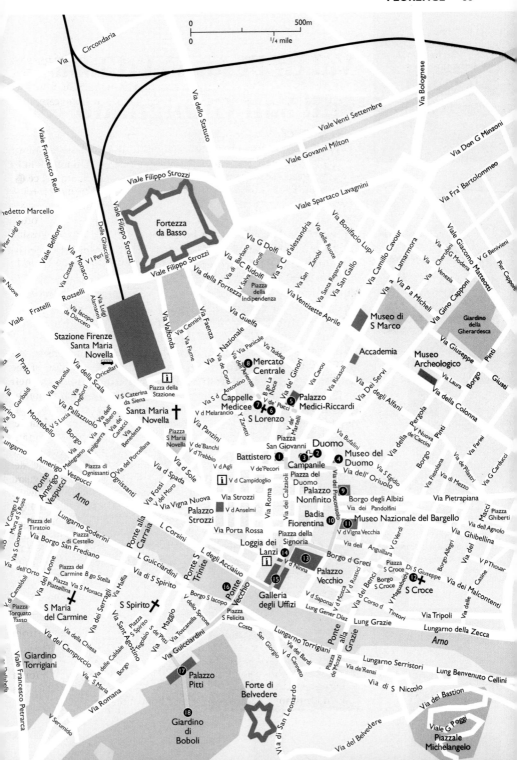

FLORENCE 55

Circondaria

Via

Viale Francesco Redi

Viale Filippo Strozzi

Viale Venti Settembre

Viale Giovanni Milton

Via dello Statuto

Viale Spartaco Lavagnini

Via Bolognese

Via Don G Minzoni

Via Fra' Bartolommeo

Viale Giacomo Matteotti

Via G Benivieni
Via G Benivieni

Pier Capponi

Fortezza
da Basso

Viale Filippo Strozzi

Via G Dolfi

Via C Ridolfi

Via S C d'alessandria

Via delle Ruote

Via San Zanobi

Via Bonifacio Lupi

Via Camillo Cavour

Lamarmora

Via a
Via P A Micheli

Cherubini
G Modena

Via Venezia

Piazza
della
Indipendenza

Via della Fortezza

Via San Gallo

Via Santa Reparata

Via Ventisette Aprile

Museo di
S Marco

Via Gino Capponi

Giardino
della
Gherardesca

Stazione Firenze
Santa Maria
Novella

Via Nazionale

Via Guelfa

Via Faenza

Via Cennini

Via Fiume

Via del Ariento

Via de' Conti

Accademia

Museo
Archeologico

Via Giuseppe

Pinti

Borgo

Giusti

8 Mercato
Centrale

Via de' Ginori

Via Cavour

Via Ricasoli

Via Del Servi

Via Laura

Via della Colonna

V S Caterina
da Siena

Piazza della
Stazione

Santa Maria
Novella

Cappelle
Medicee

7 **5**
6

S Lorenzo

Bgo La Noce

Palazzo
Medici-Riccardi

Via degli Alfani

Pergola

Via Nuova
Pinti

Via della de'Caccini

Via Farini

Piazza
San Giovanni

Via Martelli

Via Panzani

Piazza
S Maria
Novella

Battistero **1**

Campanile **3** **2**

Duomo

Museo del
Duomo **4**

Via Bufalini

Via S Egidio

Borgo

Via Fiesolana

Via di Mezzo

Via de' Pilastri

Via G Carducci

Palazzo
Strozzi

Via Strozzi

Via Roma

Piazza del
Duomo

Via dell' Oriuolo

Via Pietrapiana

Piazza
Ghiberti

Via dell'Agnolo

Ghibellina

Palazzo
Nonfinito **9**

Borgo degli Albizi

Via dei Pandolfini

Ponte
Amerigo
Vespucci

Arno

Lungarno Soderini

Palazzo
Strozzi

Via Porta Rossa

Badia
Fiorentina **10**

11

Museo Nazionale del Bargello

V d'Vigna Vecchia

Via dell' Anguillara

Loggia dei
Lanzi **14**

Piazza della
Signoria

13

Borgo d Greci

Palazzo
Vecchio

Via del Benci

S Croce **12**

S Croce

Via dei Malcontenti

Ponte
alla
Carraia

Ponte
S Trinite

Ponte
Vecchio **16**

15

Galleria
degli Uffizi

Lung Gener Diaz

Lungarno Torrigiani

Ponte
alla
Grazie

Lungarno della Zecca

Arno

Lung Benvenuto Cellini

S Maria
del Carmine

S Spirito

Giardino
Torrigiani

17 Palazzo
Pitti

Forte di
Belvedere

18 Giardino
di
Boboli

Viale G Poggi

Piazzale
Michelangelo

0   500m
0   ¼ mile

Val di Pesa, Val d'Elsa and San Gimignano

Ratings

Architecture	●●●●●
Art	●●●●○
History	●●●●○
Scenery	●●●●○
Vineyards	●●●●○
Museums	●●●○○
Shopping	●●●○○
Nature	●●○○○

The resourceful Romans built a road – the *Via Cassia* – through the valley of the Elsa river. The same road, with potholes and detours, became the Via Francigena in the Middle Ages and a war zone between Florence and Siena. The region has a series of major towns, from unprepossessing Poggibonsi to charming Certaldo. The side roads are a different story. They offer scenery to rival neighbouring Chianti, but without tourists. The ridge road leading to Montespertoli cruises a landscape that, from a distance, would have looked scarcely different during the Renaissance. The final destination is San Gimignano, almost as famous for its skyline as New York. The flood of tourists does nothing to diminish its fascination. They just make it hard to find parking.

BARBERINO VAL D'ELSA✧

ⓘ Pieve Sant'Appiano
€ Inside is a fine 12th-century relief of Archangel Michael and the dragon, which once decorated the portal.

Above
Certaldo

Right
Barberino Val d'Elsa city gate

Enter the medieval part of this town through the city gate of Porta Fiorentina from the north or Porta Romana from the south. The Piazza Barberini is a fine medieval ensemble of the Palazzo Pretorio and Romanesque Pieve San Bartolomeo. A small Museo Civico occupies a former hospice for pilgrims. However, the real artistic highlight is a couple of kilometres southwest: the **Pieve Sant'Appiano✧** is one of the oldest (10th-century) parish churches in the region. A ruined baptistry attests to its former importance.

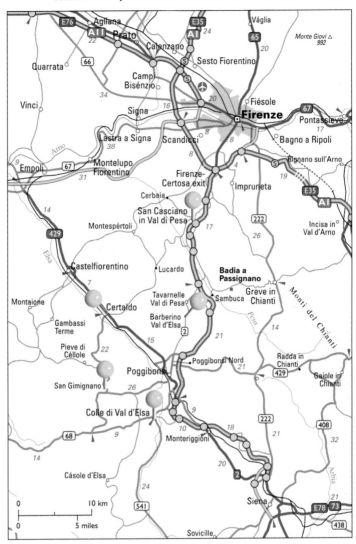

CERTALDO◆

❶ Pro Loco *Via Boccaccio 16; tel: 0571 652730.*

ⓘ Palazzo Pretorio € *Piazza del Vicariato, Certaldo Alto; tel: 0571 61219. Open daily 1000–1230, 1630–1930 (1000–1230, 1500–1800 in winter).*

The upper part of the city – Certaldo Alto – is a complete medieval town still fully encircled by its defensive walls with a magnificent view of San Gimignano from the Porta Rivellino. In the **Palazzo Pretorio**◆, built at the end of the 12th century by the counts Alberti, are a lavishly painted Sala delle Udienze and a 1490 fresco attributed to Benozzo Gozzoli that tells the story of Doubting Thomas, sticking his finger into Christ's bleeding midriff. Look for the strange *Tabernacle of the Executed* in the chapel, located near the former prison cells.

Casa del Boccaccio
€ *Via Boccaccio 18, Certaldo Alto; tel: 0571 664208. Open daily, 1030–1230, 1530–1830.*

Giovanni Boccaccio, the greatest medieval Italian writer after Dante, was born here in 1313 and lived here for the last 12 years of his life. By then he had renounced women and literature for prayer and philosophy. 'I have returned to Certaldo,' he wrote, 'and here I have begun to find consolation for my life; and to taste and feel eternal happiness.' An Allied bomb all but destroyed the **Casa del Boccaccio**✧, the house where the poet was born, in 1944. However, it has been meticulously rebuilt. His simple marble tombstone is buried in the centre aisle of the Chiesa Santi Jacopo e Filippo next door. Modern Italian writers come here occasionally, kneel down and discreetly kiss his feet.

COLLE DI VAL D'ELSA✧

Pro Loco *Via Campana 18 (Colle Alto); tel: 0577 921334; www.comune.collevaldelsa.it. Open Mon–Sat 0640–2010, Sun 0800–2010*

Museo Archeologico € *Piazza del Duomo 42; tel 0577 920490. Open May–Sept Tue–Fri 1000–1200, 1700–1900, Sat and Sun 1000–1200, 1600–1900; Oct–Apr Tue–Fri 1530–1730, Sat and Sun 1000–1200, 1500–1800.*

Colle di Val d'Elsa produces excellent glass and crystal ware. There is a glass workshop in the Vicolo della Fontanella (off Piazza Santa Caterina).

Colle is a medieval town of arcaded passageways that seem to swallow up residents and tourists alike. The brooding, monumental Porta Nuova, or Porta Salis, dominates the upper part of Colle. Designed by Giuliano da Sangallo, it is an imposing example of Renaissance architecture, built after a siege in 1479, and is flanked by two cylindrical towers with Guelph battlements.

The Duomo of Colle di Val d'Elsa is adjacent to the Palazzo Pretorio, seat of the well-organised **Museo Archeologico**✧ (lots of Etruscan urns) that occupies a former medieval prison. The Duomo itself is baroque, with a 19th-century façade by neo-classical architect Agostino Fantastici. Inside are two precious works of art – the marble pulpit, decorated with bas-reliefs attributed to Giovanni da Maiano (architect of Siena's cathedral) located in the nave; and a bronze Crucifix above the high altar thought to be by Giambologna. The Via delle Volte is a tunnel 100m long which can be reached by a path branching off from Piazza del Duomo. Locally made blown-glass lampshades arranged in a succession of colours softly illuminate its gloom.

The Torre di Arnolfo (*Via del Castello 63*) is, according to tradition, the birthplace of Arnolfo di Cambio, the great Tuscan architect who built the Palazzo Vecchio, Duomo and Santa Croce in Florence. Colle Basso, the lower district, is a 19th-century town with many small workshops and a few modern factories, the sort of place that provides most modern Tuscans with a living.

Above
Colle di Val d'Elsa

SAN CASCIANO❖

Museo di Arte Sacra € *Via Roma 31; tel: 055 8229444. Open May–Sept Sat 1700–1930 (holidays 1000–1200, 1630–1900); Oct–Apr Sat 1630–1900 (holidays 1000–1230, 1600–1900), or by appointment.*

Sant'Andrea a Percussina marks the beginning of the Chianti Classico region (*see page 66*). An office of the Chianti Classico Consorzio 2000 is located across the street from the Machiavelli Inn and Museum. It provides detailed maps showing the location of over 600 Chianti wine estates.

Below
Pressing mats used to produce olive oil

Although mostly a 19th-century town, San Casciano has some remarkable works of art from its medieval days. The 1304 **Santa Maria sul Prato**❖ is one of the most interesting churches in the region and possesses a Crucifixion by Simone Martini, part of a triptych by Ugolino di Nerio and a marble chancel by Giovanni di Balducci da Pisa. The **Museo di Arte Sacra**❖ displays religious art from a church destroyed in the Second World War. An early work by Ambrogio Lorenzetti takes pride of place alongside an enormous candelabra that was created for Sant'Antimo (*see page 92*) by a French Cistercian monk.

Machiavelli wrote *The Prince* (as well as a series of pornographic farces) while living in exile in the village of **Sant'Andrea a Percussina**❖, 2km to the north of here. The inn where he lived is still an inn and now bears his name; there is a tiny museum next door only open when the restaurateurs/owners are not making pasta.

San Casciano is known for olive oil rather than wine but the grapes that grow between San Casciano and Mercatale (5km southeast) go towards making two of the most expensive wines in Italy – the so-called 'super-Tuscans' Tignanello (80 per cent Sangiovese, 20 per cent Cabernet) and Solaia (100 per cent Cabernet). The Marchese Antinori, descended from a family of medieval silk merchants, developed them between 1971 and 1979. The family was the first large Chianti producer to depart from the 19th-century Chianti 'formula' (*see page 70*) and launch a completely new wine.

SAN GIMIGNANO✦✦

ℹ **Pro Loco** *Piazza Duomo 1; tel: 0577 940008, fax: 0577 940903; e-mail: prolocsg@tin.it; www.sangimignano.com. Open Mar–Oct 0900–1300, 1500–1900; Nov–Feb 0900–1300, 1400–1800.* A *Biglietto Cumulativo* offers admission to all museums for a single price.

🏛 **Museo Civico e Pinacoteca** €€ *Palazzo del Popolo, Piazza del Duomo. Open Mar–Oct, 0930–1920; Nov–Feb 1000–1750.*

Torre Grossa €€ *Palazzo del Popolo, Piazza del Duomo. Open Mar–Oct, same hours as Museo Civico.*

🍴 **Buca di Montaiuto** *Via San Giovanni 16; tel: 0577 940407.* Picnic supplies include salami from *cinghiale* ('wild boar').

A town of some 8000 inhabitants, San Gimignano is flooded by eight million visitors a year. During the Middle Ages, San Gimignano was an important stop on the Via Francigena, the route take by pilgrims on their way to Rome. It also made a killing in saffron. The plague of 1348 decimated the population and, in 1353, its town council agreed by a majority of one to a Florentine take-over. Its local history involved the usual suspects – Guelphs and Ghibellines – engaged in conspiracy and murder. In those days, Tuscan towns bristled with towers from every *palazzo* – 72 in the case of San Gimignano within the space of a couple of hundred square metres. In places such as Florence, towers were eventually circumcised by city ordinances against private warfare. In San Gimignano, by contrast, many of the original towers remain.

Culturally speaking, the town justly calls itself a 'museum of Tuscan art and architecture'. Too small to develop a local style, San Gimignano imported leading artists from Florence and Siena instead. The **Palazzo del Popolo✦** (town hall) houses the **Museo Civico e Pinacoteca✦** with 13th–16th-century works from Florentine and Sienese schools and offers access to the **Torre Grossa✦**, the only one of

Right
San Gimignano

Collegiata Santa Maria Assunta (and Cappella di Santa Fina) € *Piazza del Duomo. Open Mar–Oct Mon–Fri 0930–1930, Sat 0930–1700, Sun 1300–1700; Nov–mid-Jan Mon–Sat 0930–1700, Sun 1300–1700; mid-Jan–Feb for religious services only.*

Degli Srumenti di Tortura €€ *Museo Criminale Medioevale, Via Castello 1/3; tel: 0577 942243. Open daily mid-Mar–mid-Jul 1000–1900; mid-Jul–mid-Sept 1000–2400; mid-Sept–Oct 1000–2000; Nov–mid-Mar Mon–Fri 1000–1800, Sat–Sun 1000–1900.* Claiming to be the 'most disturbing exhibition in the world' this museum does offer a convincing anthology of human cruelty.

San Gimignano's towers that you can climb. The 12th-century Duomo was modified by Giuliano da Maiano. The **Collegiata Santa Maria Assunta**, though plain on the outside, conceals a majestic interior that is a revelation of fresco painting. The inner wall of the façade displays the *Martyrdom of St Sebastian* (1465) by Benozzo Gozzoli. Above it is the *Last Judgement* by Taddeo di Bartolo. The medieval equivalent of a snuff movie, it stars devils with green snake penises that rape, sodomise and disembowel the damned. In the **Cappella di Santa Fina***, frescos by Renaissance painter Ghirlandaio depict a woman – Santa Fina, San Gimignano's patron saint – being gnawed by rats. Her finely carved sarcophagus is also in the chapel. In the fresco on the left, Ghirlandaio includes a portrait of himself standing behind a bishop during Mass.

Most tourists tend to overlook the church of Sant'Agostino at the north end of town. Behind its equally plain Romanesque-Gothic façade is a magnificent collection of art, particularly the vivid fresco cycle about the life of St Augustine by Benozzo Gozzoli (in the apse). There is also a marble altar sculpted by Benedetto da Maiano in the chapel of St Bartolo and two St Sebastians by Benozzo Gozzoli from 1464, one with, and more unusually, one without, arrows. Praying to St Sebastian (or commissioning pictures of him) was the 14th-century idea of treating a plague epidemic. The second painting was executed in a year when the plague didn't reach the city.

Vernaccia di San Gimignano

Vernaccia is a type of grape, not a brand of wine. The word translates roughly as 'belonging here' and it has been cultivated around San Gimignano since the 13th century. The English began drinking it in the 16th century. There are two contrasting types of wine made from the same grape: a mass-marketed, crisp and colourless drink, almost neutral in flavour that seems ubiquitous at summer parties; and the straw-coloured vintage with a rich flavour that was one of Michelangelo's favourite wines. San Gimignano producers also make lots of Chianti Colli Senesi, which tastes much like Chianti though is rarely as good and never as expensive.

What to drink

Teruzzi & Puthold/Ponte a Rondolino *Ponte a Rondolino, northeast of Casale; tel: 0577 940143.* Outstanding oaked Vernaccia, *Terre di Tufia,* and a good Sangiovese.

Giovanni Panizzi *southeast of San Gimignano near Santa Margherita between San Gimignano and Racciano; tel: 0577 941576.* This local hero of Vernaccia tradition produces exceptional Vernaccia Riserva and Chianti Colli Senesi.

Montenidoli *southeast of San Gimignano; tel: 0577 941565.* Elisabetta Fagiuoli produces several interesting wines: *Fiore* (made with soft-pressed grapes), *Tradizionale* (macerated before fermentation) and barrel-aged *Carato. Sono Montenidoli* is a blend based on Sangiovese.

Simple fare

The food in this region is an easy-going variant on simple Tuscan cuisine rejoicing in dishes such as *penne strasciate* (macaroni tossed in sauce over high heat), watercress soup and delicately fried chicken. The Lucardo cheeses have been famous since the 13th century.

Accommodation and food

Osteria del Vicario €€€ *Via Rivellino 3, Certaldo; tel: 0571 668228; www.osteriadelvicario.it.* Built on the site of a 13th-century vicarage with a delightful terrace that has views far and wide. There are five rooms in the main building (best) and six in an annex down the road.

Il Paretaio €€ *San Filippo, Barberino Val d'Elsa; tel: 055 8059218; Cellphone: 0338 7379626; fax: 055 8059231; e-mail: ilparetaio@tin.it.* A Tuscan ranch that rents six rooms with private bathrooms to overnight guests. Ideal for anyone who likes horseback riding and rustic living.

Hotel L'Antico Pozzo €€€ *Via San Matteo 87, San Gimignano; tel: 0577 942014; fax: 0577 942117; www.anticopozzo.com.* Elegant and intimate hotel with exquisite period furnishings.

La Cisterna €€ *Piazza della Cisterna 24, San Gimignano; tel: 0577 940328.* Former cloister with 17th-century Florentine furniture and fabulous views from (some) rooms of the city and countryside.

Osteria Delle Catene €€ *Via Mainardi 18, San Gimignano; tel; 0577 941966, closed Wed.* Before tourism, saffron was San Gimignano's main source of wealth and it finds its way into many recipes of this

Below
The walled city of Certaldo

small *trattoria* – *zuppa medioevale, lingua in salsa allo zafferano* (tongue in saffron sauce) and a flat bread called *torta di farro e zafferano*. The *nana col cavolo nero* (duck with black cabbage) or *coniglio alla Vernaccia* (rabbit in white wine sauce) are just fine without saffron.

Il Frantoio €€ *Via Matteotti 33, Marcialla (near Lucardo); tel: 055 8074244. Closed Mon; also Tue and lunch in winter, last three weeks of Jan and two weeks in July and Aug.* Impeccable food served, most of the year, in a garden. From homemade *pasta alla puttanesca* and *gnocchi di patate* ('potatoes') to a signature *fritto misto* (lightly breaded and fried meat and vegetables).

C'era Una Volta €€ *Via Certaldese 11, Lucardo; tel: 0571 669162. On the road between Montespertoli and Certaldo. Closed Tue; also mid-Jan–mid-Feb.* A country *trattoria* with a view and food 'like it used to be': starters such as *pappardelle al sugo di coniglio* ('noodles with rabbit sauce') and *tagliatelle ai porcini* give way grudgingly to main courses such as a *frittura* of chicken, rabbit and vegetables. It is as good a place as any in the area for a *bistecca fiorentina* (one is enough for two people). Even the house wine is a full-bodied Chianti C'era Una Volta.

Suggested tour

Total distance: 142km; detours add 9km and 15km (both return).

Time: Two to three days at a leisurely pace. If you only have a day, concentrate on San Gimignano while still taking time to enjoy the scenery along the way.

Links: This route has the same starting point as that in Chianti Classico (*see page 72*) and runs parallel to it for some distance. You can cross over from Poggibonsi on the serpentine N429 driving east to Castellina in Chianti (and the N222). Volterra is 36km west from Colle di Val d'Elsa (on N68) (*see page 162*).

Route: The easiest way to begin this route is to leave **Florence ❶** (or circumnavigate it) via the *autostrada*, exiting at Firenze-Certosa; at the roundabout, take the *Via Cassia* in the direction of **SAN CASCIANO ❷**. From San Casciano, follow the road for Cerbaia. What follows is a succession of ridge roads, each one more captivating than the last. From Cerbaia, turn left (southwest) to **Montespértoli**, known for its wine fair, the *Mostra del Chianti* (*last Sun in May to first Sun in June*). Press on southeast part of the way towards Tavernelle. At the hamlet of **Lucardo**, follow the road south to **CERTALDO ❸**, park in the lower town and walk, or take the funicular, up to Certaldo Alto, the historic part of the city – little changed since Boccaccio lived there in the 14th century. The road out of town is clearly signposted for **SAN GIMIGNANO ❺**.

Detour: Few churches have a more poetic setting than **Pieve di Céllole** ❹, nestled in a hilltop cypress grove off the road to San Gimignano. It was the inspiration of Puccini's opera, *Suor Angelica*. A simple Romanesque building (1193–1238), it is nevertheless striking for the quality of its medieval workmanship.

Leaving San Gimignano, follow the signs for Volterra. The road runs parallel to the Riserva Naturale Castelvecchio, past a prison and ends in a T-crossing at Castel San Gimignano. Turn left (east) on the N68. An uneventful road, graced by several rows of birch trees, sneaks up on **COLLE DI VAL D'ELSA** ❻. Below the town, it drops to the Elsa river and lands you in industrial **Poggibonsi** ❼. During the Middle Ages, it was a *città imperiale* – a Ghibelline city – of some importance until one day in 1270 its Guelph neighbours (Florence, San Gimignano and Col d'Elsa) joined forces and annihilated it. If you penetrate that far, there are a couple of fine medieval buildings in its nucleus. Otherwise, follow the signs for the *autostrada* (but don't get on it) and Florence. You will find yourself on the Roman *Via Cassia* again (N2). **BARBERINO VAL D'ELSA** ❽ is on this ancient road, at the top of a ridge. **Tavarnelle** ❾ was another important stop on the Roman *Via Cassia* and its medieval successor but most of the houses you see today are from the 18th and 19th centuries. The Santa Lucia al Borghetto was once part of a Franciscan convent.

Below
San Gimignano's Piazza della Cisterna

Detour: Follow the signs for San Donato and take the turn for Sambuca. Just half a kilometre north, the **Badia a Passignano** ❿ is clearly marked. The first glimpse – 2km up a farm road – is dramatic. It would be hard to find a more picturesque and solitary corner of Chianti than the hilltop it occupies. The monastery was once one of the most important in Italy, having been founded by Benedictines in the 11th century. The 13th-century church has been done over in baroque style but the refectory still has a Renaissance treasure – Domenico Ghirlandaio's *Last Supper* (*unfortunately only open to visitors on Sun 1600–1800 in summer and 1500–1700 in winter, or by prior arrangement, tel: 055 8071622; www.passignano.org*). The monastery has an excellent wine estate, Poggio al Sole, that makes an intense Chianti Classico.

Continue north on the N2 and return to Florence.

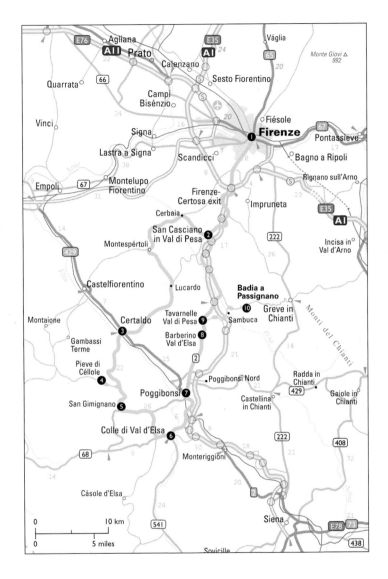

Also worth exploring

The Sienese built the fortified town of **Monteriggioni** in 1213–19 along the northern boundary of their territory in the spirit of 'good walls make good neighbours' – 570m of wall topped by 16 towers that Dante compared to 'ugly giants'.

Chianti Classico

Ratings

Scenery	●●●●●
Vineyards	●●●●●
Food and drink	●●●●○
Villas	●●●●○
Architecture	●●●○○
Nature	●●●○○
Shopping	●●●○○
Museums	●○○○○

The region between Florence and Siena is Chianti – or Chianti 'Classico' as it now calls itself, because neighbouring wine regions tend to borrow its famous name. The Chianti hills form a spine supporting a succession of steep valleys. The Chiantigiana road (N222) links them, rising and plunging through groves of silver-grey olive trees, swathes of precisely angled vines, brown chestnut woods and ridges marked by dark cypresses. Most of the castles and villas are secluded and Chianti feels surprisingly empty. Its past was so violent that no one dared to build a city. Florentine and Sienese artists, however, created a blissful mythic Chianti in some of the world's first landscape paintings and its legendary wine completed an identification with the good things in life – Chiantishire to the British. *Altro luogo come il Chianti no c'è* is what Italians say – 'there is no other place like it'.

CASTELLINA IN CHIANTI*

Bottega del Vino Gallo Nero *Via della Rocca 10. An outlet for the town's wine co-operative with a serious selection of local producers.*

The liveliest and most simpatico town on the N222 (if you can forgive it for having a fertiliser factory at one end). Furthermore, it has a worthwhile *Centro Storico* up its sleeve. From the long covered street of Via delle Volte, once part of its ramparts, you have a wide view of the green hills that surround it.

GREVE IN CHIANTI*

Viale G. da Verrazzano 59; tel: 055 8546287; fax 055 8544149; www.greve-in-chianti.com. Open Mon–Sat 0930–1330, 1530–1930; shorter hours in winter.

Greve's main square is the triangular Piazza Matteotti. In the middle stands a dramatic bronze of explorer Giovanni da Verrazzano. In many respects a more able explorer than Christopher Columbus, he explored the actual mainland of North America, Brazil and the mouth of Hudson Bay (New York, at least, honours his memory with a

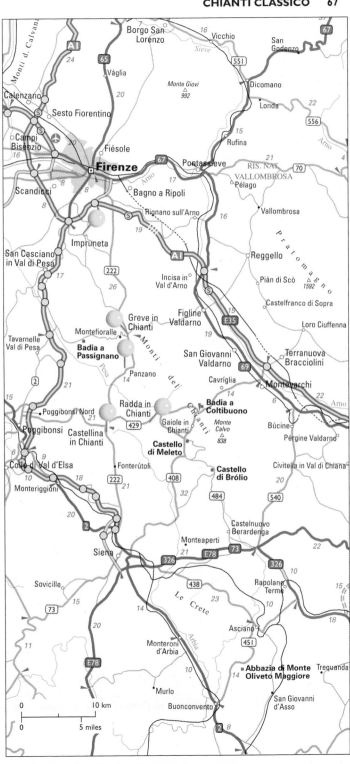

Castello di Verrazzano € *Tel: 055 854243; www.verrazzano.com. Open Mon–Fri 1100–1500 (reservations necessary).*

Castello di Uzzano €
Tel: 055 8544851; e-mail: uzzano@val.it. Call ahead for an appointment.

Villa Vignamaggio €€ *Via Petriolo 5. To visit the villa and wine estate, you must call ahead. Tel: 055 854661; www.vignamaggio.com*

Antica Macelleria Falorni *under the arcades of the Piazza Matteotti, 69–71; www.falorni.it. If there is a salami shop in heaven, this is what it looks like. It has ham cured in every way known to man, wild boar salami, finocchiona (fennel salami), pancetta ten different ways and prosciutto from a local species of pig, the brada senesi (they look like a black-faced Babe with white stripes).*

Enoteca del Chianti Classico *Piazzetta Santa Croce 8. A compendious selection of Chianti wines as well as other local products such as Vin Santo and olive oil.*

La Cantinetta di Greve in Chianti *Viale le Veneto across from the Coop supermarket. This narrow little wine shop carries quality wines from Chianti's smaller producers at prices that undercut better-known labels. Ask the owner for consiglio (advice) and you won't be sorry. It also has reasonably priced olive oil.*

Verrazzano bridge between Staten Island and Brooklyn). An impressive *Sagra dell'Uva* ('grape festival') takes place here in September.

The area's real attractions are the castles and villas in the surrounding hills: the **Castello di Verrazzano**✴ wine estate, which belonged to the famous navigator, is just north of nearby Greti. He might well have asked himself why he ever left this idyllic home as he watched cannibals prepare to slaughter and eat him in 1528 somewhere in the lower Antilles. The medieval **Castello di Uzzano**✴ was converted with ineffable skill into a Renaissance pleasure villa by the 16th-century architect Andrea Orcagna. It is also a fine wine estate and ideal for an afternoon picnic beneath ancient cedars, followed by a romp through the garden's green maze. Some 6km south of Greve and 390m high, **Villa Vignamaggio**✴ is one of the most romantic spots in Chianti. Its charm was nearly milked dry by ex-luvvies Kenneth Branagh and Emma Thompson in the film version of *Much Ado about Nothing*. It is certainly possible that it was in this villa that Lisa Gherardini stood for her portrait in 1503. The result was *La Gioconda* – the Mona Lisa.

IMPRUNETA✦

ℹ️ Pro Loco Via Mazzini 1;
tel: 055 2313729;
www.impruneta.com.

☕ The tourist office has a list of local terracotta workshops. Many of them are located along the Via Cappello such as **Mario Mariani** (No 29; tel: 055 2011950).

A working town that has been synonymous with terracotta for centuries, Impruneta was the place where Brunelleschi shopped for tiles for the dome of the cathedral in Florence. The local clay also went into the terracotta tabernacle for the Chapel of the Cross created by Michelozzo for **Santa Maria dell'Impruneta✦**. Lucca della Robbia sculpted the terracotta statues of SS Paul and Luke for the church's Chapel of the Madonna. Impruneta is also known for straw hats and an annual horse and mule fair in October.

PANZANO✦

🍷 **Enoteca del Chianti Classico** Via Giovanni da Verrazzano 8-10; tel: 055 852003. A tiny wine shop absolutely stuffed with Chianti's finest.

Bottega Carlo Fagiani Via Giovanni di Verrazzano 17; tel: 055 852239; www.carlofagiani.com. A wizard in leather who produces chic leather goods, handbags, clothing and shoes made to order.

A friendly fortified town high on a 500m hill next to the ruins of a 1260 castle. You can still see its remains behind the Chiesa Santa Maria after climbing up the village street – Via Verrazzano. On the second weekend in September, it is Panzano's turn to host a big wine festival. Panzano is the epicentre of a wine region known as *Conca d'Oro* that produces some of Chianti's best wines.

RADDA IN CHIANTI✦

ℹ️ **Pro Loco** Piazza Ferrucci 1; tel: 0577 738494; e-mail: proradda@chiantinet.it; www.chiantinet.it. Open daily 1000–1300, 1530–1900; mornings only on Sun and in winter.

Tiny, picture-perfect Radda, straddling a ridge between the Pesa and Arbia valleys in the wooded Monti del Chianti, was the capital of the *Lega del Chianti* in 1475. The League also included Castellina and Gaiole. It still has an impressive Palazzo del Podestà, a ruined castle, walls and two towers. Today, it caters to wine tourists with places to taste and buy excellent local wines such as *Vignale* (*Piazza XX Settembre 23* in the hotel of the same name) and *Vigna Vecchia* (*Sdrucciolo di Piazza*). The famous Sangiovese wine, *Le Pergole Torte*, is made by winemaker Signore Sergio Manetti in Monte Vertine, a small fortified village 3km north of Radda (*tel: 0577 738009; fax 0577 738265*). The estate's wine, grappa and olive oil all sell out fast. The castle-village of **Volpaia✦** (another 3km north) is even more perfect than Radda and boasts an even better wine – *Castello di Volpaia*.

Accommodation and food

Volpaia *Tel: 0577 738066; www.volpaia.com.* The unlikely setting for modern art exhibitions, mounted in September in the early Renaissance Commenda di San Eufrosino, a former pilgrim hospice.

There is almost no industry, light or otherwise, in Chianti Classico. Some traditional crafts are still going strong: the production of terracotta, utensils in olive wood, woven wicker baskets, wrought iron and blown glass for wine-flasks and demi-johns.

The area known as Chianti Classico has no major towns to speak of (Greve in Chianti hardly qualifies). There is a lot of *agriturismo* with a range of accommodation though much of it is at the luxury end of the spectrum. Towns along the *Via Cassia* such as Colle Val d'Elsa have more options and a wider range of prices.

Il Cenobio €€€ *Via Petriolo 5, Greve in Chianti; tel: 0558 54661; fax 0558 544468; www.vignamaggio.com.* Sumptuous apartments in Mona Lisa's villa. Mod cons include a swimming pool, tennis courts and fitness room.

Casa La Mura € *2km south of Panzano; tel/fax: 055 852138.* The gracious and warm-hearted Ciapini family rents several well-equipped apartments among their olive groves. They are available by the night when it is not high season.

Chianti cuisine is based on 'poor' but savoury dishes: *ribollita* (a 'twice-cooked' vegetable and bread soup), minestrone, grilled meats, tripe and fried zucchini flowers and the famous *cantucci* biscuits accompanied by the dessert wine, Vin Santo.

Nerbone € *Piazza Matteotti Giacomo 22, Greve in Chianti; tel: 055 853308.* A small place with slow service where workers and tourists rub elbows over Tuscan comfort food: soup, sausages, stews and *lampredotto* (stewed cow's stomach).

Badia a Coltibuono €€ *across from the abbey, Gaiole in Chianti; tel: 0577 749424; www.coltibuono.com. Closed Mon.* Gourmet food cooked the Luisa de Medici way and served, in summer, on the leafy terrace of this former monastery.

Opposite
Badia a Coltibuono

Carloni € *Via G Pucini 24, Gaiole; tel: 0577 749549. Closed Wed.* Simple restaurant on the outskirts of Gaiole. Great local food and wine.

Chianti

The Latin poet Fluvio Testi said that Tuscan wine 'kisses you and bites you and makes you shed sweet tears'. In Chianti itself, it was medieval monks at Badia a Passignano and Badia a Coltibuono who advanced the cause of the big red wine. Chianti in the strictest sense of the word, however, was 'invented' in 1835 when Bettino Ricasoli came up with a modern 'formula' based on the traditional Sangiovese grape and a special fermentation process to give it more depth.

The 1960s were the low point in the long history of Chianti; in those days, low-grade Chianti drunk from a straw-covered flask – the *fiasco* (!) – caused many a hangover. But Chianti winemakers have made an extraordinary comeback in the space of a generation and are realising its potential to be, again, one of the world's great wine regions. Areas such as Castellina, Gaiole and Radda are the source of heady red wines that only get better with time.

Suggested tour

Chianti is a region where it is hard not to lose your way. The wine estates, castles and abbeys are scattered through a surprisingly rural region where vineyards alternate with bare hillsides, dense stands of wood and shrub, and alleys of cypresses with puzzling signs at the entrance. A good map is essential. Try to get *Il Chianti* (1:70,000) from a local tourist board or the APT in Florence.

Below
Chianti country

Total distance: 115km; detours add 20km, 10km (both return) and 8km (last detour is an alternate route that rejoins the N408 south).

Time: One could follow this route as an idyllic way of getting from Florence to Siena in a single day; or explore it during an extended *soggiorno* in the hills of Chianti Classico; or sell up, move here and, like American author Frances Mayes, write a book about your 'life-transforming experience'. Where the humbler pursuits of driving and wine-tasting are concerned, count on everything taking twice as long as you would imagine.

Links: The route runs parallel, in places, to the route of the previous chapter and has the same starting point.

Route: It is hard to find your way out of **Florence** ❶ on the N222, because the signs command the driver to make simultaneous left and right turns (even Italian roads are subject to the laws of physics). It is far easier (or less fiendishly difficult) to get on the *autostrada* and exit at Firenze-Certosa; from the roundabout, take the *Via Cassia* in the direction of San Casciano and, after 1km, the narrow road towards **IMPRUNETA** ❷; in only five minutes, you will be cruising the hills of Chianti. The road joins the elusive N222 after Impruneta; press on to **GREVE IN CHIANTI** ❸. This particular stretch is full of sudden bottlenecks in the form of villages, cyclists and heavily wooded blind turns. In other words, it is utterly charming.

Detour: Upon entering Greve from the north, there is a tiny road that veers up to **Montefioralle** ❹, an almost perfectly oval fortified village with a panoramic walk that triggers the 'wannalivehere' Tuscan fantasy. For centuries, until the conquest of Siena, this was a Florentine military outpost that guarded the route north. Amerigo Vespucci – the explorer from whom America got its name – was born here in 1451 (while mapping the coast of Brazil, he thought he was in the seas of southern Asia; only later did he realise his mistake).

An even narrower road (with a traffic light for the one-lane stretch) takes you through a dreamy, hilly tableau of olive trees and vineyards towards **Badia a Passignano** ❺ (*see page 64*). It eventually turns into a quality dirt road that twists through more vineyards on its way to the 11th-century abbey. On the way back, you will cross an intersection with a road signposted for Panzano. If you take it, you won't be sorry. It has sweeping views east of Chianti's hills and west of the Val di Pesa. You can either backtrack to Greve or skip it.

A couple of wide curves soar up to the lower end of **PANZANO** ❻, which occupies a narrow ridge. As in so many places, the interesting part of town is at the top of the hill. A rigorous amount of hairpinning will take you to **CASTELLINA IN CHIANTI** ❼.

Detour: Just five minutes south of Castellina is the village of **Fonterútoli** ❽, famous for the wine estate of the Mazzei family and

The world's first brand

The black cock (*Gallo Nero*) on your typical bottle of Chianti was, arguably, the world's first 'brand', adopted in 1384 by the *Lega del Chianti* – an alliance of winemaking towns – to indicate the quality and origin of their product. Eventually, it passed into history but was revived in 1924 and is still going strong. Having said that, you can ignore it while shopping for wine. Some of the best Chianti wines depart from Chianti traditions and grape varieties, and don't even bother with the symbol. Furthermore, the black rooster has suffered terrible indignities. The producer of America's worst plonk ('Ripple' and 'Thunderbird') is also named Gallo and based in Modesto, California. This New World rooster pursued a legal cockfight in the 1990s, attacking the Chianti winemakers for 'infringing' on its name. The Italians' resistance was eventually crushed by the sheer weight of legal expenses. They agreed never to sell their wine abroad with the venerable *Gallo Nero* symbol. In the meantime, the American Gallo produces vast quantities of a dreadful wine and calls it – Chianti!

for some of the best olive oil in Tuscany. The Castello di Fonterútoli *(www.fonterutoli.it)* has an earthy Osteria with a small wine bar where you sample the estate's wine before buying it.

Turn east on to the N429 and drive 10km to **RADDA IN CHIANTI ❾**. From there, drive further east (ignoring the N408 south) up into the heavily forested hills. On a ridge (628m) in the middle of an oak forest, **Badia a Coltibuono ❿** moulders in profound peace, only rarely disturbed by modest tours. The abbey was founded almost a thousand years ago, in 1050, and Lorenzo the Magnificent was often a guest here in the 15th century. Its wine estate and restaurant are now popular among foodies and occasionally used as a venue for upmarket cooking classes by cookbook author Luisa de Medici.

There is not much to **Gaiole in Chianti ⓫** itself. No one ever even bothered to build a wall around it; it served rather as a marketplace for the surrounding area. However, it is completely surrounded by castles, monasteries and quirky mountain villages. You could easily spend a couple of weeks ferreting them all out.

Detour: The area around Gaiole was the historic fault line between the territories of Florence and Siena. Some 3km south of Gaiole, the beginning of the Strada dei Castelli ('Castle Road') is indicated by unmissable signs. The **Castello di Meleto ⓬** was, in its 13th-century heyday, an almost impregnable place behind its cylindrical towers. The 'formula' for Chianti was created by Barone Bettino Ricasoli at **Castello di Brólio ⓭** in 1835: a mixture of red (Sangiovese and Canaiolo) with an itsy bitsy bit of white (Malvasia and Trebbiano) grapes. The castle and wine estate now belong to Seagrams and its wines don't quite live up to its tradition.

Follow the signs for **Siena** to get back on the N408 and arrive in Siena after about an hour.

Also worth exploring

The hill of **Monteaperti** lies just off the N326. Sienese Ghibellines and Florentine Guelphs demonstrated once and for all that Tuscany was not big enough for both of them here on 4 September 1260. It was the bloodiest battle fought on Italian soil in the Middle Ages. A simple pyramid in a cypress grove recalls the event. Siena was victorious, killing 10,000 Florentine soldiers and capturing 15,000. The painter Duccio celebrated the victory with an impressive *Maestà* in the cathedral of Siena (now in the museum of the Duomo Nuovo). It was, however, a short-lived triumph. The Pope excommunicated the entire population of Siena while Guelph armies destroyed its forces in the decade that followed. Merchants with Guelph sympathies took power in Siena and pursued a policy of peace. The decades of their rule were marked by a period of great prosperity and artistic achievement.

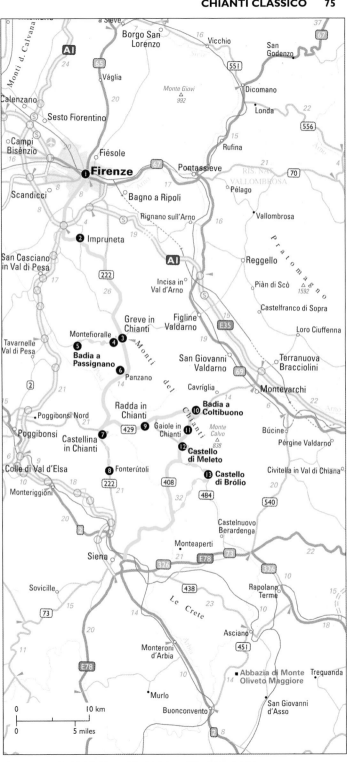

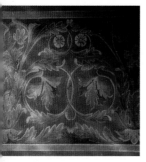

Siena

Ratings

Architecture	●●●●●
Art	●●●●○
Food and drink	●●●●○
Museums	●●●●○
Children	●●●○○
Shopping	●●●○○
Nature	●●○○○
Scenery	●●○○○

Siena and Florence, the two cities that fought bitterly in the Middle Ages to control the destiny of Tuscany, remain worlds apart. Siena is a place where the Renaissance never triumphed – an isolated hilltop floating in a Gothic time warp. Incredibly, its major monuments were built in a mere six decades between the 13th and 14th centuries, until the Black Death came to town in 1348 and swept away two-thirds of the population. Its lifeblood ebbed with the decline of the Via Francigena, the route of trade and pilgrimage to Rome. Florence conquered Siena in 1555 after a terrible siege, putting an end to the last Republican government in Italy. In 1956, Siena reasserted its liberty by saying 'no' to the 20th century and barring traffic from its ancient core.

Sights

ⓘ Informazioni turistiche *Piazza del Campo 56; tel: 0577 280551; fax: 0577 270676; www.siena.turismo.toscana.it & www.terresiena.it. Open mid-Mar–mid-Nov Mon–Sat 0830–1930; mid-Nov–mid-Mar Mon–Fri 0830–1300, 1500–1900, Sat 0830–1300*

Battistero di San Giovanni*

The Battistero (Baptistry) di San Giovanni (built in 1316) sits behind the Duomo where the crypt should be. The white marble façade and its three large doorways were added later (1382). The interior seems to rotate inexorably towards the magnificent baptismal font, attributed to Jacopo della Quercia. It also bears works by Donatello and Lorenzo Ghiberti. Many other works add to the sensory overload: bronze figures by Giovanni di Turino and Goro di Neroccio as well as frescos by Vecchietta (c. 1450), Michele di Matteo Lambertini and Benvenuto di Giovanni. The sumptuous cross-vaulted ceiling invites much craning of the neck but, fortunately, there are wood-framed mirrors that allow you to contemplate its reflection in your lap.

0 ⟞——————⟝ 200 metres
0 ⟞——————⟝ 150 yards

Porta
Camollia

Viale Sardegna

Viale Giuseppe Mazzini

Via Simone Martini

Via di Camollia

Viale Don Giovanni Minzoni

Via Camporegio

Via di Biagio di Montluc

Viale Armando Diaz

Via Giuseppe Garibaldi

Viale Rinaldo Franci

La Lizza

La Lizza

Via Simone Martini

Porta
Ovile

Via della Stufa Secca

Via di Vallerozzi

S Francesco

† Piazza
S Francesco

Via Baldassarre Peruzzi

Viale Venticinque Aprile

**Stadio
Comunale**

Via dei Montanini

Via dei Rossi

Oratorio di
San Bernardino

Viale del Mille

Viale Curtatone

Piazza
Giacomo
Matteotti

Via della Sapienza

Piazza
Salimbeni

Banchi di Sopra

**Casa di Santa
Caterina**

Via della

Via dei Termini

Via delle Terme

Via Sallustio Bandini

Via di S Caterina

S Domenico

Croce del
Travaglio

Banchi di Sotto

Porta
Fonte
Branda

**Battistero di
San Giovanni**

Fonte Gaia

**Piazza del
Campo**

Via di Pantaneto

Via dei Pispini

Porta
Pispini

ⓘ

Via del Porrione

Via di Salicotto

Via S Martino

Via Roma

**Ospedale di
Santa Maria
della Scala**

Duomo

**Palazzo
Pubblico**

**Museo
dell'Opera
Metropolitana**

Piazza
del
Mercato

Via del Fosso di S Ansano

Via di Città

Casato di Sotto

Via S Pietro

Via Giovanni Dupre

**Pinacoteca
Nazionale**

Via Paolo Mascagni

S Agostino

Piano dei Mantellini

Via delle Cerchia

Via di Fontanella

**S Maria
del Carmine**

**Orto
Botanico**

Via Pier Andrea Mattioli

Porta
Roma

Via S Marco

Via delle Sperandie

Porta
S Marco

Strada di Certosa

Via Massetana

Porta
Tufi

Via Enea Silvioni Piccolomini

Via Girolamo Gigli

Battistero di San Giovanni € *Piazza San Giovanni. Open mid-Mar–Sept 0900–1930 (Oct until 1800); Nov–mid-Mar 1000–1300, 1430–1700*

Duomo *Piazza del Duomo. Open mid-Mar–Sept Mon–Sat 0730–1930 (Oct until 1800); Nov–mid-Mar Mon–Sat 0730–1700. Sun from 1400. Free admission.*

Libreria Piccolomini € *Piazza del Duomo. (inside the cathedral). Open daily mid-Mar–Oct 0900–1930; Nov–mid-Mar 1000–1300, 1400–1700. Sun from 1400.*

Museo dell'Opera Metropolitana €€ *Piazza J. della Quercia; www.operaduomo.it. Open mid-Mar–Sept 0900–1930 (Oct until 1800); Nov–mid-Mar 0900–1330.*

Below
Siena's Duomo

Duomo✦✦✦

The Duomo Santa Maria (cathedral) of Siena is at the highest point in the city (346m). A tale of two styles, it was begun in 1200 in Romanesque fashion then, in 1258, Cistercian monks (who also worked on the monastery of San Galgano) took over and built the transept, dome and choir in a revolutionary new Gothic style. The great sculptor Giovanni Pisano worked on the marble façade between 1284 and 1297. The campanile was finished in 1313.

The interior, in the form of a Latin cross, with a nave and two aisles divided by Romanesque pillars and arches, is highly evocative. There is a cornice of the nave and presbytery overpopulated with 172 busts of popes above and 32 busts of emperors below. The floor is divided into 52 panels of inlaid, etched and coloured marble representing various tales. Unfortunately, many are under wraps on any given day. In the left (north) transept is the cathedral's greatest work of art, the pulpit (1266–8) by Nicola Pisano, only fully appreciated after multiple drops of the coin in the illumination strongbox. The **Libreria Piccolomini**✦ has a lavish Renaissance interior and is covered in frescos (1502–9) by Pinturicchio that tell the life story of Anea Silvio Piccolomini, the poet who became Pope (*see Pienza, page 100*).

Duomo Nuovo (Museo dell'Opera Metropolitana)✦✦

The cathedral is only a small part of the Duomo Nuovo (new cathedral) planned by the city fathers in 1316, which might have been completed had not the plague intervened. The sheer ambition of the Sienese builders bordered on lunacy. Their idea was to use the existing cathedral as the transept of a gargantuan new edifice that would surpass anything in Pisa or Florence. The cathedral choir was moved to the east and the baptistry constructed as part of the foundation while work commenced on the enormous façade and three naves.

The **Museo dell'Opera Metropolitana**✦✦ occupies rooms obtained by closing the first three spans of the right aisle of the Duomo Nuovo. The sculptures, paintings, gold objects, illuminated manuscripts and hangings come mostly from the Duomo: works by Giovanni Pisano, Jacopo della Quercia and, its crowning glory, Duccio's glorious *Maestà*, the supreme masterpiece of the Sienese school, painted between 1308 and 1311. You are allowed to climb to the very top of one of the walls of the Duomo Nuovo for a dizzying view over the roofs of Siena and a chance to imagine what might have been the strangest cathedral in Italy.

Palazzo Pubblico***

Henry James called this building 'Siena's Declaration of Independence' and it is one the finest examples of Gothic architecture in Italy. However, the building does not dominate the square but, rather, forms part of its harmony – one of the achievements of Sienese architecture. The 'Sienese' arch used on the town hall and other buildings in Siena looks Gothic but was probably an import from the Orient. The black and white coat of arms of the town of Siena – the Balzana – is above the tympana of the doors and windows. Its other symbol appears on a granite column – a she-wolf and twins Romulus and Remus.

One entrance leads to the courtyard of the Podestà (mayor); the other leads to the rooms where the paintings of the **Museo Civico*** are now kept, including the fresco cycles by Ambrogio Lorenzetti depicting Good Government and Bad Government. Jesus, Mary, angels and saints float in a tender *Maestà* by Simone Martini in the Sala del Mappamondo ('globe room'); however, they co-habit the room with a portrait of *condottiere Guidoriccio da Fogliano*. Between the end of the 14th century and the beginning of the 15th century the interior of the palace was altered. The Sala del Risorgimento was created in honour of Vittorio Emanuele II and filled with the heroic works of Sienese artists such as Amos Cassioli, Piero Aldi and Cesare Maccari.

The **Torre del Mangia***, one of the most striking towers in Italy, looks like a cross between a spear, a lily and a hypodermic needle. It rises from the lowest point of the Piazza del Campo alongside the Palazzo Pubblico to a height of 102m (including the lightening rod), a lasting symbol of power once wielded by the Palazzo Pubblico. Built between 1325 and 1348 (additions in 1680), it is of red brick with a travertine belfry.

Piazza del Campo***

The historic centre of Siena and perhaps the most beautiful square in Italy, sunk between the three hills the city is built on, encircled by the red brick and stone façades of medieval houses. The scallop-shaped square was the original nucleus of Siena, built to stem the rainwater and to reclaim the ground, formerly a market place that sloped downhill. A document from 1196 shows that it included today's piazza and the part known as the Mercato (market). Later a large wall was built to separate the two parts and the Campo acquired its characteristic form while the first buildings were erected. Gradually the Campo took on the full functions of a square, a public meeting place, and became the centre for social, civil and religious life. It is paved with nine bands of travertine fanning out across the square. The Palazzo Sansedoni is a complex of medieval houses joined into one palace by Agostino di Giovanni in 1339. Its façade curves around the Piazza. The windows are of the same type as those of the Palazzo Pubblico in accordance with the city's 13th-century building code.

Textbook definition of the 'Sienese Arch': a pointed arch with the double ferrule inside the archivolt, placed on a lowered arch in the architrave.

Museo Civico €€
Palazzo Pubblico, Piazza del Campo; www.comune.siena.it/ museocivico/. *Open mid-Mar–Oct 1000–1900; Nov and mid-Feb–mid-Mar 1000–1830; Dec–mid-Feb 1000–1730.*

Torre del Mangia €€
Palazzo Pubblico, Piazza del Campo. Open daily mid-Mar–Oct 1000–1900; Nov–mid-Mar 1000–1600.

In July and mid-August, the legendary Palio takes place on the Piazza del Campo, a horse race, in which every *contrada* (district) of Siena enters a horse in the race (after having it blessed in church). The colourful festival has existed since the Middle Ages, when each neighbourhood took part in the defence of the city.

Pinacoteca Nazionale**

Pinacoteca Nazionale €€ *Via San Pietro 29. Open Mon 0830–1330; Tue–Sat 0815–1915; Sun 0815–1315.*

Ospedale di Santa Maria della Scala €€ *Piazza del Duomo 2; tel: 0577 224811; www.santamaria.comune. siena.it. Open daily mid-Mar–Oct 1000–1800; Nov–mid-Mar 1030–1630.*

Siena's famous art gallery is partly housed in the Palazzo Buonsignori, donated by the nobleman Niccolò Buonsignori, and in the adjacent Palazzo Brigidi, belonging to the Province of Siena. If there is a drawback, it is the sheer number of Madonnas. If you try to look at every one, you may find yourself wishing, blasphemously, that the New Testament had never been written. Begin with the best; the *Madonna of the Franciscans* by Duccio di Buoninsegna (1255–1319), the great altarpiece by Pietro Lorenzetti (dated 1329), the refined Madonnas by Ambrogio Lorenzetti and the *Madonna and Child* by Simone Martini. Also the *Città sul Mare*, again by Ambrogio Lorenzetti, regarded as one of the first landscape paintings in modern history.

Among 15th-century works, look for the paintings of Giovanni di Paolo, the comforting Madonnas of Neroccio di Bartolomeo Landi and Francesco di Giorgio Martini, and the stylised compositions of Matteo di Giovanni. In the collection of masterpieces donated by the nobleman Spannocchi, two are of particular interest: the *Self-Portrait* by Albrecht Dürer (1514) and the *Nativity* (1521) by Lorenzo Lotto.

Ospedale di Santa Maria della Scala*

A hospital founded in the 9th century, Santa Maria was in operation until the 1980s (Italo Calvino, the author of *Invisible Cities*, died here in 1985). Most of the present building dates from the 13th and 14th centuries. It is now being transformed into a cultural centre and museum complex.

Left
Siena's Piazza del Campo

Below
The Oratorio di Santa Caterina

The frescos by Domenico di Bartolo in the great hall – Sala del Pellegrinaio – are one of the artistic glories of Siena and offer fascinating insights into the blood and guts reality of 15th-century hospitalisation. It also portrays orphans in different stages of their lives, from childishly naughty to subdued and apprenticed young men and marriageable women (with small dowries provided by the hospice). There is a frescoed chapel by the artist Vechietta and another one underground – the Oratorio di Santa Caterina della Notte – where Siena's patron saint had visions and ecstasies.

Accommodation and food

Drogheria Manganelli *Via di Città 71; tel: 0577 280002.* Gourmet delicatessen with regional specialities at elevated prices – olive oil, honey, wine, truffles, marmalade, vinegar.

Consorzio Agrario *Via Pianigiani 9/Piazza Matteotti; tel: 0577 2301; www.capsi.it.* The largest supermarket in the *Centro Storico*. It carries a large selection of wine, olive oil, *charcuterie* and other goods.

Pensione Palazzo Ravizza €€ *Pian dei Mantellini 34; tel: 0577 280462; fax: 0577 221597.* The queen of Siena's hotels has 30 elegant rooms in a restored palace, spectacular views and a garden (ask for a room overlooking the garden). But it is hard to reach by car if you don't know the city.

Villa Liberty €€ *Viale Vittorio Veneto 11; tel: 0577 44966; fax: 0577 44770; www.villaliberty.it.* Charming, intimate and only a short walk from the centre. It has 12 rooms in a restored art-nouveau townhouse with marble and parquet floors, and is easy to reach by car with parking in front. You should insist on a room overlooking the garden.

Antica Trattoria Botteganuova €€ *Via Chiantigiana 29; tel: 0577 284230. Closed Sun and Mon lunch.* Creative variations on Tuscan classics and a Michelin star in 1999 are the big draw for foodies. It is located on the road to Chianti.

Hosteria del Carroccio €€ *Via del Casato di Sotto 32; tel: 0577 41165. Closed Wed in winter. No credit cards.* Down a street just off the Piazza del Campo. The menu here changes every week and is based on fresh ingredients, Sienese tradition and owner Renata's fancy. Make reservations.

La Taverna del Capitano €€ *Via del Capitano 8; tel: 0577 288094.* Easy to find, this traditional restaurant is on a broad street near the cathedral. The menu usually includes things such as *panzanella di farro* (spelt, dried bread, herbs and vegetables), *pappardelle* ('broad noodles') with meat sauce, an outstanding veal cutlet and, on Friday, cod cooked Tuscan style.

La Chiacchiera € *Costa San Antonio 4; tel: 0577 280631.* For an informal, delicious but inexpensive meal, there isn't a better place in Siena but it is hard to get a table and service is often slow. The best strategy is to come early.

Cucina Senese

The Sienese season their food more heavily than the Florentines and rely even more on roasting and grilling. Typical dishes are *ribollita* (a 'twice-cooked' vegetable and bread soup), minestrone, grilled meats, tripe and fried zucchini flowers. The classic dessert is *cantucci* ('almond biscuits') accompanied by the dessert wine, Vin Santo. *Panforte* is a famous Sienese speciality, a cake of candied fruit, almonds, honey and orange peel compressed into a chewy, dense, delicious mass that they say never goes bad. *Ricciarelli* are biscuits made of almonds, egg white, sugar and vanilla. Tourism in Siena has had its culinary side effects and it is now possible, in the fast food places on the Via Banchi di Sopra for example, to eat a truly lousy meal.

Grattacielo € *Via dei Pontani 8; tel: 0577 289326. Closed Sun.* A humble place with just a couple of tables and a low ceiling (hence the name, 'skyscraper') where the owner hands over plates of sausage, cheese and ham across the counter along with *vino della casa* – the authentic and delicious Sienese version of a quick lunch.

Pasticceria Nannini €€ *Via Massetana Romana 42–4; tel: 0577 285208.* The Italian rock singer Gianna Nannini grew up in Siena. Her family owns a chain of shops here that make Siena's most celebrated nosh – the chewy *panforte*.

Below
Festive Siena

Suggested tour

Total distance: 2km.

Time: Two days should be a minimum for Siena. Distances are deceptively short in Siena relative to the number of its *palazzi*, museums and other things to see. If you are limited to a single day, concentrate on the two poles of the city – the Piazza del Campo and the Piazza del Duomo – and try to take in either the Pinacoteca Nazionale or the Museo dell'Opera del Duomo. The latter has a fabulous view of the city that rivals that of the town hall's famous tower and there are no queues.

Route: From the *terrazza* of the church of **San Domenico ❶**, you can take a long look at the city's two highest hills, occupied by its cathedral and town hall. The vast brick structure of San Domenico looks more like a warehouse than a church. Behind the unfinished façade, deep in the cavernous interior, is a chapel where the mummified head of St Catherine holds court, accompanied by a finger and the chain that she used to beat herself with. She is one of the most famous women in church history and the subject of chapel frescos by Sodoma that depict vivid scenes in which she faints, casts out demons, and pleads for a young man facing execution. Back outside, walk down the Via della Sapienza.

Detour: Turn right into Corta San Antonio and follow the sign to the **Casa di Santa Caterina ❷** (*open 0900–1230, 1430–1800 in summer, 0900–1230, 1530–1800 in winter*). St Catherine was born here on a back street, into a dyer's family. In her lifetime, she would dictate letters to popes and kings and helped bring about the return of the papacy from Avignon to Rome. The house attracts a mix of tourists and pilgrims. The rooms where Caterina Benincasa lived have been transformed over the centuries (but her hair shirt is still there). The inner Superior Oratory, known as '*della Cucina*' has a magnificent majolica floor beneath a coffered ceiling. A Renaissance loggia leads through a modern annex to the Oratory of the Crucifix.

The Via Banchi di Sopra is Siena's throbbing, claustrophobic shopping street where locals and tourists vie for space, particularly during the evening *passeggiata*. It is worth taking a moment to contemplate the world's oldest bank still in operation – the Monte dei Paschi di Siena – housed in the Gothic Palazzo Salimbeni and two adjoining Renaissance palaces on **Piazza Salimbeni ❸**. The bank was founded by the city in 1472 to provide cheap loans to sheep farmers. The Piazza Tolomei has the first of many Sienese she-wolf statues. The city council met in the church on the square, San Christoforo, before completion of the Palazzo Pubblico. The Palazzo Tolomei (1205–67) was the proud headquarters of yet another medieval bank.

Opposite
Siena's Piazza del Campo

ⓟ Siena is relatively easy to navigate by car compared to Florence but the *Centro Storico* is off limits (hotel guests have the right to drive into the *Centro Storico* to unload but there is no public parking there). The two largest paid parking lots (Il Pallone and Stadio Comunale) are near Piazza San Domenico. You can sometimes find free parking, particularly early in the morning or at lunchtime on Viale Vittorio Veneto (or its side streets) which leads into San Domenico. Read the street signs to make sure there is no street cleaning and that it isn't a market day (usually Wednesdays).

The **Croce del Travaglio** ❹ is the meeting point of three streets, Banchi di Sopra, Banchi di Sotto and Via di Città. Squeeze through the Vicolo di San Pietro to **PIAZZA DEL CAMPO** ❺. You will find yourself standing next to the 14th-century **Fonte Gaia** ❻ ('happy fountain'), which flows on the highest point in the square. Nineteenth-century copies have replaced the magnificent original reliefs (1414–19) by Jacopo della Quercia. The **PALAZZO PUBBLICO** ❼ occupies the lowest point in the square and its **Torre del Mangia**, perhaps the finest medieval tower anywhere, rises up to a dramatic height, as if it is going to take flight.

Return to the Croce del Travaglio and go left into the Via di Città, a street of medieval and Renaissance palaces such as the Palazzo Patrizi (No 75) and, best of all, the **Palazzo Chigi-Saracini** (No 82) with a curved façade built of brick and stone. Inside the entrance is a statue of Pope Julius II. Diagonally opposite is the **Palazzo Piccolomini**, built by Bernardo Rossellino for the sister of Pope Pius II (hence its other name, the Palazzo delle Papesse). It is now an art gallery.

Turn right when you run into another she-wolf column – this is the Via del Capitano. Walk past the 13th-century Palazzo del Capitano and its nine Sienese arches; after a few more paces, you will step into the Piazza del Duomo, which is the highest point in Siena, 30m higher than the Campo. It is only logical to visit the **DUOMO SANTA MARIA** ❽ first. Many believe it to be the most beautiful Gothic building in Italy. However, save time for the **Museo dell'Opera Metropolitana** ❾ located in the ruins of the **DUOMO NUOVO** – Siena's most ambitious work in progress that was never to be. If at all possible, climb to the top. The square's two remaining attractions are the **BATTISTERO DI SAN GIOVANNI** ❿ and the **OSPEDALE DI SANTA MARIA DELLA SCALA** ⓫.

Retrace your steps from the Piazza del Duomo down the Via del Capitano to the Piazza Postierla and walk down its continuation, the Via San Pietro. The **Palazzo Buonsignori** ⓬, containing the PINACOTECA NAZIONALE, is on the left.

Also worth exploring

Fortezza Medici (**Forte di Santa Barbara**) is located near the Piazza San Domenico. The Medici fortress built by Cosimo I (1555) has since become a park with magnificent views. The Enoteca Nazionale displays 600 wines from all over Italy in the glowing arches of the fortress's brick cellar. Upstairs is a bar where you can savour them.

0   200 metres
0   150 yards

Porta
Camollia

Via di Biago di Montluc

Via di Camollia

Viale Sardegna

Viale Giuseppe Mazzini

Viale Don Giovanni Minzoni

Via Campansi

Viale Armando Diaz

Viale Rinaldo Franci

Via Giuseppe Garibaldi

La Lizza

La Lizza

Via Simone Martini

Porta
Ovile

Via Simone Martini

S Francesco

† Piazza
S Francesco

Via di Vallerozzi

Via Baldassarre Peruzzi

Via di Rossi

**Oratorio di
San Bernardino**

Stadio
Comunale

Viale Venticinque Aprile

Viale del Mille

Viale Curtatone

Via della Stufa Secca

Via dei Montanini

Piazza
Giacomo
Matteotti

Piazza
Salimbeni

❸

Via della Sapienza

Banchi di Sopra

Via del Termini

Via delle Terme

Via Sallustio Bandini

❶
Casa di Santa ❷
Caterina

Via della

S Domenico

Via di S Caterina

Croce del
Travaglio ❹

Banchi di Sotto

❻ Fonte Gaia

❺

Porta
Fonte
Branda

**Battistero di
San Giovanni**

Duomo S Maria ✠

❿

**Piazza del
Campo**

ℹ ❼

Via del Porrione

Via di Pantaneto

Via dei Pispini

Porta
Pispini

❽ ❾

**Museo
dell'Opera
Metropolitana**

Via di Città

**Palazzo
Pubblico**

Via di Salicotto

Via S Martino

**Ospedale di Santa
Maria della Scala**

⓫

Via del Fosso
di S Ansano

Casato di Sotto

Piazza
del
Mercato

Via Giovanni Dupré

**Pinacoteca
Nazionale**

Piano
dei Mantellini

⓬

Via S Pietro

S Agostino

Via di Fontanella

Via Roma

Porta
Roma

Via Paolo Mascagni

**S Maria
del Carmine**

Via delle Cerchia

**Orto
Botanico**

Via Pier Andrea Mattioli

Strada di Certosa

Via Girolamo Gigli

Via S Marco

Via delle Sperandie

Porta
S Marco

Via Massetana

Porta
Tufi

Via Enea Silvio
Piccolomini

The Crete

Ratings

Art	●●●●●
Castles	●●●●●
Monasteries	●●●●●
Scenery	●●●●●
Vineyards	●●●●●
Architecture	●●●●○
Nature	●●●●○
Museums	●●●○○

The hillsides south of Siena are an undulating sea of clay in which thickets of oaks and *maquis* seem to float like islands. The fields have been adapted with terrible labour for use as farm and pastureland. The haunting landscape, called the *crete senese*, forms the background of many school of Siena masterpieces. All historical epochs have left their mark. There are Etruscan Cities of the Dead, and medieval castles and monasteries. Even the road system is ancient, once forming part of the Roman *Via Cassia* and the medieval *Via Francigena*. Further south, the Crete gives way to Monte Amiata, an extinct volcano and the highest peak (1 739m) in southern Tuscany.

ABBAZIA DI MONTE OLIVETO MAGGIORE❖❖

Abbazia di Monte Oliveto Maggiore €
On the N451 between Buonconvento and Asciano at 273m; tel: 0577 707611; www.ftbcc.it/monteoliveto/. Open daily 0915–1200, 1515–1745 (until 1700 in winter). The monks produce an excellent herbal liquor – Flora di Monte Oliveto – from 26 herbs grown in the monastery garden. It can be purchased in the pharmacy, where 17th-century vases are still used for keeping the herbs.

The solitary Benedictine monastery, still occupied by monks, has one of the most beautiful cloisters in Tuscany. Bernardo Giovanni Tolomei, a Sienese nobleman, renounced the world and founded the abbey in 1313. Beyond the fortified outpost, which is decorated with fine Della Robbia terracottas, a cypress avenue leads to the abbey's late Gothic church, much altered during an 18th-century baroque facelift. The abbey complex also comprises a library, guesthouse, cloisters, chapels and gardens. The intarsia (inlaid wood) of the choir stools (1503–5) unfolds a series of imaginary cities and dream landscapes – all in perspective – created with chips of oak, chestnut, olive, acorn and walnut (if it is too dark, ask the caretaker to switch on the lights).

One of the monastery's three cloisters is decorated with a magnificent series of frescos that tell the life of St Benedict in 36 panels. Five were painted by Luca Signorelli and the rest by Giovanni Antonio da Bazzo, or 'Sodoma'. Vasari claims that he 'earned' his

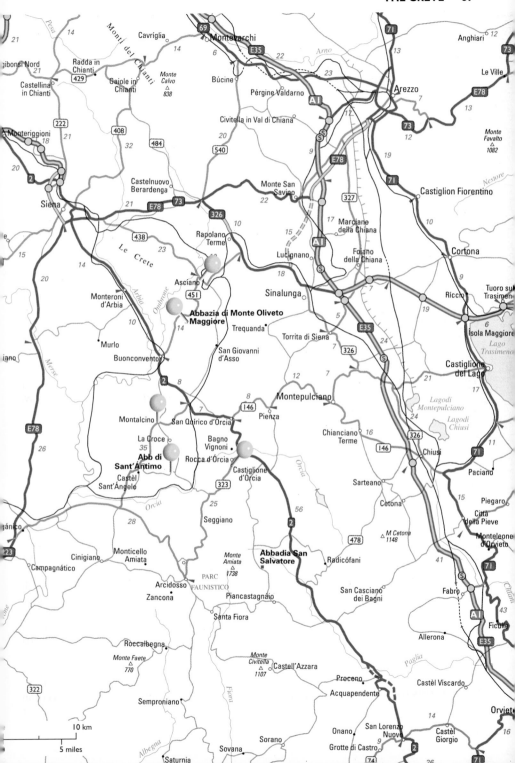

nickname. The young painter certainly didn't lack self-confidence; he inserted his self-portrait next to that of the saint in the third episode, more or less demanding equal time. For a young man, he understood a lot about temptation, corruption, greed, voluptuousness, gluttony and forgiveness: though employed by monks, he depicted them freely in his art.

ASCIANO*

ℹ Informazioni turistiche *Corso Matteotti 18; tel: 0577 719510. www.comune.asciano.siena.it. Limited opening hours.*

🏛 Museo Archeologico e di Arte Sacra € *Corso Matteotti, Palazzo Corboli; tel 0577 719510. Open Tue–Sun 1000–1800.*

Museo Amos Cassioli € *Via Mameli 36. Open 1000–1230 and mid-Jun–mid-Sept 1630–1830.*

🥖 Panificio Caselli *Piazza Garibaldi 5. A small baker that makes perfect foccacia, pizza and intense panforte.*

Asciano is the largest town in the Crete and an important centre of sheep farming and cheesemaking that remains within its medieval fortified walls. Few tourists bother to stop here, which is part of its charm. Surprisingly, it has three worthwhile museums. The main street, the Corso Matteotti, lined with neo-classical *palazzi*, ends in the Piazza della Basilica, embellished by a 15th-century fountain. The Basilica di Sant'Agata stands across from it. Nearby, housed in the restored 13th-century Palazzo Corboli, is the **Museo Archeologico e di Arte Sacra*** with several important works from the Basilica and other churches of the area. Of particular interest are the wooden panel paintings of the Sienese school (14th–15th centuries) with a stunning archangel by Ambrogio Lorenzetti and a Madonna with child by Duccio.

The museum also contains an interesting collection of Etruscan art and artefacts excavated in the nearby necropolis di Poggio Pinci (7th–4th centuries BC). The **Museo Amos Cassioli*** has a collection of 60 paintings and numerous drawings by Amos Cassioli (1832–92), the master of Risorgimento melodrama, and his son Giuseppe (1865–1942), both interesting for a look at 19th-century Italy.

Brunello di Montalcino

Brunello di Montalcino is one of the world's most famous red wines. Unlike Chianti, it is made from a single type of grape – Brunello, a clone of Sangiovese Grosso – and aged for four years. Rosso di Montalcino, aged one year, packs a similar punch and is good for uncomplicated drinking. On a different note, Moscadello is a soft, lightly sweet white wine. Producers to look for:

Il Poggione *south of Castel Sant'Angelo; tel: 0577 848412; www.ilpoggiolomontalcino.com.*

Col d'Orcia *south of Castel Sant'Angelo; tel: 0577 808001.*

Talenti *main road just to the north of Castel Sant'Angelo; 0577 444064.*

Lisini *dirt road between Sant'Ántimo and Castel Sant'Angelo; tel: 0577 864040.*

Opposite
Crete Sienese scenery

Castiglione d'Órcia*

Rocca a Tentennano € *Open Easter–Oct 1000–1300, 1500–1800; Nov–Easter Sat/Sun only 1000–1300, 1430–1630.*

13th-century human rights

Another feudal family of Castiglione, the Tignosi, did an extraordinary thing in 1207. They granted rights – in writing – to the town's population. This unheard-of document – the *Charta libertatis* – is one of the most important in medieval Italian history.

From its perch above the Val d'Órcia, Castiglione was strategically important for many centuries. It is first mentioned in a historical document in 853 and later belonged to the powerful Aldobrandeschi family that controlled a chain of castles on the Via Francigena. The town has a dipped-in-amber medieval square, the Piazza II Vecchietta, with a fanciful baroque fountain in the middle. There is a Palazzo Comunale with school of Siena frescos, and the earthy Romanesque Chiesetta di Santa Maria Maddalena, which hides behind a 17th-century façade. Its star attractions are paintings by Pietro Lorenzetti, Simone Martine and native son Il Vecchietta.

From the church, it is just a short walk to the ruined Aldobrandeschi castle, the pentagonal Rocca d'Órcia, now a park. It has a panoramic view of Castiglione and Monte Amiata. For an even more extraordinary view, guaranteed to upset acrophobes, climb to the top of the town's second castle, the trapezoidal **Rocca a Tentennano***, which was built by the hyperactive Salimbeni family in the late 13th century. A hundred years later, the fortress was used by them for a last stand during their confrontation with the city of Siena that ended with the surrender of Cocco Salimbeni in 1419. He was exiled and his castle remained an important military outpost until seized by the Florentines in the 16th century. In both cases, betrayal rather than force breached the fortress defences.

MONTALCINO✧

ℹ Pro Loco
Costa del Municipio 8;
tel: 0577 849331;
www.proLocomontalcino.it.
Open Tue–Sun 1000–1300,
1400–1800.

🏛 Rocca € *(access to the ramparts, courtyard free) Piazzale della Fortezza. Apr–Oct daily 0900–2000; Nov–Mar Tue–Sun 0900–1800.*

Museo Civico e Diocesano d'Arte Sacra
€€ in the former Convento di Sant'Agostino, Via Ricasoli; tel: 0577 846014. Open Apr–Dec Tue–Sun 1000–1800; Jan–Mar Tue–Sun 1000–1300 and 1400–1730.

Above
Montalcino's Rocca

The splendid panorama of the Sienese hills from Montalcino – as far as the mountain of Amiata – is an impressive site. It might have looked a bit different to the last of the Sienese Republics (600 families) who holed up here in 1555 in the **Rocca✧** and held out against the Florentines for four more years. To honour their memory, the procession at Siena's Palio di Contrade is always led by the Montalcino delegation. Today, the fortress is regularly besieged by coach-loads of tourists, who patrol the town for 45 minutes, buy a bottle of wine and press on to rupture the peace of nearby Sant'Ántimo monastery.

The street across from the fortress leads into the Via Ricasoli and past the Gothic marble portal and rose window of the Romanesque church of Sant'Agostino. Its former convent houses a well-endowed **Museo Civico e Diocesano d'Arte Sacra✧** displaying works by Sodoma, Sano di Pietro and Luca di Tommé, five pictures by Bartolo di Fredi (1380) and one of the earliest known works of Sienese art, a crucifixion by an unknown artist. Downhill from the fortress, the curious little Piazza del Popolo is dominated by the Palazzo Comunale (or dei Priori), which is vaguely reminiscent of Siena's famous town hall. The square also has a number of fine Renaissance buildings with double loggias.

SANT'ÁNTIMO✧✧

🏛 Abbazia di Sant'Antimo *tel: 0577 835659. Open Mon–Sat 1030–1230, 1500–1830; Sun 0915–1045, 1500–1800.*

Proud and solitary, the abbey of Sant'Ántimo is arguably the most beautiful Romanesque church in Tuscany and one of the region's finest examples of 13th-century monastic architecture. It is surrounded by fields, forest and olive groves. The present church, dating back to the 12th century, has a simple façade crowned with small arches, a massive square bell tower in the Lombard style with a 12th-century bell, and a semicircular apse. The interior – essentially a Romanesque basilica – has a nave and two aisles separated by piers and pillars whose capitals are carved with lions and mythic beasts. A lot of alabaster was used in the building of the abbey and it adds strange effects of light. The abbey, restored at the beginning of the century, is the seat of a community of canons who officiate with Gregorian chants several times a day.

Accommodation and food

Cantina

Conveniently, at Montalcino there is an **Enoteca della Fortezza** (wine bar and shop) right inside the fortress (not the place to buy in bulk). You can have a drink with a view at the Fiaschetteria Italiana or with the locals and football on the telly at the Bar Mariuccia; both are on the Piazza del Popolo.

Abbazia di Monte Oliveto Maggiore €; *tel: 0577 707611*. From Easter to Oct you can stay overnight in simple rooms in the abbey guesthouse and eat with the monks. The abbey also has a café open at lunchtime that serves good *panini* ('sandwiches') and a *menu turistico*. In summer, there are tables outdoors.

Porta al Cassero €€ *Via della Libertà 9, Montalcino; tel: 0577 847196; closed Wed*. Just two blocks from the fortress, a small establishment run by an uncle–nephew team. Homemade pasta, tripe in saffron or *scottiglia* (stew) and pungent *pecorino* cheese from Pienza paired with good house wine or a bottle of Brunello, Rosso or Moscadello.

Fattoria Taverna dei Barbi €€ *7km on the road to Sant'Ántimo just after La Croce; tel: 0577 841111; www.fattoriadeibarbi.it. Closed Tue evening and Wed*. A family-owned *agriturismo*, wine estate and restaurant with a compendious assortment of local wine and dishes such as *porcini*, *pici* or *parpadelle*, followed by sizzling grilled meat. Accommodation includes apartments near the 12th-century Villa Colombini along with two others in old farmhouses close to the taverna. All are furnished with Cinelli family furniture.

Food of the land

Local food and drink in the Crete includes *pici* (handmade thick spaghetti) with hare and garlic sauce and wines like Brunello of Montalcino and Vino Nobile di Montepulciano (*see page 98*). The best Tuscan cheese comes from the Crete. The forests of Monte Amiata also play a major role in Crete cuisine providing chestnuts, raspberries, mushrooms, wild asparagus and game. Traditional biscuits and cakes are more or less the same as in Siena – *ricciarelli*, *cavallucci*, *copate* and *panforte*, the dense, sweet cake that never goes bad.

Suggested tour

Total distance: 83km; detours to Monte Amiata and Abbadia San Salvatore add 60km; detour to Castèl Sant'Ángelo adds 16km.

Time: If you skip the detours and don't indulge in much wine-tasting, this tour of the Crete can be completed in a moderately ambitious day. Adding detours, walks and wine to the equation expands it to at least three days.

Links: The first of two routes that explore the Crete (*see page 105*).

Route: From **Siena ❶** take the N326 and turn on to the N438 to get on the road to **ASCIANO ❷**. After the village of Taverne d'Arbia, you will get your first real look at the landscape of the Crete. From Asciano, there are two roads that lead in the right direction. Either one will do and both are scenic but the one at the entrance to Asciano is more direct.

It is a lonely few kilometres to **ABBAZIA DI MONTE OLIVETO MAGGIORE ❸**; however, unless you spend the night or join the order, you will never have the abbey to yourself. It is usually beset by a couple of coach-loads of tourists. The next stretch of road is perhaps the best of the entire day. The rolling hills have been worked over the centuries into a landscape that seems timeless, embroidered by cypress-lined ridges, hillside farms and isolated stone villas.

Buonconvento ❹ is directly on the ancient *Via Cassia* and sits behind walls that the Sienese built in the Middle Ages (its Museo d'Arte Sacra contains fine works that other Sienese painted).

The road to **MONTALCINO ❺** appears about 2km outside of town. To really appreciate the hill-town, zigzag to the very top and the Rocca (paid parking is available). The monastery of **SANT'ÁNTIMO ❻** is just 13km to the south, and a right-turn down a dusty road.

Detour: On the road to Sant'Ántimo, there is an immediate left fork that leads to Castèl Sant'Ángelo. It is a wide and well-maintained dirt road that penetrates deep into the heart of Brunello vineyards. Many wine estates along the road have signs saying *vendita diretta*, inviting you to taste and buy wine.

At the end, turn left on the paved country road and carry on to **Castèl Sant'Ángelo ❼** where a couple of sharp curves climb to its main piazza. The town feels like a miniature version of Montalcino without the tourists. The Romanesque church of San Michele is well worth a look, followed by a visit to the friendly cantina across the square. The owner will wave lists and unfurl maps of local vintages, telling you everything you want to know while pouring glasses of intense Brunello.

South of Sant'Ántimo, the prosperous realm of Brunello quickly gives way to the solitary foothills of Monte Amiata. The hamlet of Monte Amiata in the Órcia valley (not to be confused with the mountain) is just a whistle-stop on a neglected railway. A couple of uphill curves end in a fork in the road near Ansidonia.

Detour: If you just can't get enough of mountain driving and medieval monasteries, turn south on the N323 and get ready for the 22km ascent of **Monte Amiata ❽**. The actual summit is a bit of an anticlimax thanks to a tacky complex of bars, car parks, ski runs and hotels. It doesn't detract, however, from the spectacular glimpses of sea to the west, Lake Bolsena to the southeast, and the towers of villages that encircle the mountain (the best lookout is the statue known as the Madonna delle Scout).

The **Abbadia San Salvatore ❾** is just 8.5km further southeast. The Romanesque monastery was constructed of brown trachite, a sombre contrast to Sant'Ántimo's travertine and alabaster. The Cistercians built the 11th-century abbey church on top of a vast and eccentrically decorated 8th-century crypt. The town itself, an ensemble of Renaissance and Gothic buildings, seems an odd place for a budding winter sports capital but that is how it sees itself. From the abbey, it is easier to rejoin the route by driving east to the N2 and turning north.

A further 12km of driving, mostly on mountain ridges, leads to **CASTIGLIONE D'ÓRCIA ❿**. It overlooks, at a distance, the *Via Cassia*, last seen in Buonconvento.

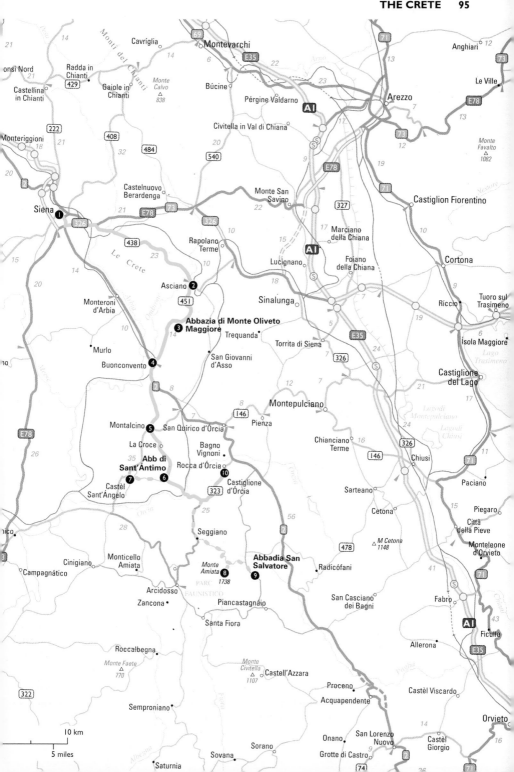

21

14

Cavríglia

59

Montevarchi

Anghiari ° 12

Monti del Chianti

73

14

E35

6

22

23

13

onsì Nord

Radda in
Chianti

429

Le Ville

Castellina
in Chianti

Gaiole in
Chianti

Monte
Calvo
△
838

Búcine

Pérgine Valdarno

Arezzo

E78

13

222

Monteriggioni

18

21

408

484

540

20

Civitella in Val di Chiana

AI

7

Monte
Favalto
△
1082

20

Siena ●1

326

21

E78

73

Castelnuovo
Berardenga

326

10

Monte San
Savino

22

327

17

Marciano
della Chiana

Castiglion Fiorentino

10

Cortona

438

Rapolano
Terme

15

AI

Foiano
della Chiana

S

19

S

73

12

71

15

Le Crete

23

10

Lucignano

18

Asciano ●2

451

Sinalunga

Riccio

Tuoro sul
Trasimeno

Monteroni
d'Arbia

20

14

Murlo

Abbazia di Monte Oliveto
Maggiore ●3

Trequanda

San Giovanni
d'Asso

Torrita di Siena

E35

24

9

Isola Maggiore

Lago
Trasimeno

Buonconvento ●4

10

8

7

326

7

Castiglione
del Lago

21

17

12

7

8

Montepulciano

Lago di
Montepulciano

Montalcino ●5

146

Pienza

24

Lago di
Chiusi

La Croce

San Quírico d'Orcia

Bagno
Vignoni

Chianciano
Terme

16

326

11

Chiusi

35

Abb di
Sant'Antimo

Rocca d'Orcia ●10

146

71

Castèl
Sant'Angelo ●7 ●6

323

Castiglione
d'Orcia

Sarteano

Paciano

E78

26

25

Cetona

15

Piegaro °

Città
della Pieve

Seggiano

56

2

478

M Cetona
△ 1148

Monteleone
d'Orvieto

Cinigiano

Monticello
Amiata

Monte
Amiata ●8
△ 1738

Abbadia San
Salvatore ●9

Radicófani

41

71

S

Campagnático

Arcidosso

PARC

Piancastagnáio

San Casciano
dei Bagni

Fabro

AI

43

Zancona

FAENISTICO

Santa Fiora

Allerona

Ficulle

E35

Roccalbegna

Monte Faete
△ 770

Monte
Civitella
△ 1107

Castell'Azzara

Proceno

Castèl Viscardo

322

Semproniano

Acquapendente

14

Orvieto

10 km

Onano

San Lorenzo
Nuovo

Castèl
Giorgio

5 miles

Saturnia

Sovana

Sorano

Grotte di Castro

74

71

3

no

3

Montalcino

ico

nico

The Crete and Val d'Órcia

Ratings

Architecture	●●●●●
Castles	●●●●●
Scenery	●●●●●
Thermal springs	●●●●●
Vineyards	●●●●●
Nature	●●●●○
Museums	●●●○○
Shopping	●●●○○

The scenic Órcia valley was one of Italy's historic fault-lines, forming the medieval frontier with the Papal State. Two of the most memorable towns in Tuscany occupy the hills above it: ancient, airy Montepulciano and Pienza, a Renaissance Pope's utopia. Strongholds such as the Rocca at Radicófani, by contrast, are dramatic examples of feudal one-upmanship. Chiusi, lying just off the modern *autostrada* near the border of Umbria, was a mysterious Etruscan capital and efficient Roman colony. The Crete has attracted health tourism for at least 2000 years in places such as Bagni San Filippo and Bagno Vignoni. The hot springs of the region have been channelled into modern thermal baths but you can still soak in naturally steaming ponds and sulphurous cascades deep in the woods.

BAGNO VIGNONI*

Terme € *Via Dante 35; tel: 0577 887365. The baths are located behind the Hotel Posta-Marucci. Open daily 0900–1300 and 1430–1800. You can soak for free in pools at the edge of town.*

In the middle of Bagno Vignoni is a steaming pool (51°C) instead of a piazza. Etruscan and Romans bathed in it. The Russian director Andrej Tarkowski used it as a setting for *Nostalgia*, an eerie film about an exiled, hydrophilic Russian poet who tries to walk across the water. The Renaissance Palazzo Piccolomini was a residence of master architect Bernardo Rossellino who built Pienza for Pope Pius II. It is now the Hotel Le Terme (*see Accommodation and food*).

In ancient times, the medical benefits of the hot springs were attributed to water nymphs. In the Middle Ages, physicians boiled the maidenhair ferns growing on its edge and had their patients drink the liquor for 40 days, to flush the 'melancholy' out of their systems so that it wouldn't concentrate in any one organ – say the spleen – for too long. It was even known to cure the 'French disease'. Lorenzo the Magnificent soaked his rheumatic body here in the company of the humanist philosopher Pico della Mirandola.

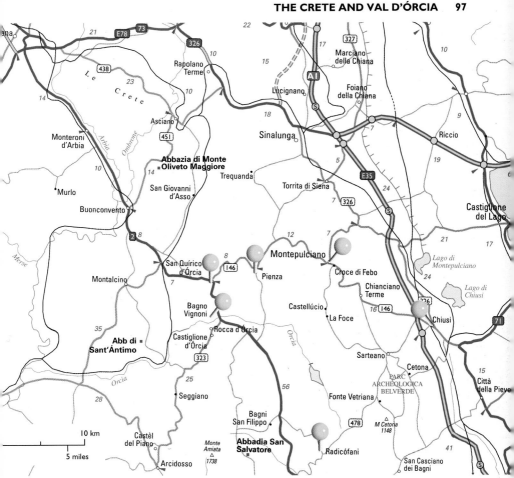

CHIUSI*

Pro Loco, *Via Porsenna 61; tel: 0578 227667.* Open Mon–Fri 0930–1230, 1500–1900, Sat/Sun mornings only.

Right
Etruscan relief

The origins of Chiusi date back to the first millennium before Christ. In the 6th century BC, *Clevsin* or *Chamars* (as the Etruscans called it) was one of the 12 most important cities in the Etruscan federation. Under King Porsenna, Chiusi reached its peak when the Etruscans fought and defeated the Romans.

ⓘ Museo Archeologico Nazionale € *Via Porsenna 93; tel: 0578 20177. Open daily 0900–1930. Charge includes admission to tombs.*

Tomba della Pellegrina € *Guided tours daily 0900–1930 (shorter hours in winter), via the Museo Archeologico Nazionale.*

Catacombe Santa Mustiola €€ *The only Christian catacombs ever discovered in Tuscany are located just outside of Chiusi; the tombs include a children's cemetery. The Museo della Cattedrale on the Piazza del Duomo arranges guided tours (tel: 0578 226490, Mon–Sat Jun–mid-Oct 1100–1600; mid-Oct–May 1100; Sun all year 1100–1600). Dress warmly and bring a flashlight.*

The Duomo San Secondiano, one of the earliest churches in Italy, is supported by 18 marble columns taken from Roman temples after the city's destruction by Goths. The altar rests on a Roman mosaic (the mosaics in the apse are 19th-century imitations of Byzantine work).

The **Museo Archeologico Nazionale****, for all its merit, is a masterpiece of disorganisation: signs placed next to display cases refer to objects that are not in the museum; the only texts are written in academic jargon that suffers further in translation; and a photocopy of a tomb gets top billing while a rare – and very real – tomb painting is half-hidden on a wall in the back. There are many cinerary urns and most of them have inscriptions; one of the most famous is the urn of Larth Sentinathes' Caesa, discovered in the grave of Pellegrina. The sculpture is represented by numerous *cippi* (remarkable is the one with wedding scenes) and by some sphinxes, xoana and lions which were placed as guardians of the graves. There are Roman pieces, too. Don't miss the powerful head of Augustus.

Chiusi was one of the most important centres for Etruscan art and, in the 19th century, produced – for the second time – finely crafted 'Etruscan' urns, vases and figurines. These fakes became the major local industry. Their quality was such that even museums and expert collectors were fooled. The museum displays some of these remarkable copies next to Etruscan originals. It also organises tours of the two Etruscan tombs near Lago di Chiusi – the Tomba del Leone and the **Tomba della Pellegrina***. The latter has been left as it was discovered, with some of the funerary urns and sarcophagi in the odd positions they were left in by tomb raiders centuries ago.

Vino nobile

The wine of Montepulciano was already held in high esteem in the 14th century. The style of today's Nobile di Montepulciano, however, only goes back a few decades. It is based on a different variety of Sangiovese than Chianti, the *Prugnelo Gentile*, which is mixed with Canaiolo (and sometimes Mammolo) and small amounts of white Malvasia and Trebbiano. By law, a Montepulciano wine is only *nobile* if it has aged two years (three if it is a *riserva*). Rosso di Montepulciano is younger and less expensive. Sangiovese-Cabernet blends are becoming very fashionable. To taste some of these wines, drop into the Enoteca del Consorzio del Vino Nobile di Montepulciano, *Piazza Grande 7*; tel: *0578 757812*; *www.vinonobiledimontepulciano.it*

Wine producers to look for

Poliziano *Via Fontago 1, Montepulciano Stazione; tel: 0578 738171; www.carlettipoliziano.com*. A wine estate with a grand tradition, Vino Nobile cru Vigna Asinone is its flagship wine. Also, Elegia (Sangiovese/Cabernet) and Vin Santo.

Avignonesi *Via di Gracciano nel Corso 91, Montepulciano; tel: 0578 757872; www.avignonesi.it*. The Avignonesi brothers make a fine Grifi (Sangiovese/Cabernet), Marzocco (barrique Chardonnay) and acclaimed Vin Santo.

Poderi Boscarelli *Via di Montenero 28, Cervognano, 5km east of Montepulciano between Cervognano and Aquaviva; tel: 0578 767608*. Small wine estate with intense wines with lots of aroma. Boscarelli is a compelling Sangiovese/Cabernet blend.

MONTEPULCIANO**

ℹ Pro Loco *Via di Gracciano nel Corso 59/a; Tel: 0578 757341; proLocomontepulciano.it & www.comune.montepulciano.si.it*

ℹ Palazzo Comunale € *Piazza Grande 1; tel: 0578 757034. Closed Sun.*

Duomo Santa Maria Assunta € *Piazza Grande. Open daily.*

Madonna di San Biagio € *Via di San Biagio 14. Open daily.*

Below
The walls of Montepulciano

At 605m, Montepulciano is one of the highest situated cities in Tuscany, straddling the Chiana and Órcia valleys. Legend has it that the famous Etruscan king Lors Porsena founded the town. Etruscans dug deep beneath the city and their chambers were later used as wine cellars. Architecturally, it is a fascinating mix of Sienese Gothic and Florentine Renaissance architecture. The ring of fortifications was erected in 1511 based on designs by Antonio da Sangallo the Elder at the behest of Cosimo I.

A long, arduous street, the Corso, winds its way from the main square up to the Piazza Grande, the highest point in the city. The **Palazzo Comunale**✦ dates to 1243, but was massively rebuilt by the Florentines in 1393 who gave it a facelift based on plans by Michelozzo, as well as a symmetrically placed tower. The building has three floors; the upper one is made as a battlement and has some similarities with the Palazzo Vecchio of Florence – a 14th-century court with loggias placed one upon another. The view from the top of the tower takes in the surrounding region and, on a clear day, Siena is visible 65km to the north. The impressive Palazzo Nibili-Tarugi, built entirely with travertine, is on the northern side of the square. The **Duomo Santa Maria Assunta**✦ is late baroque, resting on the foundations of a Romanesque church and retaining its bell tower. Behind its unfinished façade is a harmonious interior with a luminous, gilded triptych on the main altar, the Ascension of Mary (1400) by Sienese painter Taddeo di Bartolo.

Perhaps the most remarkable building in Montepulciano sits in a solitary setting just outside the city gates. The Renaissance masterpiece of **Madonna di San Biagio**✦ (1518–45) is based on designs by Antonio da Sangallo the Elder and much influenced by St Peter's in Rome. It is built entirely of travertine on a Greek-cross plan and surmounted by a central dome. The front of the church, facing north, is flanked by two bell towers. The inside repeats the Doric lines of the exterior. Near the main altar there is a huge marble missal-cover made by Giannozzo and Lisandro Albertini.

PIENZA✧

❶ Informazioni turistiche *Palazzo Comunale, Corso Rosellino 59; tel: 0578 749071; www.comunedipienza.it & www.pienza.org.*

❶ Museo Palazzo Piccolomini € *Piazza Pio II 2; tel: 0578 748503. Open Tue–Sun Jul–Sept 1000–1230, 1600–1900; Oct–Jun 1500–1800.*

Sant'Anna in Camprena *Tel: 0578 748037; www.scuolacamprena.it. Open daily. 7km north of Pienza, off the road to Castelmuzio. Benedictine monastery founded in the 14th century, with frescos by Sodoma. It provided a setting for The English Patient and offers accommodation and Italian courses.*

⬤ Pienza is in the capital of Tuscany's cheese zone. Many of its shops sell delicious local *pecorino* made from sheep's milk. The *Fiera del Cacio* – an annual cheese fair and festival – takes place on the first Sunday in September.

The scholar and humanist Aenea Silvio Piccolomini became Pope Pius II in 1458. It wasn't enough for him to build a cathedral in his birthplace, Corsignano. He wanted to turn it into utopia, a *Città Ideale*, and name it after himself. He recruited Leon Battista Alberti to create plans and Bernardo Rossellino to carry them out. The result, though never finished, was one of the most beautiful cities built during the Renaissance, a harmonious ensemble of buildings constructed of honey-coloured travertine that glows at dusk and dawn. It was the stage set for Zeffirelli's *Romeo and Juliet* long before the film crew of *The English Patient* arrived. Piazza Pio II is its core, a trapezoidal square based on the ideas of Humanistic Renaissance culture.

At the main side of the Piazza is the cathedral of Santa Maria Assunta, built over the spot where the ancient Pieve di Santa Maria was situated. The papal coat-of-arms adorns the facade. Inside, you can pace its Latin cross of travertine columns, similar to the Hallenkirche (hall churches) of central Europe. Two altarpieces, by Giovanni di Paolo and Matteo di Giovanni, compete for attention with an *Assunzione* by Vecchietta, a *Madonna con Bambino* by Sano di Pietro and a marble altar, probably by Rossellino. Under the apse there is a crypt, actually the church of San Giovanni, where it is possible to find some portions of Romanesque sculptures that decorated the ancient Pieve di Santa Maria; there also is a magnificent font designed by Rossellino.

On the left of the cathedral is the **Palazzo Piccolomini✧** (1459–62), inspired by the Palazzo Rucellai in Florence. It has a nearly squared plan with ashlar-worked façades. The three floors have mullioned windows between pilasters and views of the Val d'Órcia and Monte Amiata. Nature and architecture were meant to coexist harmoniously in the *Città Ideale*. The court is surrounded by an elegant arcade with arches placed over columns with Corinthian capitals. The Palazzo is now a museum with the library of Pope Pius II and a collection of papal paraphernalia.

RADICÓFANI✧

❶ Rocca di Radicófani € *tel: 0578 55700. Open daily Apr–Sept 1000–1900; Fri–Sun Jan–Mar 1000–1700.*

On a visit to Radicófani, Charles Dickens described the region as 'barren, as stony and as wild as Cornwall in England'. Perhaps that is why the only English pope in history, Nicholas Breakspear of St Albans (1100–59) – better known as Adrian IV – chose the site for his fortress. This **Rocca✧** ('castle'), sitting at 766m on a hill above town, was used in later centuries by the notorious Ghino di Tacco. His name is mentioned with fear and loathing by both Boccaccio and Dante.

The town has a pair of interesting churches, the Romanesque San Pietro and the Renaissance Sant'Agata. Both have glazed terracotta

Opposite
Bagno Vignoni

Below
The portal of Collegiata
di Orsenna

work by the Andrea della Robbia school. On the road from Radicófani to Siena is an abandoned-looking Medici villa called Palazzo La Posta with an imposing fountain. For a couple of centuries, it was one of the few hotels in the region between Siena and Rome, serving people on the Grand Tour.

SAN QUÍRICO D'ÓRCIA✦

Collegiata di Orsenna € *Via Dante Alighieri; tel: 0577 897506.* Open daily.

Each year in June (on the third weekend), San Quírico remembers its moment in history with a *Festa del Barbarossa*, which involves a lot of medieval pageantry, flag waving and longbow competitions.

High on its hill, San Quírico began its history as an Etruscan settlement (its original name, *Osenna*, is Etruscan for 'water', or 'brook'). From the beginning of the 11th century, it became an important stop for pilgrims on their way to Rome as well as for Holy Roman Emperors. Frederick I (Barbarossa or 'red beard') came to Italy in 1154–5 to pick up the Imperial Crown. He and his army encamped at San Quírico because it was the last town before the boundary of the Papal State. Pope Adrian IV sent three cardinals to meet him and they struck a deal: the Pope gave him the crown; in return, Barbarossa hanged the Pope's nemesis, a monk named Arnaldo of Brescia. Unlike his friend Peter Abélard (lover of Héloïse), Arnaldo had put his actions where his words were and organised a rebellion against papal greed and warmongering.

The town's single artery is the Via Dante Alighieri with the tiny 11th-century Romanesque Chiesa Santa Maria Assunta at the south end and the baroque Palazzo Chigi (1679) at the north end. Facing the *palazzo* is the **Collegiata di Orsenna**✦ – famous for its carved portals. The *portale di mezzogiorno* (south door) is carved with enigmatic symbols and mythic beasts in mostly Romanesque style, with a few hints of Gothic. It is attributed to Giovanni Pisano. Inside, the choir stools have magnificent intarsia work, based on designs by painter Luca Signorelli that were originally created for one of the chapels of Siena's cathedral.

Accommodation and food

Il Chiostro €€ *Corso del Rossellino 26, Pienza; tel: 0578 748400; fax: 0578 748440.* As the name suggests, this is a former Franciscan cloister with vaulted rooms, frescos and coffered ceilings; a swimming pool, parking and a dazzling view.

Santo Pietro € *Strada Statale 126, No 29 on the road between Pienza and Montepulciano; tel and fax: 0578 748410; e-mail: santo.pietro@libero.it. Open Mar–Dec. Three-day minimum stay, half board only.* Fine views and lots of bucolic bliss at this *agriturismo*. The farm of Felice d'Angelo and Giulia Scala provides the wine, olive oil and vegetables for their guests' dinner.

Le Terme € *Overlooking the Basin of St Catherine, Bagno Vignoni; tel: 0577 887150; fax: 0577 887497; www.albergoleterme.it.* Unforgettable location but the interior is disappointing. Reservations a must.

Castello di Ripa d'Órcia €€ *Via della Contea 1/16, Ripa d'Órcia, 5km south of San Quírico d'Órcia; tel: 0577 897376; fax: 0577 898038; www.castelloripadorcia.com. Open Mar–Nov; two-day minimum stay.* The Aluffi Pentini family offers six rooms with private bathrooms in their castle (at the end of a gravel road out of Bagno Vignoni) with all sorts of comfort without compromising its medieval character. There are sweeping views from its terrace down the Val d'Órcia, a swimming pool and tennis court. It also has a good restaurant (*closed Mon*).

La Frateria di Padre Eligio €€€ *Convento San Francesco, Cetona; tel: 0578 238015 or 238261; fax: 0578 239220; e-mail: frateria@bcc.tin.it. Closed Nov.* St Francis would not approve, but if you want to splurge, go ahead and reserve one of the six luxurious double rooms in this converted monastery, now one of Tuscany's top hotels.

Camping delle Piscine € *Via del Bagno Santo 29 (9km from Sarteano); tel: 0578 26971; fax: 0578 265889; www.bagnosanto.it. Open Apr–Sept.* 'Camping' with a difference. There are three swimming pools, hot springs, a bar-restaurant and tennis courts. Reservations advised for summer.

La Solita Zuppa € *Via Porsenna 21, Chiusi; tel: 0578 21006; www.lasolitazuppa.it. Closed Tue.* A dozen kinds of soup: try chestnut and lentil, zucchini and fresh basil.

Osteria del Leone € *Via dei Mulini 3, Bagni Vignoni; tel: 0577 887300. Closed Mon.* Right across from the old Bagni Vignoni bathhouse, this simple *trattoria* offers a blackboard rather than a menu – just a short list in chalk of seasonal dishes such as pasta with a sauce of rabbit or boar, *anatra all'uva* ('duck with grape sauce') and *scottiglia di pollo* (chicken stew with herbs).

Antico Caffè Poliziano € *Via di Voltaia nel Corso 27, Montepulciano; tel: 0578 758615; e-mail: caffepoliziano@libero.it.* The art-deco café/bar has an art gallery, magnificent view and, in July, a jazz festival.

Suggested tour

Total distance: 94km; detours add 14km (to Cetona) and 4km (to Bagni San Filippo) (both return).

Time: Three days would be a reasonable amount of time for this tour. The itinerary can be done in a day if you drive most of the time and don't dawdle in castles, hill-towns or vineyards. There might even still be time for a quick soak in the thermal springs.

Links: This route can readily be combined with the route of the previous chapter. Chiusi is only about 10km from Città della Pieve, in Umbria (*see pages 213–14*).

Above
Hilltop Pienza

Route: From **MONTEPULCIANO ❶**, proceed to **Chianciano Terme ❷** – one of the most important thermal spas in Italy, celebrated for its waters since the Roman period. It was the centre for a cult of Apollo and another temple gave equal time to Diana. Today, the spas are rather clinical, in keeping with their serious medical role in the treatment of liver and rheumatic problems.

Detour: For an alternative route from Montepulciano, take the small, desolate road at Croce di Febo and drive through an almost unpopulated stretch of the Crete brushing past the hamlets of **Castellúcio** and **La Foce**; from Sarteano (10km), turn northeast to Chiusi.

Carry on 13km to **CHIUSI ❸** where there is free parking in a field at the edge of town (*you have to drive into the centre first to get there*). After retrieving the car, drive to **Sarteano ❹**, another medieval town with an Etruscan past.

Detour: Turn left ('south') on the road to **Cetona ❺**, at the foot of Monte Cetona. The village is an oval-shaped maze built around a formidable Rocca. The Chiesa Collegiata has a fresco of the ascension of Mary by Pinturicchio. The **Parco Archeologica Belverde ❻**, 5km north of Cetona, is an idyllic natural park with a small museum displaying Stone Age finds.

Continue on the N478 for the next 18km. It crosses the upper valley of the Órcia river.

Getting out of the car: After 8km, there is a road leading to the hamlet of **Fonte Vetriana**. The trail from there that climbs up to Monte Cetona is one of the most rewarding hikes in Tuscany.

The village of **RADICÓFANI ❼** seems high enough but a brutally steep road twists even further up to the **Rocca** (720m), the most famous castle in southern Tuscany. After hairpinning back down the hill (in low gear), proceed towards Siena.

Detour: Almost immediately after getting on the N2, you will see signs for **Bagni San Filippo ❽**. There is not much to the place except a turn-of-the-century spa and a handful of modest hotels at the edge of the forest. The thermal waters here range from 25° to 52°C. Signs will direct you further up the valley to **Fosso Bianco**. This is surely one of the most surreal waterfalls in Italy. The cascade of thermal water has left brilliant white deposits that look like hummocks of snow and icicles. It has many inviting pools of hot, milky water to soak in.

The N2 rejoins the valley of the Órcia river at the village of **BAGNO VIGNONI ❾**, clearly signposted just 1km off the road. **SAN QUÍRICO ❿** is a hop, skip and 5km up the N2. From there return to the N146 going to east in the direction of **PIENZA ⓫** (*parking just outside of the walls*). It is another 12.5km back to Montepulciano.

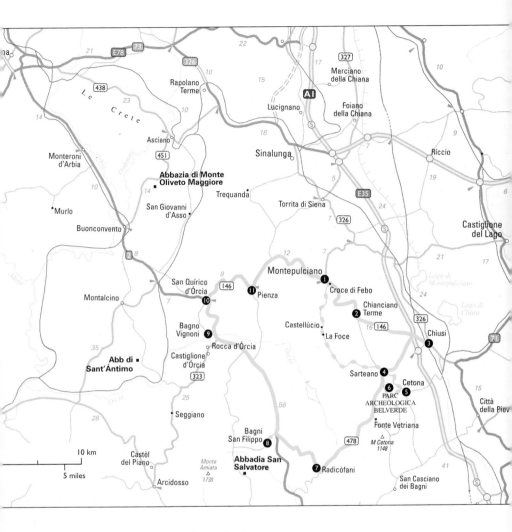

Also worth exploring

San Casciano dei Bagni is a medieval town on the southern slopes of Monte Cetona, not far from the meeting point of the provinces of Tuscany, Umbria and Lazio. The town, which attracts few foreign tourists, is surrounded by a natural park of hundred-year-old oaks, chestnuts and pines. At its core is a narrow maze of ancient streets intersecting with a Romanesque church and bell tower. The town's hot springs bubble with indubitable therapeutic properties. Not far from the town, in fact, flow 42 thermal springs, at a blissful bathtub temperature of 37–43°C.

Lucca

Ratings

Architecture	●●●●●
Shopping	●●●●●
Villas	●●●●●
Food and drink	●●●●○
Parks	●●●●○
Children	●●●○○
Museums	●●●○○
Nature	●●○○○

Lucca rivals any city in Italy for fascination and beauty. One century flows into the next – and right up to the present – as you walk past shops with medieval and art-nouveau façades, cross a Roman amphitheatre turned piazza and stroll along the magnificent 16th-century ramparts that are now a pleasure garden. This is 'the Tuscany that still lives and enjoys, hopes and works' (Henry James). Lucca is located in a plain at the foot of the high Apuan Alps and separated from the Tyrrhenian coast by a green border of pine-forest and a line of low hills. Thanks to its impenetrable walls, Lucca remained an independent city until the 19th century, long after most other Tuscan cities had became part of the Grand Duchy of Tuscany under the control of Florence.

Sights

❶ APT office *Piazza Santa Maria 35; tel: 0583 919931; fax 0583 469964; www.lucca.turismo.toscana.it & www.comune.lucca.it.*

Tourist Information *Piazzale Verdi, Porta San Donato; tel: 0583 419689; fax: 0583 442505.*

❶ Duomo San Martino *Piazza del Duomo. Open 0700–1900 in summer, shorter hours in winter*

Anfiteatro Romano❖
The Roman amphitheatre (2nd century AD) is now underground beneath this strange piazza and its former exterior is a street – Via dell'Anfiteatro. You can see one of the original arches at No 32. The amphitheatre was elliptical in shape and had two levels of 55 arches, one on top of the other.

Duomo San Martino (Opera del Duomo)❖❖
Bishop Frediano commissioned the building of the church of San Martino in the 6th century and the edifice advanced to the status of cathedral in the 8th century. Another bishop of Lucca and Pope Alexander II rebuilt it a couple of centuries apart. On the latter version, Guidetto da Como created its façade: a series of loggias resting on pillars and an atrium packed with bas-reliefs (1233) depicting the

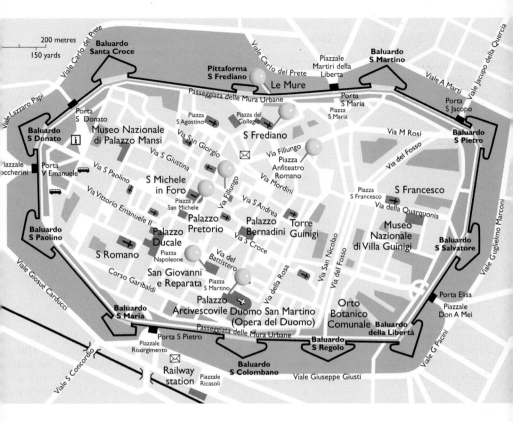

Ilaria del Carretto
€ *Sacrestia del Duomo.*
Open Apr–Oct Mon–Sat
0930–1745; Sun
0900–1000, 1300–1745;
Nov–Mar Mon–Fri
0930–1645; Sat
0930–1845; Sun
0900–1000, 1300–1700

Opera del Duomo €
*Piazza del Duomo; tel: 0583
490530. Open Apr–Oct
1000–1800; Nov–Mar
1000–1400.*

four stories of St Martin, the dispute with the Aryans and the Martyrdom of San Regolo. The great sculptor, Nicola Pisano, added a Nativity and Deposition. The porch is decorated with the tasks of the 12 months of the year, from giving a girl roses to slaughtering a pig.

Inside, the cathedral's pride and joy is the Volto Santo ('Holy Face'), an ancient wooden statue of a bearded Christ on the Cross, fully dressed, with a feminine face – said to have been carved by St Nicodemus. The people of Lucca have worshipped it for centuries. The cross is rumoured to contain relics – hairs of Christ, a phial of blood and, believe or not, Our Lord's prepuce.

The marble figure of **Ilaria del Carretto**❖❖ is Lucca's greatest monument. Ilaria, the 19-year-old wife of nobleman Paolo Guinigi, died in childbirth at the beginning of the 15th century. Short of freezing her head, there is nothing more sculptor Jacopo della Quercia could have done to immortalise her. The beautiful young woman seems to have fallen asleep on a cushion. At her feet is an alert lapdog, a symbol of fidelity. Other important works in the cathedral include: *Last Supper* by Tintoretto or his school (16th century) in the third

Volto Santo is carried out of the cathedral every year for the Luminaria di Santa Croce on the evening of 13 September. The crucifix is wrapped in its best silver and gold brocade, and paraded by candlelight through the *Centro Storico* by citizens of Lucca in medieval dress.

Every third Sunday of the month, there is a large antique market in front of the Duomo.

The 4km circuit of Lucca's walls can be done on a rented bicycle. Lucca is one of the few Italian cities that likes to 'get on its bike'. **Barbetti Cicli** Via dell'Anfiteatro 23, tel: 0583 954444; **Cicli Bizzarri** Piazza Santa Maria 32, tel: 0583 496031; **Antonio Poli** Piazza Santa Maria 42, tel: 0583 493787.

San Michele in Foro Piazza San Michele. Open 0800–1200, 1500–1800. To the right of the church is the Palazzo Pretorio, by Civitali, with a loggia containing busts of illustrious city citizens. On the left, the Palazzo del Decanato takes up the whole side of the square. Behind the tower are perfectly preserved 14th-century houses.

Opposite
Duomo San Martino

altar; *Madonna with Child* by Domenico Ghirlandaio (15th century) in the sacristy; *Resurrection* by Giambologna (16th century) in the so-called Freedom Chapel at the top of the left nave; *Madonna and Child between Two Saints* by Fra Bartolomeo (16th century) in the Madonna of the Sanctuary Chapel; and *Holy Apostle* (1416) by Jacopo della Quercia (in the left transept). There is also much fine work by Matteo Civitali, Lucca's best sculptor, including the pulpit, baptistry font and the tombs of Domenico Bertini and Pietro da Noceto in the south transept.

The Cathedral Museum, **Opera del Duomo**, next door was opened in 1992 as an act of piety and PR by a local bank. It is full of objects relating to the cult of the Volto as well as cathedral treasures: liturgical vestments, choir books, silver objects, paintings and statues.

Le Mure✷✷

Lucca is one of the few towns in Italy with a set of defensive walls perfectly intact (for what it is worth, they are, according to the Guinness Book of World Records, the largest completely preserved set of walls in Europe). The 4km circuit of wall was started in 1554 and took nearly a century to complete. Twelve metres high, it consists of 11 curtain walls, 10 bastions and 1 platform, called San Frediano. The base is 30m thick. On the bastions, the little barracks still stand that once housed guards or munitions. One hundred and twenty-four cannons defended the city until the Austrians removed them in 1799.

The walls of Lucca were so intimidating that no one ever dared to besiege the city. The only assault it was ever called on to withstand was the great flood of 1812 when the Serchio river overflowed its banks and turned the plain around Lucca into a lake. Maria Luisa Bourbon, acting on the suggestion of Napoleon's sister, Elisabeth Baciocchi, transformed the ramparts into a public garden. It is thanks to her that the people of Lucca take their *passeggiata*, the ritual evening walk, beneath the ancient plane, oak, lime and chestnut trees.

Piazza San Michele✷✷

The Piazza San Michele stands on the site of the former Roman forum. The church of **San Michele in Foro**✷✷, first mentioned in a document of AD 795, was rebuilt in the 11th century and completed in its present form in the 14th century. The brilliant white façade is a dreamy fusion of Gothic and Romanesque styles beneath a triumphant statue of St Michael the Archangel slaying a dragon (13th century).

'For the first time I now saw what medieval builders were and what they meant,' was the reaction of John Ruskin. The adjoining bell tower is the highest in Lucca. The façade is a hard act to follow (and the medieval builders ran low on funds) so the interior is less impressive. In one corner is a Madonna and Child by sculptor Matteo Civitali (it was once part of the façade). There is a glazed terracotta Madonna and Child attributed to Andrea della Robbia and a crucifix

San Frediano €
Piazza San Frediano.
Open Mon–Sat 0830–1200,
1500–1700; Sun
1030–1700.

**San Giovanni e
Reparata €** Piazza San
Giovanni; tel: 0583 490530.
Open May–Sept Mon–Fri
1000–1800, Sat–Sun
1000–1900; Oct–Apr
Tue–Fri 1000–1400,
Sat–Sun 1000–1800.

Taddeuci (Piazza San
Michele 34; tel: 0583
494933) is the best place
to buy the local speciality,
buccellato, a raisin and
aniseed cake. The shop has
an untouched 19th-century
interior of wood panels
and mosaic tiles.

**Centre of
government**

Lucca was already an
important city when
Caesar, Pompey and
Crassus met there in 56
BC to form Rome's first
triumvirate, and it
became even more
important when, under
the Lombards, it formed
the centre of
government of the
surrounding region.

by Berlinghieri from the end of the 12th century. However, the real highlight is the luminous panel by Filippino Lippi, son of the more famous Filippo.

San Frediano⁎

The oldest church in Lucca was named after the Irish saint and Lucca's first bishop, Fredianus. The mosaic façade, a kaleidoscopic Ascension of Christ, is by the picturesquely named Berlinghiero Berlinghiera. The church faces the wrong direction, east, because it was built next to a city wall. Inside, it is a monumental basilica with some of the capitals recycled from the nearby Roman amphitheatre.

The single most impressive object is the Romanesque Fonta Lustra near the front, a baptismal font upon which an anonymous artist sculpted Moses crossing the Red Sea, pursued by Egyptians in medieval armour. There is another baptismal font, still in use, carved by Matteo Civitali in 1489. The Cappella Trenta has an altar by Jacopo della Quercia. In the left nave, frescos by Amico Aspertini depict the arrival of the Volto Santo in Lucca.

The unmissable right-hand chapel is one of the most popular places to pray in Lucca – in the presence of the mummified St Zita. She accepted that bending the rules is all in a saintly day's work. A servant born in 1218, she stole bread on the job to give it to the poor and lied about it when caught in the act. But the lie became truth when the scraps of bread miraculously turned into roses.

San Giovanni e Reparata⁎

Few basilicas in Tuscany have a longer tale to tell than this one, from Roman times to the Middle Ages. It is a surreal experience to wander among the bits and pieces of Roman baths, pillars, mosaics and shops (180–100 BC) beneath the floor of the present church and then to re-emerge into natural light and look up at the baroque coffered ceiling. The stones are a vast puzzle, presented in a meticulous multicoloured map that the guardian will sell or loan out. The church dome was built in 1390 and represents a brave attempt to solve the problem of supporting such a structure, using a circle on top of a square. Brunelleschi studied it before beginning work on the cathedral in Florence.

Via Fillungo⁎

This narrow street is lined with medieval palaces and towers and shops with *fin de siècle* or art-nouveau façades: the jeweller Chioccetti (No 20); the shoe store graced with sexy art-deco nudes dating from the time when it was the Profumeria Venus (No 65); Puccini's favourite place to chain-smoke, the Caffè di Simo (No 58); Carli (No 95), in business since 1655 selling jewellery, ancient coins and antique watches; and the jeweller Pellegrino (No 111). There is also a small art-nouveau passage (No 102).

Opposite
San Michele in Foro

Accommodation and food

Don't even think of coming to Lucca without reservations. If you just arrive on a weekend or in high season, you might have to drive far before you sleep.

Universo €€€ *Piazza del Giglio 1; tel: 0583 493678; fax: 0583 954854.* The location is ideal, just inside the city walls and near the cathedral. It has an evocative, if faded, *belle-époque* atmosphere, its own parking and a good restaurant.

Hotel Stipino €€ *Via Romana 95; tel: 0583 495077; fax: 0583 490309.* The best hotel immediately outside of the walls (well, a five-minute walk from Porta Elisa), Stipino also has private parking. The owner is always busy, good-naturedly fussing over the housekeeping, his guests and his grandchildren. However, the rooms on the street are loud unless the double-glazed windows are kept shut (a disadvantage in summer) so ask for a room at the back.

Piccolo Hotel Puccini € *Via di Poggio 9; tel: 0583 55421.* A simple, friendly hotel with nostalgic, 19th-century flourishes but no 21st-century parking. Located just off Piazza San Michele in Foro.

Da Giulio in Pelleria €€ *Piazza S Donato; tel: 0583 55948. Closed Sun and Mon.* A big crowded *trattoria* great for homemade pasta and local standards such as stockfish with leeks, *bollito misto* ('stewed beef') with a sauce of herbs, and chicken roasted in a brick oven. For people who are not too PC, it also serves delicious horsemeat tartar. Mealtimes are crowded and chaotic so come early.

Buca di Sant Antonio €€ *Via della Cervia 1/5; tel: 0583 55881. Closed Sun and Mon.* A rustic place that is always crowded with people hungry for traditional dishes such as *zuppa al farro* (soup made with chicken stock, lentils and spelt) and homemade pasta such as *tortelli al sugo.*

Osteria Baralla € *Via Anfiteatro 5–9; tel: 0583 440240. Closed Sun.* An atmospheric bar/inn right off the Roman amphitheatre, popular with students, where you can eat anything from a *crostini* (toasted bread with liver pâté or tomatoes) to a full traditional meal.

Suggested tour

(P) While you are permitted to drive within the walls, you will probably regret it. There are small, paying car parks in: Piazza San Ponziano, Piazza Santa Maria Bianca, Piazza della Manifattura and Piazzale San Donato; but they fill up quickly. The free car parks just outside the walls are a better option (Via delle Tagliate or the Macelli area beside the hospital).

Left
Crostini

Below
Le Mure, Lucca's defensive walls

Total distance: 3.5km.

Time: Although compact, Lucca is not the sort of place you can easily reduce to an afternoon or even a long day. Two days is better. If time is short, walk a part of the walls, visit the Duomo and focus on the Piazza San Michele in Foro and the Via Fillungo.

Links: The route through the Garfagnana and Alpi Apuane begins and ends in Lucca (*see page 124*). It is also the starting point for the route on *page 135*.

Route: Enter Lucca from the Piazza Risorgimento through the **Porta San Pietro ❶**, the city's oldest gate. Turn left into the Via F Carrara and then right into the Via Vittorio Veneto to reach the **Piazza Napoleone**. There is a grotesque memorial to Princess Maria Luisa in the middle of the square and one of Garibaldi in the adjoining Piazza del Giglio. Walk past the latter statue and squeeze through a short lane into the Piazza San Giovanni to come face to face with **SAN GIOVANNI E REPARATA ❷**. Walk into the next piazza – the Piazza San Martino, dominated by the **DUOMO SAN MARTINO ❸** and the

Palazzo Arcivescovile. Exit the cathedral and veer right past a group of houses abutting the Duomo – built on the former colonnade of its 13th-century cemetery. The door to the cemetery is still preserved and leads to the treasures of the **Opera del Duomo** (Cathedral Museum). Continue up the same street (Via delle Trombe) a couple of paces and duck left into the atmospheric **Via del Battistero**. Proceed to Piazza San Giusto and turn right into Via Cenami. After one block it meets Via Roma. Turn left and walk into Piazza San Michele. Circle around **SAN MICHELE IN FORO ❹**, turn left into Santa Lucia then immediately right into Chiasso Barletti, an almost sunless lane which intersects with **VIA FILLUNGO ❺**. From here, join the eternal parade of this fascinating street. The walk now follows, roughly, the route taken by the annual candlelit procession of Lucca's prize relic, Volto Santo ('Holy Face'), and, in reverse, the silent procession of Napoleon's sister, Elisa Bonaparte Bacciochi, when she entered the city as princess in 1805.

Detour: At the Piazza dei Mercanti take the Via Sant'Andrea to the **Torre Guinigi ❻**. Bizarrely, it is crowned with holm oaks. However, the people of Lucca claim that all of their towers once sprouted trees. Climb the tower for a memorable view of the rooftops of Lucca and the marble-veined peaks of the Alpi Apuane to the north. On the way up and down you can study the shoe marks on the white-washed staircase walls, some as high as six feet up. No, it's not a Euro-funded art project, just a local, acrobatic form of graffiti.

Carry on down Via Fillungo to Piazza Scalpellini. Duck under the arch to the right and walk into the middle of the **PIAZZA ANFITEATRO ❼**. Exit the piazza through the gate on the opposite side (the small figure above it to the left is St Frediano). On the other side of the gate is Via dell'Anfiteatro. Follow the curve left until you reach Via Fillungo, walk left a few paces and take the first right to reach **SAN FREDIANO ❽**. After going inside, retrace your steps and, facing the church, walk left around it. Once behind it (having crossed Piazza del Collegio) take the ramp to the right of the wall. Begin your *passeggiata* along **LE MURE ❾** (city walls) going right (northeast).

Detour: Descend from the walls at the bastion of Baluardo San Salvatore, dropping down into Via della Quarquonia, to reach the **Villa Guinigi ❿**.

The Villa Guinigi was built by Paolo Guinigi in 1408 in a style that still displays some characteristics of Gothic architecture. The villa is now seat of the **Museo Nazionale di Villa Guinigi €**; *tel: 0583 496033; (open Tue–Sat 0900–1900, Sun 0900–1400)*. The museum houses important Roman and Hellenistic finds to remind the visitor how old Lucca really is. However, it is the medieval period that predominates with Romanesque, Gothic and Renaissance sculptures. There are many fine pieces by della Quercia and Matteo Civitali.

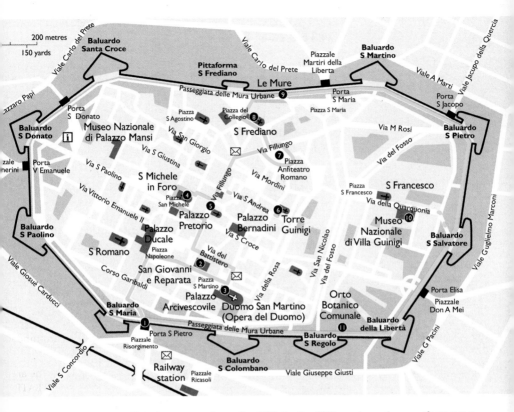

Paintings range from the 13th to the 19th century. Among them are a crucifix by Berlinghieri (13th century), two lovely altarpieces by Ugolino Lorenzetti and works by other Lucchese and Sienese masters.

Continue along the walls to the **Orto Botanico Comunale** (Botanical Garden) ⓫ at Porta Elisa (€; *open May–Sept Tue–Sun 0900–1300, 1530–1830; Oct–Apr Tue–Sat 0900–1300*), laid out by Elisa Baciocchi.

Also worth exploring

The **Museo Nazionale di Palazzo Mansi** (€ *Via Galli Tassi 43; tel: 0583 55570. Open Tue–Sat 0900–1900, Sun 0900–1400*) is worth a visit for the building alone, which is a rococo riot inside, culminating in the sumptuous *Camera degli Sposi* overflowing with Lucca-style embroidered silk. The Palazzo's Pinacoteca Nazionale has some 80-odd paintings, including a portrait of a pouting Alessandro de' Medici by Pontormo and one of Cosimo I by Bronzino. There are also works by Tintoretto, Fra Bartolomeo, Andrea del Sarto, Sodoma, and Beccafumi.

Garfagnana

Ratings

Caves	●●●●●
Geology	●●●●●
Mountains	●●●●●
Nature	●●●●○
Scenery	●●●●●
Food and drink	●●●●○
Architecture	●●●○○
Museums	●○○○○

The Garfagnana is as far from Chiantishire as you can travel, and still be in Tuscany. The mountainous region was once notorious for witches and its landmark is a grotesque medieval bridge supposedly built by the devil. Except for the hill-town of Barga, there isn't much here for the medievalist but it is a paradise for the walker, naturalist and spelunker. The Serchio river has cut a dramatic course between the heavily forested Apennines on the east and the geologically older Apuan Alps to the west. Although both ranges are beautiful, the Alpi Apuane stand out as one of the most original landscapes in Italy. Its peaks appear snowy because of the gleaming white fissures left by quarrying marble. Narrow roads switchback between the white-veined summits, plumbing forests of chestnuts and skirting alpine meadows.

BAGNI DI LUCCA❖

ⓘ **Informazioni turistiche** c/o Chiesa Anglicana; tel: 0583 805745; fax 0583 809937; www.provincia.lucca.it & www.alpiapuane.com. Bagni di Lucca is organising an annual opera festival that will take place from late July to early Aug.

Right
Bagni di Lucca

This little spa town has seen better days, for example, when literary types such as Shelley, Byron and Heinrich Heine stayed here. However, it is still a good place for people who like to wallow in faded elegance. In springtime, the surrounding sub-alpine meadows are covered with wild flowers. The casino has the oldest gaming licence in Europe, though it is not of much use since it is semi-permanently closed for restoration.

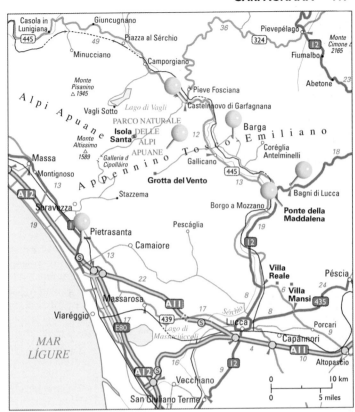

BARGA❖❖

Pro Loco *Piazza Angelio 3; tel: 0583 723499.*

Duomo San Cristofano € *Propositura. Open daily.*

It has been a long, strange trip for Barga. It evolved from Roman fort to Lombard castle-town to Lucchese bishopric and became a gleam in the expansionist eye of the Medici, who ruled it from Florence for centuries. In the hard times after the Second World War, Barga exported more people per capita than any other town in Italy.

The impressive **Duomo San Cristofano❖❖** dominates not only the town but also the surrounding valley. Architecturally, the cathedral is a Romanesque masterpiece. The lion-mounted pulpit inside is one of the most important medieval works of art in Tuscany (attributed to Guido Bigarelli), rivalling more famous work in Pisa. It evokes an early Christianity with eccentric figures portraying the familiar stories of the birth of Jesus, Adoration of the Magi, and so on. The enormous wooden figure in the choir is St Christopher, patron saint of travellers.

The people of Barga have no doubt prayed to him often in the last century as they boarded ship for America, Argentina and Scotland. The town is proud of its expatriates and its links to Scotland, in particular. Don't be surprised if you stumble across a fish and chips festival or a Highlands marching band.

CASTELNUOVO DI GARFAGNANA*

ℹ Informazioni turistiche *Via Cavalieri Vittorio Veneto; tel 0583 641007; e-mail: pro-Lococastelnuovog@libero.it; www.corrieredigarfagnana. com. Open Mon–Sat 0930–1230, 1530–1900; Sun 1000–1230.*

It was Castelnuovo's fate to be both an important base for Italian partisans during their guerrilla war against the German occupation and a part of the retreating Germans' line of defence. Allied bombing destroyed much of it. However, it is a friendly town that offers provisions and resources for all sorts of excursions into the surrounding mountains. The Renaissance poet Ariosto, author of *L'Orlando Furioso*, complained bitterly about his job as governor of this modest fortress. His former study is open to the public.

PARCO NATURALE DELLE ALPI APUANE**

ℹ Centro Accoglienza Visitatori *Piazza Erbe 1, Castelnuovo di Garfagnana; tel: 0583 644242; e-mail: grfvz@garfprod.it and Via Corrado del Greco 11, Seravezza; tel: 0584 756144; fax: 0584 756144; www.parks.it & www.parcapuane.it. Both centres open daily Jun–Sept 0900–1300, 1500–1900; Oct–Easter 0900–1300, 1530–1730; Easter–May 0900–1300, 1530–1830. Information and maps about excursions in the park (also on horseback).*

The Apuan Alps, the mountain range between the Serchio valley and the Versilian Riviera, only became a Parco Naturale in 1992, after much agitation and petition gathering. Now the struggle is on to give it the more protected status of Parco Nazionale. There is a good network of trails leading up to Pania di Croce (1858m) and Monte Forato (1223m), and the range of vegetation is amazingly wide.

Within the park are hundreds of kilometres of trails marked out by the local chapters of the Italian Alpine Club (CAI). The vast complex of caves beneath these mountains is a spelunker's paradise. The deepest, Antro del Corchia, reaches 1210m underground. Marble quarrying has contributed to the strange appearance of the mountains by leaving enormous open gashes. It remains important to the local economy and is not likely to stop anytime soon.

PIETRASANTA*

ℹ Museo Civico di Marmo € *Via XX Settembre 85, Massa Carrara; tel: 0585 845746. Open Mon–Fri 1000–1230, 1530–1830.*

Museo dei Bozzetti € *Via Sant'Agostino; tel: 0584 795500; fax 0584 795588; www.museodeibozzetti.com. Open Sept–Jun Tue–Sat 1400–1900; Jul–Aug Tue–Sun 1800–2000, 2100–2400.*

Few tourists ever bother to visit Pietrasanta ('blessed stone') and the other marble towns in the region with the partial exception of Carrara. Pietrasanta still practises the industry that was behind much of the great art in Tuscany. Once the marble quarried here was turned into heroic statues by Renaissance sculptors, but today the lion's share of the marble is earmarked for kitchens, kitsch and export to the Middle East.

The history and mining of marble is documented in the **Museo Civico di Marmo*** while the **Museo dei Bozzetti*** displays 280 works (dating from the beginning of the 20th century to the present time), created by artists from all over the word. The sketches (on a small scale) and the patterns (in actual size) represent the original idea before the work is executed. The museum, housed in the huge cloister of Sant'Agostino, also hosts travelling exhibitions.

PONTE DELLA MADDALENA❖

Ponte della Maddalena *Near the hamlet of Borgo a Mozzano.*

Above
The Ponte della Maddalena (Devil's Bridge)

Previous page
The Parco Naturale delle Alpi Apuane

The 93m-long bridge thrusts a bizarre parabolic stone arch 19m above the Serchio river, supported by three smaller arches. The existing bridge was probably built in the 13th century. Locals also call it the Ponte del Diavolo ('devil's bridge') since, presumably, only he would build it – in one night, according to the legend. Another legend claims that Satan merely helped in return for the first eight legs to cross the bridge (he was more interested, one assumes, in the souls attached to them). The architect, to fulfil his part of the bargain, sent chickens and a dog over the newly completed bridge.

Accommodation and food

Cucina in the Garfagnana

The diet in the mountains is somewhat like Lucca fare with more emphasis on frugality and ingredients such as chestnuts and mushrooms. For example, *polenta di neccio* was traditionally made with chestnut flour and served with pork bones, sausages and maybe a little ricotta cheese. Stewed rabbit is a standard, as are, in season, mushrooms and *cinghiale* ('wild boar'). Spelt, an ancient grain and staple of the Romans, is ubiquitous. Requiring hours to cook, it has never caught on in the supermarkets of the world. But in the Garfagnana it appears in many courses, including soup and pasta.

Right
Barga

Pietrasanta is a working man's town that also pulls artists from around the world in search of stone. They rub elbows in the cafés with the local masons.

Accommodation in this region is among the least expensive in Tuscany.

Roma €€ *Via Umberto I 110, Bagni di Lucca; tel and fax: 0583 87278.* A great hotel for romantics where Puccini used to be a regular. Most rooms have balconies overlooking its park and views of the Apennines.

Villa Libano €€ *Via del Sasso 6, Barga; tel: 0583 723059; fax: 0583 724185; www.hotelvillalibano.com.* The best address for Barga with a leafy garden, outdoor restaurant, swimming pool and stunning views of the Apuan Alps.

La Posta € *Piazza Antelminelli 2, in the village of Coréglia Antelminelli; tel: 0583 78027.* Rooms with a view (but shared bathroom) in an airy mountain village, with places to park and an earthy *trattoria* downstairs. The price is about the same as a campground.

La Mora €€€ *Via Sesto di Moriano 1748, in the village of Ponte Moriano, 9km north of Lucca on the N12; tel: 0583 406402.* Often described as Lucca's best restaurant though it is not in Lucca at all but to the north. A former coach station that has earned a Michelin star, La Mora triumphs with local ingredients such as eel and trout, pigeon, lamb and goat.

Locanda Le Monache €€ *Piazza XXIX Maggio 36, Camaiore; tel: 0584 989258; fax: 0584 984011; www.lemonache.com.* An inn/tavern on the ancient Via Francigena, the road used by pilgrims on their way south to Rome. They dish out a fine *frittura* of delicately fried meat and vegetables and standards such as *bistecca fiorentina*. Otherwise, the short menu depends on the season – minestrone with mushrooms, perhaps, or *coniglio* ('rabbit') *alla cacciatora*.

Da Giaccò € *Via di Arni 2, Camaiore; tel: 0583 667048.* In the heart of the Apuan Alps on the reservoir of Lake Isola Santa, this *trattoria* has a small terrace for summer eating but is perhaps at its best in autumn when they serve homemade pasta with truffles, *capretto alla brace* ('grilled goat') and *funghi* ('mushrooms'), grilled on polenta. For dessert, there are puddings made with mountain raspberries and chestnut flour.

Suggested tour

Total distance: 127km; detours add 10km (return) to Villas Reale and Mansi, 20km (return) to Coréglia Antelminelli, and 26km to the gorge of Orrido di Botri.

Time: This route can be appreciated as a long, interesting mountain drive. Getting out of the car to climb a peak in the marble mountains or descend into its caves would extend it to couple of days or more.

Links: This route does not overlap with any other. However, it would be easy to combine it with a drive down the coast (*see page 154*).

Route: From **Lucca** ❶, drive north along the meandering Serchio river on the N12.

Below
Duomo San Cristofano

Detour: The village of Marlia is signposted to the right after only 6km. From there, follow the signs for Villa Reale. The nobility and merchants of Lucca have always invested their money in land. Their villas allow you to compare 16th-century conspicuous consumption with the 18th- and 19th-century varieties. One of the best is **Villa Reale** ❷ (*open for guided tours only Mar–Nov Tue–Sun 1100–1800, with tours beginning each hour; or by booking, tel: 0583 30108*). The former summer residence of Elisa Bonaparte Bacciochi, it also belonged to the king of Italy, Vittorio Emanuele, hence its claim to be 'royal'. The main draw is a legendary baroque garden at the back with green rooms formed of clipped shrubs, potted citrus trees, a vast pool embroidered with flowers, statues of Harlequin and Columbine, and trick fountains that spray water on unsuspecting visitors. The Renaissance villa was redecorated in First Empire style by Elisa and she had another garden, English-style this time, laid out in front.

The **Villa Mansi** ❸ (*open Tue–Sun 0900–1300, 1500–1800, winter until 1700*) is only 2km away, in the direction of Segromigno. The baroque villa is in a perfect state of preservation and filled inside with Pompeii-style Mannerist décor and imposing porcelain and plate. The garden is a somewhat less impressive motley of styles – French, Sicilian and English.

The **PONTE DELLA MADDALENA** ❹ spans the Serchio river near Borgo a Mozzano. Further up the valley, take the right fork in the road towards **BAGNI DI LUCCA** ❺ into a long, leafy funnel of plane trees. Just before the edge of town to the left, a remarkable 19th-century bridge, the Ponte delle Catene (1840–60), spans the Lima river (a kind of Brooklyn Bridge in miniature).

Getting out of the car: Scale the road that rises from Bagni di Lucca above the valley of the Lima river to the high mountain village of Montefegatesi (842m). It then plunges down to a spectacular wild canyon – the Riserva Naturale dell'Orrido di Botri. The gorge has a couple of well-marked trails and nesting eagles, which you are more likely to hear than see. The adventurous mountain road continues to Abetone via the pass of Face a Giovo (1 647m).

From Bagni di Lucca, return to the Serchio river road and follow the N445, continuing north in the direction of Barga.

Detour: The mountain village of **Coréglia Antelminelli** ❻ is 10km off the N445 up a steep and scenic road. It has the curious little **Museo della Figurina di Gesso e dell'Emigrazione** (*Palazzo Vanni, Via del Mangano 17; tel: 0583 78082; open Mon–Sat 0800–1300, also Sun 1000–1300, 1600–1900 Jun–Sept*). The production of Plaster of Paris figures goes back to the 17th century here. The craftsmen, known as *figurinai*, fell on hard times and were eventually forced to emigrate to places all over the world – hence the juxtaposition of themes. If it happens to be closed, ask at the Pro Loco (*Via Roma 8*) and they will open it.

There is free parking at the entrance to Porta Reale in **BARGA** ❼. The steep walk up to its cathedral leads through a maze of houses built on the slopes over many centuries. The church terrace has one of the finest views in Tuscany sweeping over the woods of the Apennines and across the Serchio valley to the flinty crest of Pania di Croce (1 858m) in the Alpi Apuane.

Getting out of the car: Cross the Serchio river at Barga to Gallicano and press on west for 9km to reach the **Grotta del Vento** ❽ at the foot of Pania di Croce. It is one of the largest stalactite caves in Europe. There are three different tours several times daily lasting one, two or three hours that venture progressively deeper into the cave (*all three tours daily Apr–Oct and Sun year round; Nov–Mar Mon–Fri only the first tour is available; tel: 0583 722024; www.grottadelvento.com*). They

Above
Marble quarry in the Alpi Apuane

explore its crystal-incrusted lakes, natural curtains of alabaster and subterranean waterfalls. The third tour, taking in the entire cave, involves a dizzying climb down into an abyss that leaves you clutching at the handrails. Dress warmly regardless of the time of year. The normal temperature is 10°C.

Continue on the N445, skirting the Serchio river until you reach **CASTELNUOVO DI GARFAGNANA ❾**. If it isn't lunchtime, this is the best town (along with Seravezza) to find maps and information about outdoor activities. From here, take the road that leads through the narrow valley of Túrrite Secca (be careful not to get on the road to Caréggine by mistake) and you will find yourself driving through the heart of the **PARCO NATURALE DELLE ALPI APUANE ❿**.

Getting out of the car: Several trails of the Garfagnana trekking circuit pass near the small lake of **Isola Santa ⓫**. A rewarding but brutally steep trail climbs 8km (return) to the summit of Monte Sumbra (1 764m). An easier walk leads towards Lago di Vagli.

After the reservoir of Isola Santa, choose the left fork at the hamlet of Tre Fiumi. Shortly afterwards, you will pass an abandoned marble quarry (belonging to Henraux). Through a massive fissure in the rock gleams a vast, neatly carved expanse of grey-veined marble. (A rusty sign, now fallen to the ground, warns that you set foot on the area at your own risk.) The road passes through a natural rock tunnel. When you burst into the light at the exit, pull over for a look at **Monte Altissimo**, where the illusion of snow is striking. It's like a ski resort with a couple of inviting *pistes* running down the middle. (There is a road leading up to the quarry but it is strictly off-limits and signs in multiple languages warn of multiple dangers including falling rock and the use of explosives.)

A long descent now begins, through perhaps the most beautiful stretch of the Apuan Alps. For the next 45km, you will be travelling in the footsteps of Michelangelo. He spent the two most frustrating years of his life in the region (1518–20) engaged in road engineering and the transport of marble (because his patron, Pope Leo X, had a disagreement with the marble suppliers of Carrara). Quarrying marble has always been a hazardous occupation; the road is lined with small chapels in memory of those who have died in mining accidents. One of them records the death of 22-year-old Giulio, followed by his father Carlo, 15 years later.

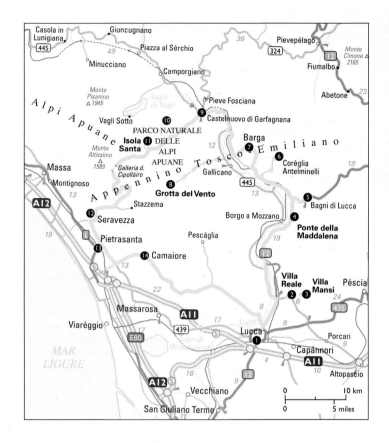

Outside **Seravezza** ⑫, a left fork in the road heads to **PIETRASANTA** ⑬ although the rusted blue sign only mentions '...SANTA'. If you miss it, it is no big deal. The next major left turn (south on the N1) also takes you there. However, when leaving town, avoid the N1, instead following the signs for **Camaiore** ⑭. From there, a pleasant country road leads back to **Lucca** with views, to the left, of the Alpi Apuane.

Also worth exploring

For people who plan ahead, there is a village worth seeing – at the bottom of Lago di Vagli. The village of **Fabbricca di Carrégine** was evacuated and flooded by a newly built reservoir in 1953. Every ten years (2004 will be the next time), the reservoir is drained for cleaning and the village rises from the protean muck as if by miracle. The former residents and a few curious tourists stand on the shore and watch.

Parco di Pinocchio
ingresso

Lucca to Florence

Ratings

Children	●●●●●
Thermal springs	●●●●●
Architecture	●●●●○
Shopping	●●●●○
History	●●●○○
Museums	●●●○○
Scenery	●●●○○
Nature	●●○○○

The lower valley of the Arno river forms a broad green trough, a notable exception to Tuscany's hilly geography. It has a dense concentration of agri-business, light industry and people. The A11 *autostrada* – one of Italy's main traffic arteries – covers the distance (74km) between Lucca and Florence in 40 minutes, unless there is a traffic jam. People who prefer travel to transit, however, will find that the valley's historic towns are rewarding for their art and architecture. Pistóia's marketplace has scarcely changed since the Middle Ages and Prato has something for both the art historian and the fashion victim. The valley's byways quickly lead to places where there is neither industry nor tourism, such as the deep woods and high mountain valleys of the Apennines, dotted with castles and medieval villages.

MONTECATINI TERME❖

❶ **APT office** *Viale Verdi 66/68; tel: 0572 772244; fax: 0572 92761; e-mail: apt@montecatini. turismo.toscana.it; www.montecatini-alto.it.*

❶ € A funicular begins a few hundred metres above the spa and climbs up the mountain to **Montecatini Alto**, an ancient fortified town.

The most elegant spa in Tuscany and the largest in Italy, Montecatini has played host to the Medici, Verdi, the Duke of Windsor, Spencer Tracy, the Shah of Iran and Princess Grace of Monaco. They all came here to cure their livers and upset stomachs, putting themselves and their organs under the care of doctors, dieticians, masseurs and polished hoteliers. While the place still pulls a few rich and famous, it is becoming more scientific and less chic. The traditional thermal treatment of the liver, digestive tract and disorders of a creaking metabolism are now supported by modern medicine and rehabilitation. Therapy might mean simply gulping the water, taking salty baths and being massaged; or, more ambitiously, mud baths, inhalations, physiotherapy and medical gymnastics. If that doesn't restore the 'psycho-physical balance', there are also naturally hot 'sweat-caves' in nearby Monsummano Terme.

Montecatini's eight spas are set in the vast, well-manicured Parco

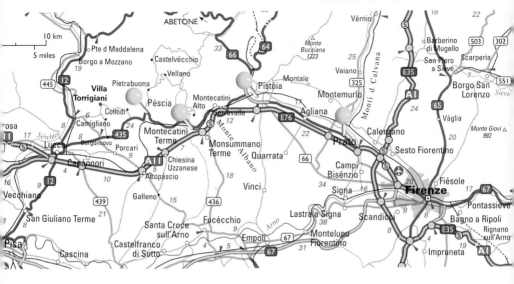

delle Terme. Since 1926, the entire complex has belonged to the State. The most elegant of them is Tettuccio. If the spa looks familiar, perhaps it is because you've seen it before in Fellini's film *8 ½*. The central protagonist, Marcello Mastroianni, oscillates between his soft-porn fantasy world and real-life encounters in the spa with wife and friends among neo-classical marble pools, fountains and loggias.

PÉSCIA✦

ⓘ Informazioni turistiche *Piazza Mazzini 11; tel: 0583 978205; www.comune.pescia.pt.it*

Below
Péscia's market

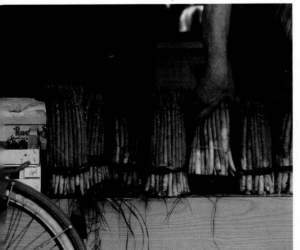

Italy's flower capital, Péscia harvests a couple of million blooms daily from its rows of vast glasshouses; it is also a major producer of olive oil and asparagus. The Piazza Mazzini is a historic, elongated square on the east side of the Péscia river packed with shops, bakers and bars.

The parish of Péscia is mentioned for the first time in a 10th-century document as being a religious complex of remarkable importance. The cathedral was, however, completely rebuilt in the baroque style in 1726. Among its treasures are a triptych by Luca della Robbia and, in the Cappella Turini, a copy of *Our Lady of the Canopy*, by Raphael (the original was appropriated by Ferdinand, Duke of Tuscany, and is now in the Pitti Palace in Florence). The altar of the austere church of San Francesco reveals the earliest known portrait of St Francis, painted in 1235, only a decade after his death.

PISTÓIA✤✤

APT office *Piazza del Duomo I; tel: 0573 21622; fax: 0573 34327; e-mail: aptpistoia@comune.pistoia.it; www.comune.pistoia.it.*

Duomo San Zeno € *Piazza del Duomo. Open daily.*

Capella di San Jacopo € *Piazza del Duomo; tel: 0573 25095. Open Mon–Sat 1000–1200 and 1600–1745, Sun 1130–1200 and 1600–1750.* If the chapel is locked and no church service is underway, ask the church guardian to open it. He might insist on locking you in, but will return, sooner or later.

The annual *Giostra dell'Orso* is a knight's tournament in Renaissance dress (25 July), in which each knight has to kill the figure of a bear – Pistóia's heraldic animal – with a heavy lance in the presence of his lady.

Pistoia Blues An international blues festival held every Jul. E-mail: info@pistoiablues.com; www.pistoiablues.com.

The Romans founded the city of Pistóia in the 2nd century and it was near here that Rome's famous conspirator, Catiline, lost his life in battle. In the Middle Ages, Pistóia was caught between the overlapping spheres of influence of Florence and Pisa, until the former took over in 1254. Pistóia had a reputation for all sorts of evil-doing, promoted mostly by the Florentines who blamed them for splitting Florence into factions of Bianchi ('Whites') and Neri ('Blacks'). In any case, Pistóia was the place where you could get the latest weapons, such as the *pistole*, originally a combination dagger and hand-held gun.

The city's Piazza del Duomo is the secular and religious rolled into one: the cathedral, bell tower and baptistry, and the Palazzo del Comune, Palazzo Pretorio and Palazzo Vescovile are all here. The **Duomo San Zeno✤**, founded in the 5th century, is one of the oldest in Tuscany. The present building dates mostly from the 12th century. An unusual porch was added to the façade in 1311. The central pillars form the opening of a barrel vault decorated with vivid coffers of shiny, pastel-painted terracotta by Andrea della Robbia (15th century). The interior is simple and imposing with a nave and two aisles divided by columns. The entrance wall has a font sculpted by Benedetto da Maiano. On the wall of the right aisle is the tomb of poet Cino da Pistóia, a contemporary and friend of Dante's. The monument to Cardinal Niccolò Forteguerri is by Verrocchio and pupils.

The most remarkable object is the luminous silver altar of the **Cappella di San Jacopo✤✤**. Generations of artists worked on it in gold and silver between 1287 and 1456 and created 628 figures. It is interesting to compare the figures on the left side, by Brunelleschi and Leonardo di Giovanni, to the nine principal scenes from the saint's life on the front, sculpted centuries earlier. Opposite the cathedral is the octagonal baptistry built in only 20 years, starting in 1338, of green and white marble.

Just two blocks off the square, the Ospedale del Ceppo is perhaps the world's most beautiful functioning hospital. It was founded in 1277 and expanded during the 1348 plague. Its storybook 15th-century frieze in glazed terracotta by Giovanni della Robbia shows the Seven Merciful Works of founder St Buglioni. It is well worth seeking out Sant'Andrea as well. Inside, is a pulpit sculpted by Giovanni Pisano (1301), and on the right in a niche, his statue of Sant'Andrea.

Above
Pistóia's market

Opposite
Pistóia's Duomo San Zeno

PRATO❖❖

ℹ Informazioni turistiche *Piazza Santa Maria delle Carceri 15; tel:/fax: 0574 24112; www.prato.turismo.toscana.it. Open Mon–Fri 0900–1300, 1400–1830; Sat 0900–1330, 1400–1800.*

🏛 Museo del Tessuto *€ Viale Santa Chiara 34; tel: 0574 611503; www.po-net.prato.it/tessuto. Open Mon, Wed–Fri 1030–1830; Sat 1000–1800; Sun 1100–1900.*

Museo dell'Opera del Duomo *€€ Piazza del Duomo 49; tel: 0574 29339. Open Mon, Wed–Sat 0930–1230, 1500–1830; Sun 0930–1230.*

Centro per l'Arte Contemporanea Luigi Pecci *€€ Viale della Repubblica 277; tel: 0574 5317. Open Mon and Wed–Fri 0800– 2000, Sat–Sun 1000–1900.*

Prato, the second largest city in Tuscany, has been in the shadow of Florence for all of its history. It even suffered the indignity, in 1351, of being sold to its wealthy neighbour by absentee rulers from the Neapolitan House of Anjou. Then, as now, the town's main concern was producing and selling cloth. Today, Prato accounts for the lion's share of Italian textile production and provides cloth to the big names in Italian fashion.

The 6 000 exhibits at the **Museo del Tessuto** (Textile Museum)❖ are a useful introduction to Prato's business and a homage to damask, silk, brocade, velvet and even polyester. However, Prato is a historic and artistic city as well as a commercial one. Its star attraction is the 13th-century cathedral of **Santo Stefano**❖❖, inspired by Pisa and Lucca in its use of limestone and green marble, which gained cathedral status in 1653. It still attracts pilgrims from all over the world to see a precious relic – Mary's girdle, which she threw down to St Thomas on her way to heaven. The outdoor pulpit on the right corner of the façade was purpose-built to show it off (designed by Michelozzo with panels sculpted by Donatello). The girdle is actually kept in the 14th-century Cappella della Cintola at the beginning of the left-hand aisle.

One of the signature paintings of the Renaissance is in the choir. The fresco of *Herod's Banquet* is the work of native son Fra Filippo Lippi, a priapic monk and great painter. He seduced a nun in a Prato convent, and immortalised her as a sensual, black-eyed Madonna in many paintings. Thin veils billow around the body of Salome as she does her veiled dance – Botticelli's beauties owe much to her (he was Lippi's apprentice); in the meantime, the head of John the Baptist arrives on a platter like the *pièce de résistance*. Architecturally, the interior is a muscular Romanesque style, lightened by the two-colour scheme, used here for the first time indoors.

The **Museo dell'Opera del Duomo**❖ has the (weathered) original Donatello panels from the pulpit of the sacred girdle and *The Death of Jerome* by Filippo Lippi. On the edge of town, near the Firenze-Mare *autostrada* exit, is Prato's progressive modern art museum and cultural centre, the **Centro per l'Arte Contemporanea Luigi Pecci**❖, created by the industrialist Signor Pecci in memory of his dead son.

Opposite
Prato's Piazza del Comune

Left
The cathedral's external pulpit

Accommodation and food

Il Convento €€€ *Via San Quírico 33, Pistóia (Pontenuovo district), 4km in the direction of Prato; tel: 0573 452651; fax: 0573 453578.* Pistóia's best hotel – 23 rooms in a former Franciscan convent with an excellent restaurant.

Stella d'Italia € *Piazza Duomo 8, Prato; tel: 0574 27910; fax: 0574 40289.* The perfect location with a view of Prato's cathedral and main square. Friendly and comfortable in a fits-like-an-old-shoe sort of way.

Below
Montecatini Terme spa

Lo Storno € *Via del Lastrone 8, just off Piazza Sala, Pistóia; tel: 0573 26193. Closed Sun and Mon–Wed evenings.* There is a wonderful price-quality ratio at this small *trattoria*. The menu is limited (no *antipasta* and only two house wines) but delicious and changes almost daily depending on what's fresh in the market and the whim of owner-chef Aldo Bugiani.

Il Pirana €€€ *Via Valentini 110, Prato; tel: 0574 25746. Closed Sat lunch and Sun.* One of the top fish restaurants in Tuscany. The décor is postmodern.

La Vecchia Cucina di Soldano € *Via Pomeria 23, Prato; tel: 0574 34665. Closed Sun and in Aug. No credit cards.* A good place to try the local *minestra di pane* ('vegetable soup'), *sedani repieni* ('stuffed celery') – a signature Prato dish – and *biscotto di Prato*, a hard biscuit that is often dipped in wine or coffee.

Shopping in Prato's factory outlets

Some of Prato's *fabbriche* (factories) sell clothing directly and the savings can be substantial. Their hours vary and are subject to change. Some of them will only accept cash.

Lanificio Cangioli *Via del Bisenzio a San Martino 6; tel: 0574 693925. Open Mon and Sat 0930–1230, Tue and Thu–Fri 1530–1830. No credit cards.* Specialists in cashmere.

Gruppo Osvaldo Bruni *Via Galcianese 67–69; tel: 0574 607591; www.gruppoosvaldobruni.it. Open Mon 1600–2000; Wed–Fri 0900–1300, 1530–1930; Sat 1000–1300. Credit cards – Visa accepted.* Classic knitwear, and high-class T-shirts.

Maglieria Artigiana *Via del Mandorlo 19–21; tel: 0574 550384; www.maglieriaartigiana.it. Open Mon–Fri 0930–1300, 1500–1900, Sat morning by appointment only. Credit cards accepted.* Classic designs and a broad range of colours.

Maglificio Denny *Via Zarini 261; tel: 0574 592191; www.denny.it. Open Mon–Fri 0900–1300, 1500–1930; Sat 0930–1300 by appointment. Credit cards – Visa, Mastercard accepted.* A vast selection of knitwear is sold here – pure wool, merino, shetland and cashmere or blends with natural and synthetic fibres.

Suggested tour

Total distance: 74km; detours add 22km (return) to Villa Torrigiani, 4km to Collodi (return); 35–60km, depending on circuit, for La Svizzera Pésciatina; 44km to Abetone, Montagna Pistoiese.

Time: This route could be considered as an alternative to the *autostrada* for reaching Florence. Or you could stay in one of the towns for a couple of nights and visit Florence by train, reserving the car for excursions into the Apennines and spending the money you save in Prato on a cashmere sweater.

Links: Lucca is also the starting point for a tour of the Garfagnana (*see page 124*).

Route: The N435 road from **Lucca ❶** (*see page 108*) to Péscia is often congested and runs the gauntlet of roadside light industry and retail. You could have your hair cut, cat spayed, shoes and tyres replaced, and furniture re-upholstered many times over in the first couple of kilometres.

Detour: Take the left fork at Borgonuovo after 9km. Drive to the village of Camigliano and follow the signs from the village to **Villa Torrigiani ❷**.

Below
Collodi's Villa Garzoni

A long avenue of cypresses leads from here to one of the most famous Medici villas in Tuscany (*open Mar–mid-Nov 1000–1230,1500–1830, mid-Nov–Dec groups by appointment only – tel: 0583 928041. Closed Tue and Jan–Feb*). The villa was the 16th-century dream home of the Buonvisi family. Alfonso Torrigiani remodelled it in the 18th century and created an English garden. The baroque garden is the biggest draw with occasional demonstrations of trick fountains used for 18th-century 'soak-the-guest' water games.

The road leaves the plain as the N435 approaches Péscia, near the foothills of the Apennines.

Detour: 4km before Péscia, the road to **Collodi ❸** is clearly marked.

Wooden Pinocchio puppets dangle by the hundred from souvenir stands in a bend in the road just before the **Parco di Pinocchio** (*tel: 0572 429342; www.pinocchio.it; open daily 0830–dusk*). The theme park recreates 21 scenes from the adventures of Pinocchio in mosaics, mazes and statues (no virtual reality yet). The author, Florentine Carlo Lorenzini, wrote the celebrated children's story in 1881, and adopted the name of his mother's village, where he had spent part of his childhood, as a pseudonym.

The town's other star attraction is the fabulous garden of the Villa Garzoni, a manmade Eden planted in the 17th century and inhabited by topiary animals and strange terracotta creatures. It is one of the finest baroque gardens in Italy. Above the garden is the medieval hamlet of Collodi that has stupendous views and relatively few visitors – perhaps because it is a steep (but short) uphill walk.

The road twists into **PÉSCIA ❹** and then out again after crossing the river of the same name.

Detour: Only a few kilometres north of Péscia, above the local paper mills, is so-called La Svizzera Pésciatina ('the Pescian Switzerland') a rugged and heavily forested range of hills and mountains divided by two high valleys. Monte Battifolle (1 109m) is their highest point. Ten tiny, fortified villages dating from the 11th century dot the area, all of them with walls and castles at least partly intact. Few tourists make their way up here and the facilities are limited so inquire in advance about accommodation. **Pietrabuona ❺** (**Pro Loco** *Via del Campanile 7, tel: 0572 408013; fax: 0572 440540*) is normally the starting point for a tour of the area, which usually includes **Castelvécchio ❻** and Pontito, and **Vellano ❼** as the final destination.

Once you reach **MONTECATINI TERME ❽**, follow the signs for Parco delle Terme. After the leafy park, the road to **Montecatini Alto ❾** zig-zags 5km and several hundred metres up to the mellow old hill-town that overlooks the Val di Nievo. On the way back down, stop at the first intersection, follow the signs for Serravalle (passing a co-operative that sells local olive oil on the right) and descend into the Val di

Nievo. At the end of the valley is the unmistakably medieval profile of **Serravalle** ⓾, where you will rejoin the N435. The *Centro Storico* has several well-preserved towers (and an optimistic tourist office that calls it 'a miniature San Gimignano'). The road to **PISTÓIA** ⓫ is uneventful except for the occasional traffic jam and a couple of fine old villas that seem stranded by the roadside. There is a car park near the *Centro Storico* and, generally, parking is available on the street as well (but check the signs).

Detour: The mountains above Pistóia – the Montagna Pistóiese – are reached via the N66, N632 and N12. This is the route Hannibal and his elephants travelled on their way to crush the Romans at Lake Trasimeno (the elephants didn't make it: *see page 217*). The area is popular for skiing in winter and trekking in summer. The highest peak is Cimone (2165m). **Abetone** ⓬ is the main ski resort.

From Pistoia, follow signs for Montale and Montemurlo to **PRATO** ⓭. The road between Prato and Florence is almost solid light industry so one might as well take the *autostrada* to get to **Florence** ⓮.

Also worth exploring

The town of **Vinci**, as in Leonardo (1452–1519), is 24km south of Pistoia along a charming road that climbs over Monte Albano. The great artist, scientist, inventor, architect and engineer was born out of wedlock in the nearby village of Anchiano. The **Museo Leonardiano** (*tel: 0571 56055; open Mar–Oct daily 0930–1900; rest of year 0930–1800*) has a fascinating collection of his inventions – the bicycle, an armoured tank, helicopter, swing and suspension bridges, a parachute and machine guns – that never made it any further than his sketchpad. Vinci is in the middle of a Riserva Naturale and the starting point for many rewarding hikes.

Pisa

Ratings

Architecture	●●●●●
Art	●●●●●
History	●●●●○
Seafood	●●●●○
Museums	●●●○○
Children	●●○○○
Shopping	●●○○○
Nature	●○○○○

Few cities, even in Italy, have known such a burst of creativity as Pisa in the 11th century. The Pisans expelled Saracen invaders and launched a new era in trade and commerce. They did the same for architecture and sculpture, contributing to the rebirth of the classical spirit in Italy. The Renaissance itself might have taken place in Pisa rather than Florence had it not been for the city's disastrous naval defeat of 1284 and the silting up of its port. The group of medieval buildings in Pisa's Campo dei Miracoli (Field of Miracles) is one of the most remarkable in the world. Its Leaning Tower, as Charles Dickens observed, leans enough 'to satisfy the most demanding tourist'. However, there is another Pisa, where few tourists go: the *Centro Storico*, not a museum but a throbbing city, humming with traffic and thousands of university students.

Sights

ℹ Informazioni turistiche *Piazza del Duomo, tel: 050 560464; www.pisa.turismo.toscana.it. Open Mon–Sat 0900–1800; Sun 1030–1630.*

🏛 Campo dei Miracoli *sights, including Museo delle Sinopie, are open daily Nov–Feb 0900–1640; Mar, Oct 0900–1740; Apr–Sept 0800–1940. Combined tickets (€€) available. For campanile see page 140.*

Battistero❖❖❖
The reason for a separate baptistry here, as in Florence, was the early Christian taboo against an unbaptised person setting foot in the Lord's house. Begun in 1152, it was essentially the work of the father and son team of Nicola and Giovanni Pisano. The hexagonal pulpit by Nicola Pisano (1260) launched a new style of sculpture in Italy. The building has remarkable acoustics. If you test it by snapping your fingers in the centre, a loud echo replies.

Campanile (Torre Pendente or Leaning Tower)❖❖❖
Surely the most bizarre fact about the Leaning Tower is that most of it was built after it had started to lean. The Pisans who began this tower in 1173 only completed 10m before things went awry. The 13th-century architects made the best of it by lengthening the south-side

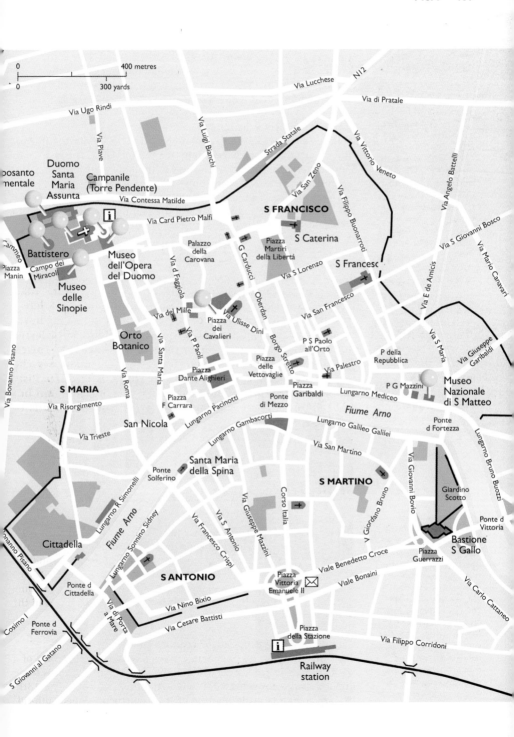

0
400 metres
0
300 yards

Via Lucchese   N12

Via di Pratale

Via Ugo Rindi

Via Luigi Bianchi

Via Piave

Via Vittorio Veneto

Via Angelo Battelli

posanto
mentale

Duomo
Santa
Maria
Assunta

Campanile
(Torre Pendente)

Via Contessa Matilde

Strada Statale

Via San Zeno

Via Filippo Buonarroti

S FRANCISCO

Via Card Pietro Malfi

Via S Giovanni Bosco

Via Mario Canavari

Campino

Battistero

Piazza
Manin

Campo dei
Miracoli

Museo
delle
Sinopie

Museo
dell'Opera
del Duomo

Palazzo
della
Carovana

G Carducci

Piazza
Martiri
della Libertà

S Caterina

Via S Lorenzo

S Francesc

Via d Faggiola

Via del Mille

Via P Paoli

Via Ulisse Dini

Oberdan

Via San Francesco

Via E de Amicis

Via S Maria

Via Giuseppe Garibaldi

Orto
Botanico

Piazza
dei
Cavalieri

Borgo Stretto

P S Paolo
all'Orto

Via S Santa Maria

Via Roma

Piazza
delle
Vettovaglie

Via Palestro

P della
Repubblica

Museo
Nazionale
di S Matteo

S MARIA

Via Risorgimento

Piazza
Dante Alighieri

Piazza
F Carrara

Ponte
di Mezzo

Piazza
Garibaldi

Lungarno Mediceo

P G Mazzini

San Nicola

Via Trieste

Lungarno Pacinotti

Lungarno Gambacorti

Fiume Arno

Lungarno Galileo Galilei

Ponte
d Fortezza

Lungarno Bruno Buozzi

Santa Maria
della Spina

Via San Martino

Cittadella

Lungarno R Simonelli

Ponte
Solferino

Via Giuseppe Mazzini

Corso Italia

Via S Antonio

Via Giuseppe Mazzini

S MARTINO

Via Giovanni Bovio

V Giordano Bruno

Giardino
Scotto

Ponte d
Vittoria

Lungarno Sommino Sidney

Via Francesco Crispi

Piazza
Guerrazzi

**Bastione
S Gallo**

Bonanno Pisano

Lungarno Arno

Ponte d
Cittadella

Via di Porta a Mare

S ANTONIO

Via Nino Bixio

Viale Benedetto Croce

Viale Bonaini

Via Carlo Cattaneo

Cosimo I

Ponte d
Ferrovia

Via Cesare Battisti

Piazza
Vittoria
Emanuele II

S Giovanni al Gatano

Piazza
della Stazione

Via Filippo Corridoni

**Railway
station**

Leaning Tower of Pisa

The symbolic importance of the Leaning Tower of Pisa rivals that of the Eiffel Tower or the Statue of Liberty. But how much longer will it stand – or rather lean – for Italy? The 55m-high Tower of Pisa, after threatening to collapse for centuries, was a full 5m out of plumb in 1990; furthermore it was actually rotating in the soft subsoil.

Around the millennium, Italian engineers began the ambitious project of removing soil from beneath its foundations opposite the lean. By late 2001, the angle had been reduced by 10 per cent. You can once again climb its 294 steps for the stunning view of the Arno, the Tyrrhenian Sea and the Apuan Alps, confirming that this is indeed the 'field of miracles'.

Campanile €€
Campo dei Miracoli. Book in advance via the website: www.opapisa.it or purchase tickets from the ticket office just behind campanile. For further information contact the **Museo dell'Opera del Duomo**, *Piazza del Duomo 17; tel: 050 560547; fax: 050 560505. Guided groups of 40 depart every 40 minutes 0800–1920 (also mid-Jul–Aug Fri–Sat 2030–2300). No children under eight.*

columns by 70mm, giving it a slight banana shape. This is the origin of the myth that it was built to tilt on purpose. Galileo put the tower's tilt to good use in 1589 by dropping assorted objects, comparing their speed, and formulating the theory of the constancy of gravity.

Camposanto Monumentale❖❖

During the Crusades, the Pisans imported 50 ships filled with earth from Golgotha for their cemetery, the Camposanto. The city's most prominent citizens were laid to rest in the holy earth until the 18th century. It is decorated with Roman tombs and sarcophagi.

Florentine artist Bonamico di Martino, nicknamed 'Buffalmacco', has been attributed as the creator of the alarming frescos that depict *Il Trionfo della Morte* ('Triumph of Death'), *Last Judgement* and *Inferno*. It is impossible fully to understand them without taking into account the plague epidemics that swept across Italy, beginning in 1348, and the sadistic visions of Hell that become a trademark of the Dominican order. A stray American bomb destroyed the other frescos during the Second World War (their ghostly remains can be seen in the Museo delle Sinopie). Beside the Camposanto, the old city wall forms an abrupt angle, leaving a rectangle free for the Cimitero Ebraico (Jewish Cemetery). Jews were allowed to bury their dead in the holy earth but not within the city walls.

Duomo Santa Maria Assunta***

The cathedral was begun in 1063 at the high point in Pisa's history after its defeat of the Saracens (about the same time that the Venetians were building San Marco). Perhaps it is only fitting that it was also the high point in Pisan-Romanesque architecture. It was the first church in Italy to use a Latin-cross floor plan with a dome over its intersection. The architect (according to Vasari) was a Greek named Buscheto. His models were the Byzantine basilica (perhaps the Hagia Sophia in Constantinople) and the Islamic mosque. The magnificent set of bronze doors was cast in 1180 by the architect of the Leaning Tower, Bonanno Pisano.

If possible, enter through the Portale di San Ranieri, opposite the Leaning Tower. The tomb of Emperor Henry VII is located to the right in the transept. The huge mosaic of Christ in the apse, by Cimabue, holds an open book with the words *Ego sum lux mundi* ('I am the light of the world'). The pulpit by Giovanni Pisano (1302–11) abbreviates the New Testament in stone, starting with the Annunciation and ending in the Last Judgement, adding enigmatic symbols like a lion goring a horse. Beneath the pedestal of Caritas is the figure of Venus covering her vagina with both hands. The two figures in medieval dress on the pedestal supported by Christ are self-portraits of Giovanni Pisano and his patron, Burgundio di Tado.

Below
Pisa's Campo dei Miracoli

Museo dell'Opera del Duomo*

The most striking thing in this museum is the dramatic view of the Leaning Tower from its courtyard and upper floors. Formerly a Dominican cloister, it forms a good setting for the original reliefs of the façade by Guglielmo and Rainaldo, sculpture by Nicola and Giovanni Pisano and Islamic objects that were brought back by Crusaders. Look for the ivory Madonna by Giovanni Pisano, carved around 1299, in the cathedral treasury (rooms 9–10).

Museo delle Sinopie*

Despite the destruction of frescos that once decorated the Camposanto – by Gozzoli, Buffalmacco, Gaddi and Spinello Aretino – their *sinopie* survived. These are preliminary drawings made with a special kind of red chalk manufactured in the town of Sinope on the Black Sea. They have been brought here, to a former hospice of the Order of Santa Chiara. The drawings reveal the original intentions and the second-guessing of the artists. Etchings of the lost frescos are shown next to them for comparison, allowing you to push backwards through the creative process. However, it can leave your imagination aching for the real thing.

Museo delle Sinopie *Campo dei Miracoli. For opening times, see Campo dei Miracoli,* p138.

Museo Nazionale di San Matteo €€ *Piazza San Matteo 1 (Lungarno Mediceo); tel: 050 541865; fax: 050 500099. Open Tue–Sat 0900–1900, Sun 0900–1400.*

Museo Nazionale di San Matteo**

Few tourists find their way from the Leaning Tower to this museum, located in a former Benedictine monastery on the bank of the Arno river, though it is one of the most important art collections in Tuscany. Look for the *Madonna del Latte* ('Madonna of the Milk', or the nursing Madonna) with a breast shaped like a coke bottle. She was carved for the Santa Maria della Spina in 1345 by Andrea Pisano and his son Nino.

There are paintings by Francesco Traini, Pisa's most important medieval painter, and a polyptych by Simone Martini. The Apostle *Paulus* by the great Masaccio (room 6) is so vigorous and expressive that it stands out, even though it is only a fragment of the altar he painted for Pisa. The other 11 (!) pieces are scattered all over the world. There is an ineffable Madonna by Fra Angelico (1423) and one by Michelozzo (1430), too. Donatello's naturalistic bronze bust of San Rossore is here, as well as a crucifixion by Benozzo Gozzoli and the *Sacra Conversazione* by Domenico Ghirlandaio.

Above
Pisa's Leaning Tower

Piazza dei Cavalieri*

The Roman forum was probably located on this square. It was the commercial nexus of medieval Pisa. Much to the humiliation and disgust of the Pisans, their Medici rulers built the massive Palazzo dei Cavalieri in 1560 and decorated it with coats of arms and busts of Florentine dukes. Napoleon would later turn it into a school (and so it remains). The Santo Stefano church, designed by Vasari, belonged to the armed Order of St Stephen, a special force created by Cosimo I to capture pirates. In practice, its members spent much of their time spying on Pisans and engaging in piracy themselves against Turks. The church has some of their Islamic booty on display.

The whimsical **Palazzo dell'Orologio*** (designed by Vasari; *not open to the public*), tacks together an archway and a pair of ancient towers, one of which has a gruesome history. Count Ugolino della Gherardesca, the admiral of Pisa's fleet in their terrible defeat at Meloria, was made a scapegoat and allowed to die of hunger with sons and grandsons while locked up in the Torre della Fame. In an ultimate posthumous insult, Dante placed him in the lowest level of Hell where burning is too good for sinners and they are frozen instead.

Right
The church of Santa Maria della Spina

Accommodation and food

Villa di Corliano €€€ *San Giuliano Terme (Rigoli district); tel: 050 818193; fax: 050 818897; www.villadicorliano.com.* The villa and its large park have been in the possession of the Count of Strido since the 15th century. In an annex, Sergio Lorenzi, acclaimed Pisan chef and refugee from city life, runs a restaurant *(tel: 050 818858).*

Royal Victoria Hotel €€€ *Lungarno Pacinotti 12; tel: 050 940111; fax: 050 940180; www.royalvictoriahotel:it.* Pisa's top hotel since 1839.

Hotel Verdi €€€ *Piazza della Repubblica 5; tel: 050 598947; fax: 050 598944.* Comfortable, quiet, just a few steps from the river.

Amalfitana € *Via Roma 44; tel: 050 29000; fax: 050 25218; www.hotelamalfitana.it.* Central yet quiet. The best rooms look out on the garden of a former convent. Booking recommended.

Osteria dei Cavalieri €€ *Via San Frediano 16; tel: 050 580858. Closed Sat lunch, and Sun and in Aug.* Extremely popular for simple, creative food. The short menu includes a couple of items each under *terra, mare, verdure* ('earth', 'sea', 'greens') and wine by the glass.

Trattoria La Mescita € *Via Cavalca 2 at the corner of Piazza delle Vettovoglie; tel: 050 544294. Closed Sat lunch and Sun.* Located near the market, this family restaurant serves savoury dishes such as *spaghettoni con lardo di Colonnata* (thick spaghetti with herbed lard), *baccalà bollito* ('stewed cod') and *trippa alla Pisana* ('tripe Pisan style').

Suggested tour

Total distance: 2km.

Time: Pisa is, for most visitors, a day trip. It would be easy to pass an entire day wandering around the buildings of the Field of Miracles where the masses of tourists seem to occupy a parallel universe apart from the actual city of Pisa. It is well worth saving a couple of hours to see the other side of Pisa. It is also better to eat there than in any of the restaurants in the immediate vicinity of the Leaning Tower.

Links: Lucca *(see page 108)* is only 22km from Pisa. Livorno *(see page 151)*, is 18.5km to the south. The Garfagnana route *(see page 124)* comes within 33km, when it passes through Pietrasanta.

Route: Anyone is spoiled for choice in the Campo dei Miracoli ('Field of Miracles') but precedence should be given to the **DUOMO SANTA MARIA ASSUNTA ❶** . You can climb up the **CAMPANILE ❷** to survey the surrounding landscape. There is more to the **BATTISTERO ❸** than first meets the eye. To appreciate fully the size of the building, climb to its upper galleries. It is almost the same height as the Leaning Tower and the glimpses through its narrow windows offer fragments of a view. The **CAMPOSANTO** ❹, for all the wartime damage, holds its own among the monuments. The two museums on the Field, the **MUSEO DELL'OPERA DEL DUOMO** ❺ and the **MUSEO DELLE SINOPIE** ❻, are rewarding but not unmissable.

From the Campo dei Miracoli, go down Via Santa Maria and duck left into Via dei Mille brushing past the 11th-century church of San Sisto on the right before stepping into **PIAZZA DEI CAVALIERI** ❼. Take Via Ulisse Dini to broad Borgo Stretto – Pisa's main shopping street – to Piazza Garibaldi. Walk out to the middle of the **Ponte di Mezzo** ❽. This was/is the oldest bridge in Pisa with a fine view of river and city. It was destroyed in the Second World War but rebuilt using much of the original stone.

Detour: Continue across the bridge and turn right (west). Walk along the river (Lungarno Gambacorti) until the church of **Santa Maria della Spina** ❾ ('thorn') comes into sight. It was a simple oratory for fisher folk and the odd traveller until it was transformed, in 1323, by a man who had acquired a true thorn from the crown of Jesus and the wealth to display it in style. The church was dismantled in 1871 and reassembled stone by stone at a point higher up the riverbank to save it from flooding. People interested in modern Italian history might be tempted to veer right, on the way back, into Via Mazzini. Giuseppe Mazzini, the man who did more than even Garibaldi to reunite Italy, died at No 29 on 8 March 1872. The house is now a museum of the Risorgimento (*see Setting the scene, page 34*).

Return to the Piazza Garibaldi, turn right (east) and stroll along the river going upstream. Like Florence, Pisa has erected magnificent palaces along the shore of the Arno over several centuries such as the 14th-century Palazzo Toscanelli, based on plans by Michelangelo and the 13th-century Palazzo Medici. The church at Piazzetta San Matteo was built in 1027 and given the full baroque treatment six centuries later. Its former convent is now the **MUSEO NAZIONALE DI SAN MATTEO** ❿.

Rather than retracing your steps after the museum, walk back as far as the first square on the Arno, the Piazza G Mazzini. Cross it and take the first left into Via Buscheto, cross Piazza della Repubblica and press on in the same direction by way of Via Palestro and tiny Via Vernagalli. You will find yourself at Piazza Garibaldi again. Walk back under the arcades of Borgo Stretto and make the first left into the **Piazza delle Vettovaglie** ⓫. The square and its surroundings are a lively area of arcades, ancient lanes used for street markets and small shops and restaurants that cater to students and locals. The square itself has a market each weekday (*open 0930–1230; Sat 0930–2000*). Press on down Via di Cavalca, cross Via S Frediano and walk along

Piazza Dante Alighieri. Take the left-hand lane, the Coll Ricci, to Piazza F Carrara, coming face to face with **San Nicola** ⑫, then rounding the corner to the Via Santa Maria. The church's 13th-century campanile is Pisa's second Leaning Tower, consisting of a hexagon on top of a cylinder (had it been the other way round, it would have collapsed by now). Inside the tower is a brilliantly designed spiral staircase. According to the not always reliable Giorgio Vasari, it influenced Bramante when he was building his Belvedere staircase in the Vatican.

A short distance up the Via Santa Maria is the Domus Galilaena (No 26). At Piazza Cavalloti, turn left into the small lane of L Ghini. The **Orto Botanico** ⑬ is the oldest botanical garden in Europe, planted in 1543 by a Luca Ghini on the shores of the Arno, and moved here in 1591. It has a corner full of 16th-century pots, arranged geometrically, and a delightful mini-*palazzo* decorated with seashells and mother-of-pearl. The star botanical attraction is a magnolia planted in 1787. This garden is only a few metres from the Campo dei Miracoli.

Also worth exploring

Five kilometres west of Pisa, the church of **San Pietro a Grado** seems to appear out of nowhere on a plain that was once full of water and ships entering the old port of Pisa. It marks the spot near the mouth of the Arno river where St Peter is said to have first set foot in Italy (in AD 44) during his journey from Antioch to Rome. The odd basilica has an embarrassment of apses – two at one end and three on the other. Inside its hoary sandstone walls are faded frescos of the life of St Peter and portraits of the popes. There are also recycled Roman columns from older buildings.

Nearby excavations have uncovered the oldest (4th century) Christian site in the region. The best way south from here is to follow the shore of the Arno river through a long alley of plane trees, the straight road to the sea and the coast towards Livorno. It is not all charming but still a lot more interesting than the ugly stretch of the *Via Aurelia* *autostrada*.

Above
Baptistry doors, Pisa

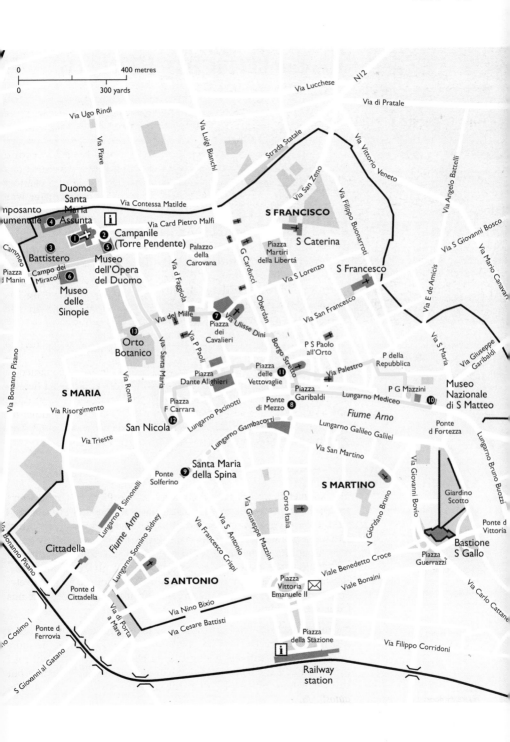

0 — 400 metres
0 — 300 yards

Via Ugo Rindi
Via Lucchese
N12
Via di Pratale
Via Piave
Via Luigi Bianchi
Strada Statale
Via San Zeno
Via Vittorio Veneto
Via Filippo Buonarroti
Via Angelo Battelli

Via Contessa Matilde

Duomo
Santa
Maria
Assunta
S FRANCISCO

nposanto
umentale ④
i
Via Card Pietro Malfi
Campanile
(Torre Pendente)
②
⑤
Palazzo
della
Carovana
Piazza
Martiri
della Libertà
S Caterina
Via S Giovanni Bosco

③
①
Camneo
Piazza
d Manin
Battistero
Campo dei
Miracoli ⑥
Museo
dell'Opera
del Duomo
Via d Faggiola
G Carducci
Via S Lorenzo
S Francesco
Via E de Amicis
Via Mario Canavari

Museo
delle
Sinopie
Via del Mille
⑦
Piazza
dei
Cavalieri
Oberdan
Via San Francesco
Via S Maria
Via Giuseppe Garibaldi

Via Bonanno Pisano
Orto
Botanico
Via Santa Maria
Via P Paoli
Via Ulisse Dini
Borgo Stretto
P S Paolo
all'Orto

S MARIA
Via Roma
Piazza
Dante Alighieri
Piazza
delle
Vettovaglie
⑪
Via Palestro
P della
Repubblica
Museo
Nazionale
di S Matteo

Via Risorgimento
Piazza
F Carrara
⑬
Lungarno Pacinotti
Ponte
di Mezzo ⑧
Piazza
Garibaldi
Lungarno Mediceo
P G Mazzini ⑩

San Nicola ⑫
Lungarno Gambacorti
Fiume Arno
Lungarno Galileo Galilei
Ponte
d Fortezza

Via Trieste
Santa Maria
della Spina ⑨
Via San Martino
Lungarno Bruno Buozzi

Ponte
Solferino
Corso Italia
S MARTINO
Via Giovanni Bovio
Giardino
Scotto

Lungarno R Simonelli
Via S Antonio
V Giordano Bruno
Ponte d
Vittoria

Cittadella
Fiume Arno
Lungarno Sonnino Sidney
Via Francesco Crispi
Via Giuseppe Mazzini
Piazza
Guerrazzi
Bastione
S Gallo

Ponte d
Cittadella
S ANTONIO
Piazza
Vittoria
Emanuele II
Viale Benedetto Croce
Viale Bonaini
Via Carlo Cattane

o Cosimo I
Ponte d
Ferrovia
Via di Porta a Mare
Via Nino Bixio
Via Cesare Battisti
Piazza
della Stazione
Via Filippo Corridoni

S Giovanni al Gatano
o Bonanno Pisano
i
Railway
station

The Etruscan Riviera

Ratings

Archaeology	●●●●●
Seafood	●●●●●
Beaches	●●●●
Scenery	●●●●
Nature	●●●
Architecture	●●
Museums	●
Shopping	●

Driving down the 'Etruscan Riviera', it is easy to wish that its reclaimed swampland had never been drained and the concrete of its holiday bunkers never poured – they clutter much of the northern coastline. However, the coastal road from Livorno has its moments and they become more frequent further south: there are still fishing villages, stretches of sand dune and *pineta* – coastal pine woods. The coast lives up to its name at Populónia, the remains of a vast Etruscan port city (most of it unexcavated) on one of the most beautiful bays in Italy. The coastal mountains are a welcome, neglected alternative to the seaside litter and throngs. They offer fascinating detours that could take you as far the geothermal realm of the Colline Metallifere (*see page 156*). The vegetation of woods and *maquis* is broken by cultivation and a couple of famous wine estates.

CAMPIGLIA MARÍTTIMA✥

ℹ Informazioni turistiche *Piazza della Vittoria; tel: 0565 838958; e-mail: apt7campiglia@livorno. turismo.toscana.it; www.comune.campigliamaritt ima.li.it.*

Standing on the terrace beside the city gate of Campiglia Marittima, Porta a Mare, you can see a wide stretch of Tuscany's coast: the Golfo di Baratti, the bay of Follónica, the peninsula of Piombino and the high mountain ridges of Elba island. Inland the first thing the eye encounters is the Pieve di San Giovanni built in 1170 by Matteo 'the sinner' on the site of an earlier church. It is surrounded by a desolate cemetery with weathered medieval tombstones. Below it are the flatlands around Venturina. Campiglia was also built as a castle in 1000 by the counts of Gherardesca; Pisa controlled it from 1158 to 1406 before Florence took possession.

Porta a Mare leads to a narrow cluster of streets. One of them, the Via Roma, links it to the Piazza della Repubblica and its hoary Palazzo Pretorio (12th–15th century). Down the Via Curtatone and past another city gate stands the Teatro dei Concordi, a 19th-century theatre that is still in use. The 12th-century Rocca is in ruins.

Opposite
Coastal *pineta*

GOLFO DI BARATTI AND POPULÓNIA✦✦

Ⓘ Parco Archeologico di Baratti e Populónia €€€ *Tel: 0565 29002; fax:0565 29107; e-mail: parcobp@parchivaldicornia.it; www.parchivaldicornia.it. Open July–Aug daily 0900–2000; June and Sept Tue–Sun 0900–1900; Oct Tue–Sun 0900–1800; Nov, Jan–Feb Tue–Fri 0900–1400, Sat–Sun 1000–1600; Mar–May Tue–Sun 0900–sunset; Closed Dec. The price of admission includes a tour of one complex of tombs (in Italian).*

Populónia or *Fufluna*, as the Etruscans evocatively called it, was the only town on the sea that belonged to the legendary League of 12 cities. The Romans borrowed a lot from the League – magistrates' insignia, a cut of toga and a technique for interpreting sacrificial chicken livers.

The Golfo di Baratti, with its halo of parasol pines, is one of the most beautiful sights on the Tuscan coast. Divers continue to find important Roman and Etruscan objects in the bay. The beach itself is not great for swimming but is still crowded in the middle of summer.

In general, Etruscans preferred to live on the heights of inland hills. During the golden age (7th–6th centuries BC), Populónia had a flourishing trade with Volterra, Vetulonia and Chiusi; its population was perhaps 25,000. The inhabitants worked the iron ore from Elba as well as zinc, lead and copper from Campiglia Marittima and the Colline Metallifere. A period of relative decline began after a siege by the Roman general Sulla in the 1st century BC. However, Populónia became a bishopric 400 years later and managed to hang on until AD 835, when the spread of malaria drove the population inland to Massa Maríttima.

During the Etruscan period, the city produced enormous quantities of iron and, in a surprising lapse of respect for their ancestors, the inhabitants used the necropolis as a dump for the slag. The tombs were discovered when Italy began to mine for iron ore in the area during the arms race that preceded the First World War. In the **Parco Archeologico di Baratti e Populónia**✦✦, it is possible to study an entire catalogue of Etruscan tomb types and periods.

Above the Gulf of Baratti (180m) is an impressive castle (mostly for its location) built in the Middle Ages. An ambitious family, the Appiani, fortified it in the 14th century to defend their independence from Florence. Two of the towers still stand and offer sweeping views up the coast to Livorno. Nearby are the remains of an important Etruscan-Roman city – belonging, no doubt, to the port of Populónia – that is still being excavated. Most of it, and its impressive Cyclopean walls (you can see one section just before you enter town), are still underground.

Above
Etruscan tomb at Populónia

LIVORNO✧

ℹ **APT office** *Piazza Cavour 6; tel: 0586 898111, fax: 0586 896173; www.livorno.turismo.toscana.it.*

Acquario Comunale €€ *Piazza Mascagni1; tel: 0586 805504. Open daily 1000–1200, 1600–1900, in winter 1600–1700.*

Livorno, or 'Leghorn' as the English insisted on calling it for centuries, is Tuscany's largest port and third largest city. Although founded by Pisans, it was the Medici and their architect Buontalenti who created a new Livorno in 1571, with some help from an English knight named Sir Robert Dudley. The Medici, having achieved control of all Tuscany, needed a new outlet on the sea. Although it was built as a harbour and fortress, it nevertheless adhered to Renaissance principles, becoming a city of broad squares, arcaded passageways, fortresses and canals. The Second World War left gaping holes in the design but it is still possible to recognise some of the original scheme.

A set of 1593 laws known as the *Leggi Livornine* made the city a haven for Jews and Turks. Even Protestants gained refuge and Italy's first Protestant cemetery (*at Via Verdi 63*) is located here – the most famous stiff is Tobias Smollett. However, this 'perfect' city was also used as the port of arrival for slaves who were bought and sold on its wharves. The city's most powerful work of art, in Piazza Micheli (by Pietro Tacca, 1615), is a statue of Medici ruler Ferdinand I who is completely upstaged by *quattro mori* – four black galley slaves – at his feet. The men in chains, straining every muscle in an unbearable posture, possess a massive dignity absent from the figure of Ferdinand.

Few tourists come to Livorno except to take a ferry to Elba, Sardinia or Corsica. However, the **Acquario Comunale**✧ offers a fascinating look at life under water in the Mediterranean. If you would rather eat fish than watch it, Livorno has great seafood. As for atmosphere, it is a lively city with a large foreign population and baby-faced cadets from the Accademia Navale (Italy's largest military academy). The dock workers are well organised and, politically speaking, Livorno is the 'reddest of the red'.

Below
Livorno's New Venice quarter

PARCO ARCHEOMINERARIO DI SAN SILVESTRO*

Parco Archeominerario di San Silvestro €€ 3km below Bampiglia on the road from Campiglia to San Vincenzo; tel: 0565 838680; fax: 0565 838703; www.parchivaldicornia.it. Open Jun–Aug daily 0900–2000; Sept Tue–Sun 0900–1900; Oct Sat–Sun 0900–1800; Nov, Jan–Feb Tue–Sat 0900–1400, Sun 1000–1600 (by reservation only); Mar–May Sat–Sun 0900–sunset; closed Dec. There is a discount on admission for people who have also visited the Parco Archeologico di Baratti. The price includes a tour (highly recommended) of the medieval mining town of San Silvestro. It is in Italian but an English-language audio commentary is available.

A mining region whose origins go back to the Etruscans, San Silvestro first appears in a written record in 1004. The British were still mining the area at the beginning of the 20th century and called it – Etruscan Mines. From its ruined castle, the mining 'ghost town' of Rocca San Silvestro, there are dramatic views of the Mediterranean. The castle changed its name many times: Castelnuovo, Castel Moncalvo, Rocca a Palmeto and Rocca di San Silvestro. It seems that the name Rocca is linked to the ancient owners: the Della Rocca from Pisa. San Silvestro was the name of its patron saint. The entire area is now part of the Parco Archeologico Minerario di San Silvestro.

Right
Etruscan landscape

SAN VINCENZO*

Informazioni turistiche Via Beatrice Alliata 2; tel: 0565 701533; e-mail: apt7sanvincenzo@livorno.turismo.toscana.it.

Opposite
Livorno's Monumento dei Quattro Mori

The Pisans fortified the fishing village of San Vincenzo in 1304 and their tower still overlooks the marina. The 5km-long beach extends north and even further south of the centre of town. Via Vittorio Emanuele II is a classy seaside boulevard with cafés, boutiques and a couple of art-nouveau buildings – the best place on the Etruscan Riviera for a self-absorbed *passeggiata*. The funny-looking cable car at the end of the beach is not part of the amusement park. It is used to transport chalk from the local hills to a factory, where it is crushed up and used in making fizzy carbonated drinks.

Accommodation and food

Cucina on the Etruscan Riviera

Livorno is famous for *triglie alla Livornese* (mullet in tomato sauce) and *cacciucco*, a shellfish stew that usually contains (at a minimum) tomatoes, red wine, olive oil, garlic, croutons, mussels, clams, octopus, and *calamari*. They are complemented by wines from the region such as Aleatico from Portoferraio and Muscatel and Passito from the island of Elba.

Alba € *Baratti; tel: 0565 29521.* Modest seaside hotel on the Bay of Baratti.

Paradiso Verde € *Via del Forte 9, Marina di Bibbona; tel and fax: 0586 600022.* Small, friendly beach hotel with garden.

L'Antica Venezia € *Piazza dei Domenicani 15, Livorno; tel: 0586 887353. Closed Sun and Mon.* Right in the *Centro Storico* in the Venezia quarter (so-called for its many canals), this *trattoria* specialises in *cucina marinara* and the menu reflects what is fresh and available.

Vecchia Livorno € *Via Scali delle Cantine 34, Livorno; tel: 0586 884048. Closed Tue.* Skip the pizza at this small place, though it's good, and just go for the seafood starters and main courses: *linguine al baccalà* ('with cod'), *riso nero* (rice cooked in squid ink), *cacciucco* or grilled catch of the day.

Il Canovaccio € *Via Vecchio Asilo 2, Campiglia Marittima; tel: 0565 838449. Closed Tue (except for summer).* A ledge just off a small square provides space for the outdoor tables with a view. *Zuppetta di frutti di mare* is a house speciality.

Gambero Rosso €€€ *Piazza della Vittoria 13, San Vincenzo; tel: 0565 701021. Closed Tue.* Widely regarded as the best fish restaurant on the Etruscan Riviera (by Michelin among others) with an unforgettable *menu degustazione*. It comes at a price but the wine list is surprisingly affordable.

Il Cappelaio Pazzo €€ *2km from San Vincenzo on the road to Campiglia Marittima; tel: 0565 838358. Closed Tue.* An extraordinary range of delicious seafood is conjured up by chef Denny Bruci in the dining room of the 'The Mad Hatter'. It is located in a turn-of-the-century villa built by an English mining engineer with a few modestly priced rooms for overnight gourmands.

Suggested tour

Ferries from Livorno

There are regular ferries from Livorno to Capráia (3 hrs), Corsica (4 hrs), Elba (4 hrs), Sardinia (10 hrs) and Sicily (19 hrs).

Corsica Ferries *Nuova Stazione Maríttima; tel: 0586 881380; www.corsicaferries.com.* Corsica and Sardinia.

Moby Lines *Stazione Maríttima; tel: 0586 826847; www.mobylines.it.* Elba and Sardinia.

TOREMAR *in Porto Medíceo; tel: 0586 896113, fax: 0586 887263; www.toremar.com. Open 0800–1200.* Piombino, Elba and Capráia.

Below
Beach huts near
Forte dei Marmi

Total distance: 82km; detour add 10km (return).

Time: Purely from a driving perspective, this route is a day-trip. Add in quality time on the beach (but not, heaven forbid, in July–Aug), detours to the coastal hills and oenophilic reconnaissance in the vineyards and it quickly becomes more.

Links: The tour overlaps part of the one that takes in Volterra (*see page 162*). Drive further south, from Piombino, to join the route through the Maremma (*see page 171*).

Route: From **LIVORNO** ❶ drive south on the coastal road, trying to avoid the *Via Aurelia* as much as possible. The promontory of **Castiglioncello** ❷ was once the site of an Etruscan settlement. During the Middle Ages, pirates nearly put an end to its existence. In defence, Cosimo I de Medici added a fortified tower in 1560. By the 19th century, it was already a popular seaside resort and artists' colony. From **Vada** ❸, take the coastal road. There is a fine stretch of beach along the 8km between here and the Marina di Cécina. In places there are pine woods near the shore and peaceful enclaves. Ancient **Cécina** ❹ was an important city to the Etruscans and Romans, trading with Volterra, Pisa and Rome. Today's Cécina is a modern town created by draining the area in the 19th century and is entirely missable. The wide beach at **Marina di Bibbona** ❺ is 4km long with an 18th-century French fortress to admire in the middle, sand dunes and stands of pine. However, much of it is off limits and one of the best bits belongs to Club Med.

Detour: The mother of all cypress alleys – almost 5km long – was planted in 1801 by local aristocrat Camillo della Gherardesca. It forms a beeline for **Bólgheri** ❻. The fortified town is also famous for a red wine, Sassicaia, and another wine cultivated nearby – Ornellaia.

A wide road leads to the popular sea resort of **Marina di Castagneto-Donorático** ❼, a white beach of fine sand with a ruined fort reduced to one tower. Walking south, you will find the beach less crowded. **SAN VINCENZO** ❽ is just 8km down the coast. From there, carry on to the **GOLFO DI BARATTI** and **POPULÓNIA** ❾.

Retrace the route going north a couple of kilometres and take the right fork down a country road that leads into **Venturina** ❿. There is no reason to linger unless you are in the mood for a sulphurous soak in baths in use here since Roman times. The ancient Terme Caldana is at the north end of town. A large *piscina* ('pool') bubbles behind the nearby pizzeria with a constant water temperature of 32°C. The most picturesque spring is the Calidario at the east end of town, a walled basin of fresh water that flows out of the ground beneath a cliff at a temperature of 35°C (*www.termevalledelsole.it; open June–Sept daily 0830–2400; rest of year 0900–2300*).

The road into the coastal mountains is clearly marked for **CAMPIGLIA MARÍTTIMA** ⓫. From there, it is a short drive down the valley to the **PARCO ARCHEO-MINERARIO DI SAN SILVESTRO** ⓬.

Also worth exploring

If you drive on to **Piombino**, it is probably for its ferry service to Elba. It is an industrial port with a less than poetic name – *Piombo* means lead – where noxious odours mingle with the sea air. However, it has its share of history, a fine old harbour and some streets with a morbid, turn-of-the-century elegance. Its main street, Corso Italia, is excellent for shopping and ends in a 13th-century Pisan tower. From there, the Corso Vittorio Emanuele II coils its way through the *Centro Storico* past the Gothic Palazzo Comunale to the old harbour. The Via Panoramica justifies its name with views of Elba and the sea.

Volterra and the Colline Metallifere

Ratings

Geology	●●●●●
Scenery	●●●●●
Architecture	●●●●
History	●●●●
Nature	●●●●
Art and craft	●●●
Children	●●●
Museums	●●●

Volterra is the most oddly self-contained hill-town in Tuscany. Once a massive Etruscan stronghold, it is set in the clouds on a ridge (550m) raked by howling winds. Over time, landslides have claimed pieces of the ancient city. By contrast, Devil's Valley – the hottest piece of the earth's crust on the European continent – is only a few kilometres to the south. The lava below the surface here is on the boil and generates violent jets of steam. Dante believed, like many medieval Tuscans, that it was the entrance to Hell. Devil's Valley is part of the Colline Metallifere ('metal hills') a stretch of wild hills between Volterra and the medieval mining town of Massa Maríttima. To the west, the coastal mountains above the Etruscan Riviera offer views of the sea and a roller-coaster ride through microclimes of chestnuts, pine trees, vines and cactus.

Bólgheri*

Count Ugolino, the ill-fated scion of the Gherardesca family, died with his sons and grandsons of starvation in Pisa's Hunger Tower in 1288.

From a point near the coast of the Etruscan Riviera, Italy's most famous avenue of cypresses leads almost 5km to Bólgheri. It was planted in 1801 by local aristocrat Camillo della Gherardesca and is the subject of a gloomy poem that is massaged into the memories of Italian schoolchildren. This was the seat of one of the most important families in Tuscan history, the Gherardesca. Most of the architecture dates from the 16th to 18th centuries.

Castagneto Carducci*

A dense network of streets surrounds the 11th-century Castello of the Count della Gherardesca. There is a stunning view from the Piazzale Belvedere of the sea and the surrounding hills. The bust on the square is of Giosuè Carducci (1835–1907), the Nobel prize-wining poet who

Museo della Geotermia *Piazza Paolina, Larderello; tel: 0588 67724. Open in summer Mon–Fri 0900–1800; Sat–Sun 1000–1900; winter Mon–Fri 0800–1700; Sun 0900–1800. Free admission.* Information is available in English. If you call ahead, you can also rejoice in your first look at a *soffione* (a hole bored into the ground to let off the earth's steam) and a reconstructed *lagone coperto* from 1830 – a covered lake in which the steam is harnessed for heat and salt.

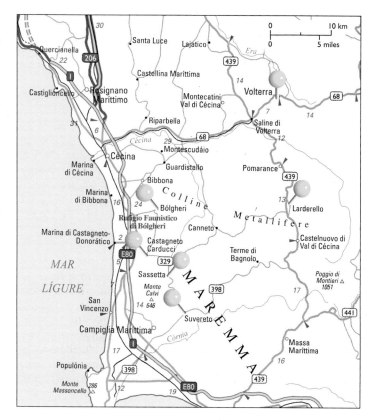

spent part of his childhood here and in Bólgheri. The village decided to honour the poet by adding his name to that of the village in the year that he died. Today Castagneto is equally renowned for its olive oil, which is among the best in Tuscany.

LARDERELLO*

For people with an interest in modern architecture, Larderello boasts a church built in the 1950s by one of Italy's better modern architects, Michelucci (he also designed the train station in Florence).

The surreal town of Larderello rests at the foot of Aia del Diavolo ('Devil's Wing') in the middle of Valli del Diavolo ('Devil's Valley'). It was named after a Frenchman, François de Larderel, who discovered a process in 1818 for producing large quantities of boric acid from the valley's *soffioni* ('geysers'). Adding to the infernal atmosphere is an odour of sulphur and rotten eggs. Still, it is nothing compared to the sewers of Paris, which people pay good money to visit.

The **Museo della Geotermia*** is free and its exhibits will explain the ins and outs of geothermalism. Minerals first brought the Etruscans to the area, which was also heavily mined for mercury and iron in the

Middle Ages. The world's first and largest geothermal complex was constructed here in the 19th century. Shiny steel pipes snake through the landscape and converge on Larderello from all directions. They carry steam from beneath the earth, which generates enough energy for almost half the homes in Tuscany.

SASSETTA✧

At its October festivals, the entire village sits at long tables eating grilled thrush and other local specialities such as *sassetana* – wild boar stewed with olives – *pecorino* cheese and chestnut jam.

Sassetta (340m) is perched on a ridge that divides the Val di Cornia, an up and coming wine region, from the Sterza, a tributary river of the Cecina. The steep hills below it are dense with old growth chestnuts. In the church of Sant'Andrea Apostolo, there is a Roman baptismal font decorated with the Orlandi coat of arms, a family that ruled here until the Medici took over. On the first three Sundays of October, the village holds the Festivals of Ottobre ('October'), Tordo ('thrush') and Castagno ('chestnut').

SUVERETO✧

Tua Rita *Notri 81 near Suvereto in Val di Cornia; tel: 0565 829237; www.tuarita.it.* The perfectionist winemakers of this small estate produce excellent reds – particularly the *perlato di bosco* from the Sangiovese grape – as well as *grappa* and olive oil.

Right on the border between the territories of Siena and Pisa, Suvereto is at least a millennium old. The ubiquitous Aldobrandeschi built a fortress here 1000 years ago and a ruined fortress still looms over the city. Through the Porta alla Silici you reach the Piazza Gramsci and a cluster of Romanesque buildings, the Palazzo Comunale, the church of Sant'Agostino (1313) and the Torre del Ghibellino. The town walls were built by the Pisans in the 14th century.

VOLTERRA✧✧✧

Informazioni turistiche *Piazza dei Priori 20; tel: 0588 87257; fax: 0588 87257; e-mail : info@volterratur.it; www.comune.volterra.pi.it & www.volterratur.it*

Museo Etrusco Guarnacci € *Via Don Minzoni 15; tel: 0588 86347. Open daily mid-Mar–Oct 0900–1900; Nov–mid-Mar 0900–1400.*

Opposite
Volterra's cathedral belltower

The city of 'wind and stone' as D H Lawrence called it, Volterra is isolated and forbidding but not without charm. Etruscan walls and tombs are sliding into the abyss at one edge of town while its exquisite medieval town hall is still open for business in the centre. Volterra was one of the major Etruscan *lucumoni* or city states, as demonstrated by vast archaeological finds. At its height, the town supported a much larger population than today. The city played an important part in the Roman civil war and was subjected to a two-year siege in AD 82 by Sulla. An impressive Roman theatre was unearthed in 1951 and its excavation was finally finished in 1997.

The **Museo Etrusco Guarnacci**✧✧ houses one of the most important Etruscan collections in Italy. There are 600 funerary urns of carved sandstone, alabaster and terracotta, dating as far back as the Hellenistic era. It is best to begin at the top floor, which has many of

the best pieces and the best explanations as well as a view of the rooftops of Volterra. Work your way down one floor to *Gli Sposi*, a terracotta tomb cover that depicts an 'old' married couple with astonishing realism; there are also bronzes such as the elongated figure *Ombra della Sera ('Shadow of the Evening')*, which greatly influenced the work of Swiss artist Giacometti (frankly, it is hard to see what he added that the original Etruscan artist hadn't already invented).

ⓘ Museo Civico e Pinacoteca € *Via dei Sarti 1; tel: 0588 87580. Open daily mid-Mar–Oct 0900–1900; Nov–mid-Mar 0900–1400.*

⬤ Alabaster workshops

Fabula Etrusca *Via Lungo le Mura del Mandorlo 8–10; tel: 0588 87401. Closed weekends.* Reproductions of Etruscan jewellery.

Paolo Sabatini *Via Matteotti 56/a; tel: 0588 81515.* Traditional work in alabaster.

Auro Grandoli *Via di Sotto 4; tel: 0588 87107.* Sculptor in alabaster who specialises in animals.

Società Cooperativa Artieri dell'Alabastro *Piazza de Priori 5; tel: 0588 87590.* Wide range of local work in alabaster.

Laboratorio Rossi *Via del Mandorlo.* Alabaster workshop open to visitors.

In the Middle Ages, Volterra was a major stop on the road linking the Po river valley and Rome, the route taken by the pilgrims from Compostela to Jerusalem. This medieval prosperity created many superb artistic and architectural treasures. The Palazzo dei Priori (1208) is the oldest municipal palace still in use in Tuscany. The well-preserved façade has a lower part decorated by the enamelled coats-of-arms of the Florentine commissioners and by other marble or stone coats-of-arms. Near the Piazza dei Priori is the **Museo Civico e Pinacoteca*** in a 15th-century building designed by Antonio da Sangallo. It displays art work from the church of San Giusto al Bostro (wrecked in a landslide). The art gallery exhibits notable works by Sienese painters such as Taddeo di Bartolo and Florentine artists including Ghirlandaio. Two star attractions are the masterful *Annunciation* by Luca Signorelli and the *Descent from the Cross* (1521), representing Mannerist genius Rosso Fiorentino at his most colourful and bizarre. The Duomo is a Romanesque-Pisan style basilica with unsubtle Renaissance additions such as a gaudy coffered ceiling and *trompe-l'oeil* marble pillars. The altar *Deposition*, carved in wood by an unknown Pisan artist, is an expressive and powerful work executed in the 12th century.

At the highest point of the hill of Volterra, broods its Fortezza, really two castles in one: the trapezoidal 14th-century Old Fortress with an elliptic tower and the squat 15th-century New Fortress with five turrets. For connoisseurs of Renaissance military architecture, this is fortification at its finest – a fact that probably goes unappreciated by the men locked up inside (today, it is a maximum-security prison).

Accommodation and food

San Lino €€€ *Via San Lino 26,Volterra; tel: 0588 85250; fax: 0588 80620; www.hotelsanlino.com.* Volterra's top hotel is a converted monastery. It has its own pool and garden and is conveniently located near the Porta San Francesco.

Opposite
Volterra's rooftops
Below
The streets of Volterra

Seminario Vescovile € *Viale Vittorio Veneto 2, on the road leading out of Porta Marcoli, Volterra; tel: 0588 86028.* Old monks' cells with big brass beds rented for a song. On the edge of town but still within walking distance.

Trattoria del Sacco Fiorentino €€ *Piazza XX Settembre 18, Volterra (just a few steps from the Museo Etrusco); tel: 0588 88537. Closed Fri and Jan–Feb.* The restaurant's odd name recalls the brutal sacking of Volterra by the army of Lorenzo de Medici in 1472. But it is not the place to eat on the run. Everything is worth savouring: a plate of *gnocchi con le verdure novelle* ('gnocchi with baby vegetables'), *penne ai formaggi toscani piccanti* ('pasta with spicy Tuscan cheese') or *coniglio in salsa di aglio e Vin Santo* ('rabbit cooked in garlic and Vin Santo').

Da Badò € *Borgo San Lazzero 9, Volterra; tel: 0588 86477. Next to the Esso petrol station in the lower city. Dinner only. Closed Wed and a few weeks in summer.* A local restaurant with homemade pasta and dishes such as *coniglio in umido* ('rabbit stew').

Alabaster

A diaphanous gypsum stone, alabaster has been worked by craftspeople in Volterra for at least two and a half thousand years. It is easier to work than marble and ideal for portraying fine portraits and intricate detail. Etruscans used it to create a look-alike portrait of the deceased and scenes from his or her life on funerary urns and sarcophagi. Alabaster was a flourishing local industry until the 19th century, when the demand for it declined. The *alabatrai* ('sculptors of alabaster') took long road trips, some as far as the Near East, to find customers, trading their wares for anything of value, including opium and spices. Today, alongside the bread-and-butter souvenir trade (such as copies of Michelangelo's *David*), many *alabatrai* continue to produce work of real artistic value.

Suggested tour

Total distance: 148km; the detour to Guardistallo adds 5km (return).

Time: Volterra really merits a day, which should include the Museo Etrusco and Le Balze (*see Detour below*). The rest of the route can also be covered in a day.

Links: The western part of this route runs parallel with the Etruscan Riviera (*see page 154*) and overlaps it at Bólgheri and Marina di Bibbona.

Route: Leave **VOLTERRA** ❶ on the road that is signposted to Çecina.

Detour: The Volterra experience is only complete with a visit to its northeast edge, where you can see massive fragments of the ancient city's embankment far out upon the now uninhabited plateau. Then you look down into the yawning void of eroded sandstone created by Le Balze ('cliffs'). These crevasses, up to 100m deep, seem to form spontaneously but are actually the result of a type of underground erosion caused by rain. In geological time, the phenomenon of Le Balze doesn't even merit the tick of the second hand. But for Volterra, a piece of its 3 000-year history (Etruscan walls and tombs, a monastery) is already lost forever. Despite the intervention of modern technology, Le Balze are still a threat to the future of Volterra. The abandoned monastery on the edge and the alabaster mines below, some of which date back to Etruscan times, add to the desolate scenery.

Drive through the broad, green valley that bears few traces of its long past as a highway for Etruscans, Romans, medieval Volterrans and Pisans, and modern travellers. Turn left (south) following signs for Montescudáio and Guardistallo, cross the valley and take the grandiose turns up to **Guardistallo** ❷.

Detour: A complicated web of narrow streets holds together the ancient town of **Montescudáio** ❸. From the broad piazza before the Abbadia Santa Maria Assunta, there are wide-ranging views of the woods and hills around Volterra and the coastal plains of Cecina.

Press on past Casale Marittima, another medieval village with views of the sea. The road drops for three lush kilometres before entering **Bibbona** ❹ where you can linger to walk along the ancient city wall, inspect the Pieve San Illario (11th–14th centuries) and the Renaissance Santa Maria della Pietà. Take the south fork in the road to Bólgheri. It also identifies itself as the Strada del Vino at regular intervals. When you reach the grand avenue of cypresses, turn left to enter **BÓLGHERI** ❺.

Opposite
Bólgheri's town gate

Getting out of the car: At the opposite end of the alley of cypresses, beyond the *Via Aurelia*, stretches one of the best beaches on the

Etruscan Riviera at the **Marina di Bibbona**. If it is crowded, walk south from Forte di Bibbona. The further you go, the more white sand you'll have to yourself.

Drive just a few hundred metres beneath the cypresses in the direction of the coast and turn left, following the signs for Castagneto Carducci (and the Strada del Vino again). This is a blissfully empty stretch of road shaded in many places by *pineta* ('umbrella pines'). It ends in a T-crossing. Turn left on the N329 and drive up to **CASTAGNETO CARDUCCI ❻**. The road climbs and plunges while views oscillate between the sea and steep densely wooded hills. After the village of **SASSETTA ❼**, the vegetation changes and lush chestnut forest gives way to dusty hillsides, olive groves and even cactus at **SUVERETO ❽**. Turn left (east) on the N398 and drive along the Córnia and Secco rivers up to the spa town of Terme di Bagnolo and, shortly beyond, the clearly marked junction with N439. Turn left (north) again to cruise this almost uninhabited stretch of the Colline Metallifere. The landscape begins to erupt at many points in *soffioni* ('geysers') that form tall plumes of steam. Flowing lengths of silvery pipe criss-cross the hillsides in patterns reminiscent of a Keith Haring poster.

The N439 skirts **LARDERELLO ❾**. If you want to enter the city centre (say to visit the Geothermal Museum) follow the bulls-eye sign down into the valley. Another lonely stretch brings you to **Pomarance ❿**, which was heavily bombed in the Second World War and doesn't offer

La Strada del Vino

The Strada del Vino is aggressively signposted on the coastal cliffs between Cecina and Castagneto Carducci. The route leads through hilly expanses of olive groves, dense fragrant shrub, beneath gargantuan umbrella pines and down an elegant avenue of cypress. So where are the vines? In fact, they are mostly around Bólgheri although there are also promising, newer wine estates around Montescudáio and the Val di Cornia. The estates at Bólgheri produce Tuscany's most exclusive and expensive wines, eclipsing even Chianti or Brunello. During the Second World War, Bordeaux was unavailable so Marchesa Incisa, a local noblewoman, planted Cabernet grapes on her Tenuta San Guido estate. In 1968, it produced Italy's first pure Cabernet, Sassicaia, widely regarded as one of Italy's best reds ever and priced accordingly.

Above
The Marina di Bibbona

much atmosphere. However, east of the town still stands the ruined fortress, Rocca di Sillano. After that, you pass the Saline di Volterra, an old salt mine that was once the major supplier for the province of Tuscany, before returning uphill again to Volterra.

Also worth exploring

The **Rifugio Faunistico di Bólgheri** contains many habitats: seashore, dunes, grassland, some of the oldest cypresses in Tuscany and marshes. Thousands of birds gather here – lapwings, cranes, grey herons, storks, the osprey and even eagles – to make it a birdwatcher's paradise. The only drawback is that this paradise requires advance reservations (*tel: 0586 778111; www.bolgheri.com; open mid-Oct–mid-Apr, Fri and third Sat of the month, 0900–1000 and 1400–1630*). The entrance to the nature reserve is on the south end of the avenue of cypresses that runs to Bólgheri (the road that crosses the railway line and continues in the direction of the sea: *see page 154*).

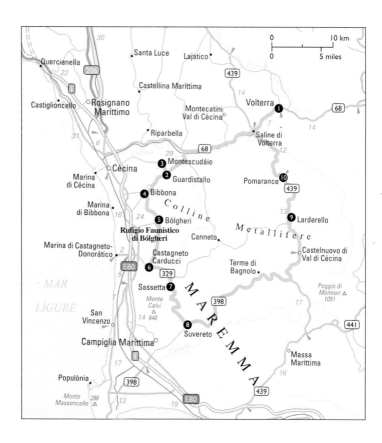

Maremma

Ratings

Beaches	●●●●●
Nature	●●●●●
Scenery	●●●●●
Architecture	●●●●○
Children	●●●●○
Food and drink	●●○○○
Museums	●●○○○
Shopping	●○○○○

Maremma means 'by the sea' and Tuscany's largest province has miles of sandy beaches. The plain around its capital, Grosseto, was actually under water in ancient times. The Etruscans made the waterlogged region one of the most fertile places on the Mediterranean: Vetulonia, Roselle and Sovana were all flourishing cities. However, by late Roman times, malaria (*mal aria*, or 'bad air', still the world's most common serious infectious disease), was spreading death. During the Middle Ages, castles, monasteries and entire cities were abandoned and most of the land fell into disuse except for winter cattle grazing. 'Siena made me, Maremma undid me,' sighs a noblewoman in Dante's *Purgatorio*. Malaria wasn't brought under control until the 1930s when Mussolini engaged in massive land reclamation. Spraying DDT in the 1950s finished the job.

CASTIGLIONE DELLA PESCÁIA**

ⓘ APT office *Piazza Garibaldi; tel: 0564 933678, fax: 0564 933954; e-mail: infocastiglione@ grosseto.turismo.toscana.it Open summer Mon–Sat 0900–1300, 1600–2000; winter Mon–Fri 0900–1300, 1500–1900: Sun 1000–1300 all year.*

Castiglione is really two places: the fishing village and holiday resort at the mouth of the Bruna river and a severe old city above it enclosed by a fortified wall with 11 watchtowers and crowned by a partly ruined 14th-century Rocca. In between, the narrow streets are lined with bars and small restaurants – it's hard not to have a good time here, though the resort manages to remain quieter and less frenetic than some of the more popular seaside towns further north. A lagoon – the Romans called it the *Lacus Prilius* – once stretched from Castiglione to the area around Grosseto. The last remnant of it, the Padule di Castilgione to the southeast, is still one of the largest swamps in Italy, and as such is a haven for all kinds of wildlife, including rare birds, reptiles, mammals and bigger beasts, including wild boar. Wide sand beaches and stands of *pineta* ('umbrella pines') stretch north and south of town.

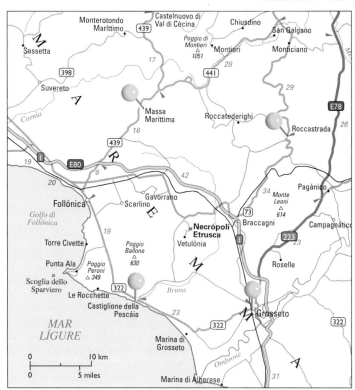

GROSSETO✣

APT office *Via Monterosa 206; tel: 0564 454510, fax: 0564 454606; www.grosseto.turismo. toscana.it & www.cittadigrosseto.it. Open Mon–Sat 0900–1300; also Apr–Oct 1630–1830 (Aug until 1930)*

Museo Archeologico e d'Arte della Maremma *€ Piazza Baccarini 3; tel: 0564 488750; email: maam@gol.grosseto.it. Open Tue–Sun Mar–Apr 0900–1300, 1600–1800; May–Oct 1000–1300, 1700–2000; Nov–Feb Tue–Fri 0900–1300, Sat–Sun 1600–1800.*

The capital of Tuscany's largest province is a mix of scruffiness and morbid charm. Unsurprisingly, the old city is the best part, encircled by fortifications that form a hexagon of six bulwarks. Its structure reflects the canons for fortified cities as put forth by architects between the 15th and 16th centuries, with the fortress representing 'reason' and the cathedral, 'heart'. Like Lucca, Grosseto converted its fortified walls into a public garden – hence its nickname *'piccola Lucca'*.

Sienese architect Sozzo di Rustichino built the Duomo between 1294 and 1302 on the ruins of a more ancient building. It was aggressively restored in the 19th century and the façade added. In the 20th century, Mussolini settled poor peasants from the Veneto region in the city and constructed new buildings for the town including the world's most pompous post office – the Palazzo delle Poste. The Corso Carducci, between the Piazza Nuova at the north end and the Porta Vecchia at the south end, is the main shopping street with the lively arcaded Piazza Dante in the middle. The **Museo Archeologico e d'Arte della Maremma**✣ has a significant collection of Etruscan and Roman objects, as it should, given the wealth of finds from Vetulónia and Roselle.

MASSA MARÍTTIMA*

APT office *Via Norma Parenti 22; tel: 0566 902756, fax: 0566 902062; www.massamarittima.it.*

Massa Maríttima's **Balestro del Girifalco** (first Sun after 20 May) is one of the most colourful festivals in Tuscany, pitting three *terziere*, or neighbourhoods, against one another.

Time and silt have made a mockery of the city's name – Massa 'on the sea'. Now it feels like an inland island. It was the most important city in the Maremma in the Middle Ages with 10,000 inhabitants. Plague and malaria decimated the population to a few hundred for several centuries and, today, the population has again reached its medieval level.

The Piazza Garibaldi in Massa Maríttima is one of the most fascinating squares in Italy and frequently shows up on slides in courses on urban planning. It is an ellipse with five-pointed stellar projections and a commanding fountain. The square is dominated by the Pisan-style Romanesque-Gothic cathedral dedicated to San Cerbone, Bishop of Populónia (570–3) and patron saint of Massa. Its construction goes back to the beginning of the 12th century, but it has been radically restored and added to over the centuries. The whole structure is decorated with lots of blind arches and enigmatic figures – man, beast and things in-between. The Latin-cross interior divides three naves with majestic travertine columns surmounted by sculptured capitals – no two are alike. The 13th-century Palazzo Pretorio houses the Museo Archeologico. After conquering the city in 1335, the Sienese built the Fortezza dei Senesi, now a ruin, in the upper city – Città Nuova.

However much Massa is admired today for its art and architecture, its historical reason for being was mining. Massa Maríttima lies embedded between two hills that were once rich in iron (Colline Metallifere) – it was a major 'industrial' town in the Middle Ages. It was here that the first European mining code was drawn up. The Museo della Miniera is a reconstruction of a mine with displays about the long evolution of mining methods and technology (*closed, at present, for restoration*).

Opposite
Massa Maríttima's San Cerbone church

ROCCASTRADA*

On the hilltop in **Sticciano** (an unspoilt village off the N73 south of Roccastrada) is a fine 13th-century Romanesque church.

Driving up to Roccastrada is like approaching an island of brown rock, floating between the sky and the wheat-covered plain around Grosseto, stretching southwest to the sea. It belonged to those lovers of heights, the Etruscans, became part of the territory of Siena in 1317, and fell to the Medici in 1559. The Castello di Montemassi dates back to the 10th–11th centuries and belonged to the Aldobrandeschi. The fortress is composed of two square blocks, a large walled yard and an octagonal-shaped tower on the western escarpment. There is also a lower set of walls. This is essentially the same rock monster portrayed in a fresco by Simone Martini in the Palazzo Pubblico in Siena. He shows how the Sienese won the day with the *battifolle*, a siege engine that looks like a portable wooden fortress.

Accommodation and food

Cucina in the Maremma

Maremma's gastronomy can't decide between turf and surf. Will it be wild boar or *cacciucco* ('fish stew')? Grilled fish or grilled goat? A dish of snails seems to occupy middle ground. Massa Marittima has an interesting *rosé* called Monte Regio.

Massa Maríttima and Castiglione della Pescáia both make a good base for the Maremma; however, there are not many hotels in either place so make reservations in advance. The tourist offices keep lists of country pensions and *agriturismo*.

Il Sole €€ *Corso della Libertà 43, Massa Maríttima; tel: 0566 901971; fax: 0566 901959.* The city's top hotel (out of only four) occupying a converted *palazzo*; it has parking. All rooms are comfortable but those at the back are quieter.

Corallo € *Via Sauro 1, Castiglione della Pescáia; tel: 0564 933668. Closed Tue (except in summer and Nov).* A *pensione*, with the town's best homemade pasta. Booking recommended.

Vecchio Borgo € *Via Parenti 12 (just behind Piazza Garibaldi), Massa Maríttima; tel: 0566 903950.* One of the best cheap eats in the entire Maremma.

Suggested tour

Total distance: 146km; detours to Vetulónia add 10 km (return), to Le Rocchette 14km (return), to Torre Civette 38km (return) and to Roselle 12km (return).

Time: The route can be done in a day, with time for a short swim, if you skip Grosseto and the detours. Massa Maríttima and Castiglione della Pescáia both have a lively evening *passeggiata*.

Links: For a more complete tour of the Maremma, this route should be combined with the other Maremma route (*see page 180*).

Route: Drive south of **MASSA MARÍTTIMA** ❶ on the N439 for 6km and follow the signs for Grosseto. After another 13km, follow the signs for Castiglione della Pescáia.

Detour: The ruins of **Vetulónia** ❷ are on the way (signposted Necrópoli Etrusca), an uphill deviation of 5km. This was the site of another one of the Etruscan League of 12 cities. Vetulónia prospered as a mining town near the shore of the ancient lagoon, the *Lacus Prilius*. Unlike the other cities in the League of 12, Vetulónia was never settled by the Romans. It was destroyed at an unknown date and 'lost' until its discovery at the end of the 19th century underneath the hilltop village named Colonne di Buriano. All that is left are piles of stones from its original 5km wall, a couple of tombs and a small museum that is rarely open. However, it is a romantic setting and can have a strong effect on people with the imagination to conjure up life from rubble. Among the tombs, look for the site of the Tomba della Pietrera, one of the largest ever found. It once contained life-size statues of gods and goddesses that are regarded as among the earliest examples of Etruscan plastic art (they are now in Grosseto).

Continue along the plain, skirting wheat fields, canals and the Bruna river to **CASTIGLIONE DELLA PESCÁIA** ❸.

Detour: Castiglione has acceptable beaches but the best ones are a short drive northwest, on the N322 then forking left along the narrow coastal road to **Le Rocchette** – excellent for swimming, swish beachside hotels and well-appointed camping-sites. For a wilder beach, drive further north on the N322 (15km) and take the road to **Torre Civette.**

Getting out of the car: There are fine walks to be had along one of the most unspoilt stretches of Tuscany's coast between Torre Civette and Follónica, or around Castiglione della Pescáia, further south. Whichever you choose, you can be sure of enjoying a fabulous panorama of the island of Elba and of the Mare Tirreno.

The N322 going south out of Castiglione della Pescáia crosses the harbour and follows a ruler-straight road through a 9km-stand of coastal pines, the Pineta del Tombolo. There are a number of picnic places beneath the trees and a couple of trails to the beach. At the next intersection, take the road northeast to **GROSSETO** ❹ that skirts the flat riverbed of the Ombrone river. Exit the town on the N1 *autostrada* going north.

Detour: To visit the ruined city of **Roselle** ❺ (Zona Archeologica di Roselle: €; *tel: 0564 403043; open May–Aug daily 0900–1930; in winter 0900–1730, rest of year 0900–1900*), take the road to Siena, N223, and follow the signs (avoiding the exit for modern Roselle, which you will see first). It is a fascinating but confusing pair of hills and a vale covered with early Etruscan to medieval ruins that are still being excavated. There is a polygonal ring of Etruscan walls that is almost completely preserved – as high as 7m in places – and, most rare, an intact Etruscan home.

Roselle also belonged to the Etruscan League of 12 cities, having been founded in the 7th century BC. After fierce resistance, it fell to the Romans in the 3rd century BC. Like Vetulónia, it was on the shore of *Lacus Prilius*, a lagoon that began to silt up late in the Roman period. The town became a diocese seat in 499 and, at the end of the 6th century, was one of the last Byzantine strongholds in Tuscany. Invading Saracens destroyed it in 935.

To return to the route, drive 2km back in the direction of Grosseto and turn north on to the *Via Aurelia autostrada* (N1).

Turn off the *autostrada* at Braccagni. The road north to Roccastrada is clearly marked. It begins as a peaceful country lane lined with cork trees then banks smoothly upwards through uninhabited hills. You will come to an abrupt T-crossing near the top of a ridge. Turn north (left) for Roccastrada (not right to Strada di Roccastrada). **ROCCASTRADA** ❻ is at the top of the ridge.

Carry on 5km north and watch for signs that say Sassoforte where you will turn east (left). A peaceful, leafy mountain road zig-zags to **Roccatederighi** ❼, which overlooks a valley of dense *maquis* and chestnuts. It was first mentioned in the 13th century as the Rocca Filiorum Guaschi (the name of the ruling family) and as Filiorum Tederigi or Tederigoli. It warred against Volterra and Massa Maríttima before becoming the property of the Republic of Siena at the end of 1200. The original fortress has been incorporated into later stone buildings. None of that really lessens the impact of this strange place, hewed directly out of the cliff with an amazing, bird's-eye view of the Maremma and the Mediterranean. The effect is bizarrely organic – like a human coral reef.

After the town is a Y-crossing. Take the right fork 8km to the hamlet of Gabellino and turn southwest (left) to reach Massa Maríttima. The

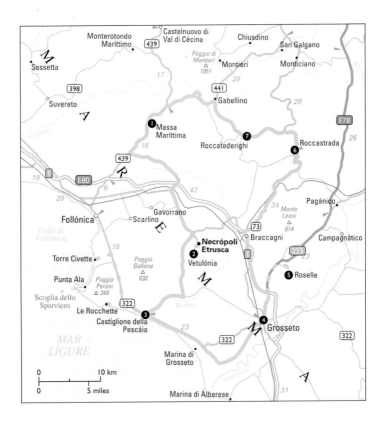

road winds through more green shrub and stands of forest that survived the axes of woodcutters who migrated here from the Apennines.

Also worth exploring

San Galgano is the oldest Gothic church in Italy and Tuscany's most haunting ruin. Cistercian monks, master builders who translated the theological principle, *God is light*, into architecture built it in the 13th century (they worked on the cathedral in Siena during the same period). In the 16th century, a greedy abbot sold off the lead from the roof. Two centuries later, the campanile collapsed. Today, it is open to heaven and paved with a meadow. On top of a nearby hill, the lonely **Oratorio di San Galgano al Montesiepi** is a rare Romanesque church for its shape – it is perfectly round. Inside are faded 14th-century frescos by Ambrogio Lorenzetti, and a sword embedded in a stone by St Galgano who renounced military life to become a hermit – a pacifist contrast to the Arthurian myth of the Sword in the Stone.

Maremma: Monti dell' Uccellina to Pitigliano

Ratings

Beaches	●●●●●
National Parks	●●●●●
Nature	●●●●●
Scenery	●●●●○
Wildlife	●●●●●
Children	●●●●○
History	●●●○○
Museums	●○○○○

The nature reserve of Uccellina is the wildest corner of Tuscany. *Pineta* – sparse forests of umbrella-pine – alternates with moorland and *macchia*, fragrant and almost impenetrable masses of brush and scrub, bristling myrtle, rosemary and broom. Thousands of birds use the park as a place to rest on their journey between Europe and North Africa (its name means 'of the little birds'). Wild boar, foxes and deer cross paths here with Italy's only wild horses. Uccellina even has cowboys – *butteri* – who tend livestock in the marshy areas that cannot be reached by any other means. Just 15km further down the coast, the circular peninsula of Monte Argentário offers Tuscany's most dramatic piece of coastline. Inland, the Maremma is a chequerboard of olive groves, fields of grain and surpassingly lush, heavily wooded hills, particularly around the ancient Etruscan cities of Pitigliano and Sorano.

MONTE ARGENTÁRIO**

ⓘ **Informazioni turistiche** *Archetto del Palio 1, Porto Santo Stefano, tel: 0564 814208; fax: 0564 814052; www.provincia.grosseto.it.*

ⓕ Porto Santo Stéfano has ferries (€€) to the island of Giglio, and (in summer) to the privately owned island of Giannutri (*day trips only*). Ferry information is available at the **TOREMAR** *office, Piazzale Candi 1; tel: 0564 810827; www.toremar.com or the tourist office.*

For all its long history of human settlement, much of this former island, particularly the interior, remains uninhabited and almost wild. Il Telegrafo (635m) is its highest point. Monte Argentário was in Spanish hands for many centuries, which accounts for the Spanish architecture and forts. It was an island until the 18th century when silting caused two sandy fingers of land to appear – the Tombolo di Gianella and Tombolo di Feniglia – gradually connecting it to the mainland and creating the Laguna di Orbetello. In 1842, a dyke was built to connect the town of Orbetello to the mainland.

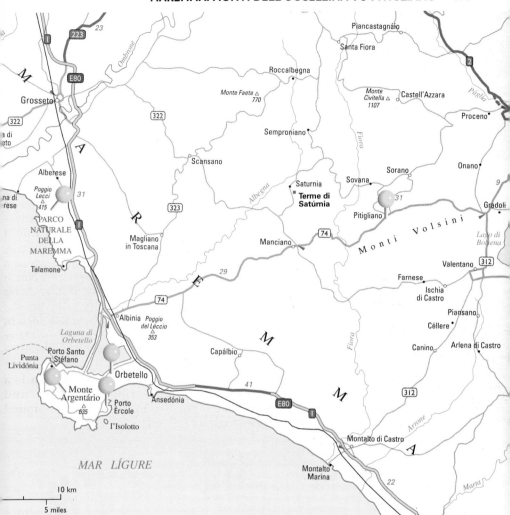

ORBETELLO✤

ⓘ **Pro Loco** *Piazza della Repubblica; tel: 0564 861226; fax: 0564 860648; www.comune.orbetello.gr.it & www.turismaremma.it. Open Apr–Oct, Dec 1000–1230, 1600–2000 (Jul–Aug 1630–2030); Nov, Jan–Mar 0900–1230, 1600–1900.*

Orbetello was an Etruscan harbour and still preserves a piece of its Etruscan walls. But what you see today dates mostly from a period of Spanish occupation that lasted almost 300 years. It was the capital of Presidio, a small Spanish principality, between 1557 and 1808. The city gate of the Porte del Soccorso still bears the arms of the Spanish king on it.

The **Duomo Santa Maria Assunta✤** was built in 1376 by the Sienese during the time of Niccolò Orsini, though often remodelled by the Spanish. Its sloping, weathered façade has a rose window and a quatrefoil frieze with eccentric figures; for example, the rampant lion

Museo Archeologico Guzman € *Piazza della Repubblica; tel: 0564 860447. Open Apr–Oct, Dec 1000–1230, 1600–2000 (Jul–Aug 1630–2030); Nov, Jan–Mar 0900–1230, 1600–1900.*

Nature Reserve € *Tel: 0564 820297. Guided tours only Sept–Apr Sun and Thu 1000 and 1430.*

Below
Maremma beach

spearing a fish – the coat of arms given to the city by Siena. Inside, perhaps the most interesting object is the *antependium* that decorates the altar. It reflects the early Christian fixation with certain animals: lions, horses, snakes and doves.

Across from the Duomo, in a former convent, the **Museo Archeologico Guzman**✦ displays the *Frontone di Talamone*, an Etruscan temple frieze of terracotta excavated at Talamone and meticulously reconstructed. It tells the mythic story of the 'Seven against Thebes', with blind Oedipus in the centre.

Orbetello is bordered on both sides by lagoons: the one to the north is a **Nature Reserve**✦ under the protection of the World Wide Fund for Nature (WWF) and of special appeal to birdwatchers, who have sighted almost half of Italy's bird species within the boundaries of its eight square kilometres.

PARCO NATURALE DELLA MAREMMA✦✦✦

Parco Naturale della Maremma
Centro Visite del Parco in Alberese; tel: 0564 407098, fax: 0564 407278. Contact the Azienda Agricola Alberese (tel: 0564 407180) if you are interested in riding with the butteri ('cowboys'). Every year in August there is a rodeo in the park.

Maquis and forest, impenetrable in places, covers the slopes of a coastal range – Monti dell' Uccellina – that looms 400m above a shore of grottoes and small bays. The 100-sq km park stretches from Principina a Mare in the north to Talamone in the south. The north part includes the mouth of the Ombrone river, sand dunes, swamps, reeds and pine groves. Wild horses and white, sharp-horned cattle roam free when they are not being herded by cowboys on horseback – welcome to the Italian Wild West. Wildfowl and flamingos live in its swamps. The ruined abbey of San Rabano, located deep in the coastal bush, is a reminder of the fact that the park has a long history of human settlement. The park has a series of trails 4–12km long.

PITIGLIANO✦✦

Pro Loco *Via Roma 6; tel: and fax: 0564 614433.*

Costanza Giunti *Via Zuccarelli 31 (near the synagogue). A herbalist shop with herbal cosmetics, infusions, honey and marmalade.*

Few towns have quite the same impact on first sight as Pitigliano. The city seems to have been grafted by time rather than built on to stone cliffs rising above the deep river valleys of the Lente and Meleta. The base of the town is honeycombed with Etruscan tombs – some now used as wine cellars or garages. The Orsini family controlled the region in 1293 and left behind palaces, a fortress designed by Antonio Sangallo and an amazing aqueduct. The baroque Duomo Santi Pietro e Paolo is worth a look but it is essentially the whole medieval ensemble and its atmosphere that are unforgettable. The Via Zuccarelli and obscure lanes running out of it such as Vicolo Goito and Vicolo di Riforme – the former Jewish Quarter – give way to terraces that have dramatic views of the Meleta valley.

Tuscany's Little Jerusalem

For almost 400 years, Pitigliano had such a thriving Jewish community that it came to be known as *piccola Gerusalemme* – 'Little Jerusalem'. Today, there are three families left, a reconstructed synagogue used as a museum and the Jewish cemetery. In the 18th and 19th centuries, more than 20 per cent of Pitigliano's inhabitants were Jews. A 1938 census lists Jewish bus drivers, doctors, factory workers, bankers, farmers, merchants and teachers. By the end of the war, they were all gone. Edda Servi-Machlin, the daughter of Pitigliano's last rabbi, published a book in 1981, *The Classic Cuisine of the Italian Jews* (Giro Press, NY). In it, she points out that the local dialect uses Hebrew words such as *Adonai* ('God') and *Zona* ('whore') and that Pitiglianese cuisine offers *billo*, a kind of 'ham' that is made of turkey.

PORTO ÉRCOLE❖

The town is wedged higgedly-piggedly between the bay and a pair of grim Spanish forts, Stella and Filippo, now condominiums for yuppies from Rome. On 18 July 1610, Michelangelo Merisi, better known as Caravaggio, was found dead here on the beach. Depending on whom you read, he died of malaria, pneumonia, sunstroke or from the clinical knife-thrust of a baroque-era hit man. He had been in hiding, having killed one of his lovers in a duel four years earlier. Ironically, Caravaggio did much of his best work while on the run. Three days after his death, a document arrived from Rome granting him clemency.

Below
Porto Ércole

Cucina in the Maremma

Anguille ('eel') is a local delicacy that comes from the Orbetello lagoon and is smoked, grilled or marinated. Bianco di Pitigliano is a white wine that has much in common with Orvieto Classico. Far and away the best known wine in the Maremma is the red Morellino di Scansano. It contains at least 85 per cent Sangiovese and tastes somewhat like Chianti.

Above
Parasol pine

Accommodation and food

Il Pellicano €€€ *4km west outside Porto Ércole; tel: 0564 833111; fax: 0564 833418; e-mail: info@pellicanohotel:com.* One of Tuscany's most expensive hotels, occupying its own piece of the coastline.

Terme di Satúrnia €€€ *off the side of the road, Via delle Terme 1; tel: 0564 600800; fax: 0564 600863; www.termedisaturnia.it.* Guests have free access to the baths. The hotel has a good restaurant, beauty salon and other comforts – enough to satisfy the most demanding hedonist.

La Conchiglia € *Via della Marina, Porto Ércole; tel: 0564 833134.* Small and surprisingly quiet *pensione* near the harbour.

La Lampara € *Lungomare Andrea Doria, Porto Ércole; tel: 0564 833024.* Friendly *trattoria* with pizza, a seafood menu and the best prices on the harbour.

Il Canto del Gallo €€ *Via Giuseppe Mazzini 29, Grosseto; tel: 0564 414589. Closed Sun, no lunch. No credit cards.* Located in the old Medici quarter near the *Centro Storico*, the 'cock's crow' has the best quality-price ratio in town. Chef Nadia Svetoni never misses a beat, from vegetable lasagne to grilled meats and game dishes such as *cinghiale alla cacciatora*. She even makes her own sorbet.

Il Tufo Allegro € *Vicolo della Costituzione 1, Pitigliano; tel: 0564 616192. Closed Tue, and Jan and Aug.* Homemade soups and pasta such as superb *pappardelle gialle al sugo di agnello* ('broad noodles with lamb sauce'); there are also some *piatto ebraico* ('Jewish dishes') based on traditional recipes.

Suggested tour

Total distance: 131km. The detour on Monte Argentário adds a lot of time but almost no distance; detours to Talamone and Sovana both 8km (return); detour to Terme di Satúrnia is 25km (return).

Time: Three days would probably be the minimum for an exploration of Monti dell'Uccellina, Monte Argentário and the hinterland around Pitigliano, assuming a couple of walks, a soak in Saturnia's hot springs and a visit to an Etruscan tomb or two. The driving can be done in a day.

Links: This route begins at a point near the circuit that includes Grosseto (*see page 171*). The two routes taken together provide an extended tour of the Maremma.

Route: Turn off the *Via Aurelia autostrada* (N1) at the exit for **PARCO NATURALE DELLA MAREMMA ❶** and carry on to Marina di Alberese.

Getting out of the car: An easy 4-km trail begins at the parking lot. Walk back up the road 100m and turn left into the path marked 'A7'. The trail leads to the mouth of the Ombrone river and returns to the parking lot along a trail through sand dunes.

The coastal mountains in the park are only accessible by foot. First of all, you have to drive further south to the town of **Alberese**. The price of admission includes a bus ride (*it runs every hour*) to the hamlet of Pratini (*no private cars allowed*), which is the point of departure for trekking in the park. There are trails to San Rabano (6km); the guard tower of Castel Marino and Torre Lungo (both 5km); and to the bay of Cala di Forno (12km).

Detour: Just 4km off the N1, **Talamone ❷** is the stuff of legends. It seems that Talamone, the father of Ajax, died here and the high hill that juts out into the sea and which the town rests on, is his tomb. Of Etruscan origin and inhabited by the Romans, it is now a fishing village gradually being taken over by tourism. The almost windowless castle that overlooks it was designed by Vecchietta in the 15th century. Talamone's modern claim to fame is that Garibaldi landed on its shores in 1860 with his 3 000 followers.

Getting out of the car: Three hiking trails lead out of Talamone into the southern part of the Parco.

Get off the N1 at Albinia and follow the finger of land that joins the mainland to **MONTE ARGENTÁRIO ❸**; the view of the bay on both sides is mostly blocked by umbrella pines.

Arriving on the island, turn right and follow the signs around the bay for **Porto Santo Stéfano ❹**. Once in town, avoid the Porto to the right (unless you want a ferry to the island of Giglio) and turn left up the steep main street following elusive signs for the Strada Panoramica. Prepare yourself for some of the most beautiful coastal scenery in Tuscany and some of the hairiest driving, particularly in the afternoon. The people of Santo Stéfano use this narrow road for the ritual of *passeggiata*. For the first few kilometres, you will have to manoeuvre between couples in various stages of courtship, families pushing prams, and old men and women on canes. After a few kilometres, there are turn-offs for a bread, salami and wine picnic. You will catch, out of the corner of your eye, the tantalising gleam of diminutive beaches nestled among the cliffs below; sadly, most of them are inaccessible or privately owned. The Strada Panoramica advances to a Y-crossing.

Detour: Turn right to continue on the Strada Panoramica. The road circles the entire peninsula and more than lives up to its name. There are fantastic views of the Giglio and Giannutri islands. The landscape is so inspiring you might be tempted to go for it. The beginning is solid enough despite the potholes. Warning signs appear thick and fast including one that warns of a lack of warning signs. Roman yuppies who live on the island cruise along with an *autostrada* nonchalance. However, the further you go, the more it feels like a place for paragliding rather than motoring.

Go left (north). Carry on along the lagoon side of Monte Argentário to the picturesque **PORTO ÉRCOLE** ❺. From there, retrace the route 4km and turn right on the N440. **ORBETELLO** ❻ is in the middle of the lagoon. If there is time, take a walk beneath the palm trees along Viale Mura di Levante. Exit the city through the triple-corniced gate with matching obelisks built by the Spanish in the 17th century. Turn left on the *Via Aurelia* (N1) and then right on the N74 at Albinia. The road is a straight shot through a plain beneath endless alleys of birch and plane trees. After the hamlet of Marsilian it curves in sync with the Elsa river before mounting a ridge and circling around **Manciano** ❼. The town is little visited by tourists, though it has an authentic medieval core, a Sienese castle (1350) and a museum with prehistoric finds from the Fiora valley.

Detour: Drive north on the N322 and take the right fork at Montemerano, another fortified town. Depending on the season and time of day, you can see the steam from a distance, rising up from the **Terme di Satúrnia** ❽, to say nothing of a lot of parked cars. Legend would have you believe that the spring was founded by Saturn, the Roman god of sowing. More than two million litres of 37.5°C carbon-sulphur-boric water flows out of it each hour. The water is said to be an effective treatment for rheumatism, bronchitis and constipation.

The **Cascate del Mulino**, a set of cascades near a ruined mill that form pools in the travertine rock below, is an ideal place to soak. On weekends and in summer, you will share it with a horde of people –

Above
Pitigliano

big extended families, luvvies, picnickers, flower children – it's all like the crowded finale of a Fellini movie. The source of the water is a little further upstream and is monopolised by a luxury spa and resort where you can soak for a day (with optional mudbath or massage) or stay overnight in its hotel for a price.

Arriving on the road from Manciano, the first look at **PITIGLIANO** ❾ is one of the most impressive sights in Tuscany.

Detour: Drive north and follow the signs to **Sovana** ❿. The town rotted away for centuries and barely clawed its way back to life in the 20th century. It is utterly quaint and, for people who don't mind their history in a dustbin, fascinating. Sovana sits on top of a vast Etruscan City of the Dead that stretches further than the eye can see or, thus far, the archaeologist can dig. It belonged to Etruscan Suana and straggles along for 3km outside of the city. Most of the tombs are from the 3rd to 2nd century BC and many of them are linked by a mysterious network of ancient roads that were either hewed through rock or built as deep ditches. The number of tombs on view is small but at least they are easy to find – just follow the yellow road signs.

In the Middle Ages, the town's fortunes were closely linked with the Aldobrandeschi family. Pope Gregory VII, its most successful son, was born here in 1021. Gregory was the Pope who forced Henry IV to come to Canossa on his knees. The building where he was supposedly born survives and, oddly enough, now houses a 'museum' full of giant snails that ooze up and down the walls of their aquariums. The wonky cathedral at the end of the diminutive town dates from the 12th to 14th centuries with a portal and capitals decorated with strange medieval symbols.

A number of fine craftspeople, some of them escaped townies, now have shops in Sovana. One of them, an artisan named Francesco di Pinto, makes handmade paper and stationery of a quality you would normally only find in places such as Florence or Venice (**Il Leone Dipinto** *Via del Duomo, 20; tel/fax: 0564 615552*). There is also a terracotta workshop near the car park, which turns out magnificent Etruscan reproductions.

Also worth exploring

North of Pitigliano (9 or 18km depending on the road), **Sorano** is as fascinating as Pitigliano and perhaps even more dramatic for its

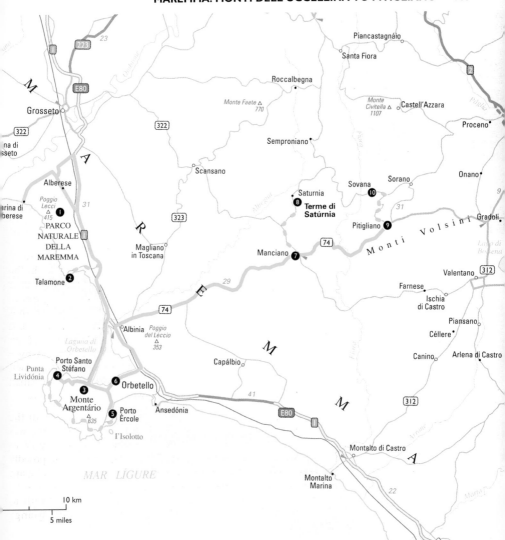

position at the edge of a green-gold gorge formed by the River Lente. Sorano rests on a sandstone cliff riddled with caves and tombs and was also part of the Orsini empire. Many of its buildings are stamped with the family heraldic symbols – the bear, the lion, the rose and the stripes. The Orsini built its proudest monument, the perfectly preserved Renaissance Fortezza. If for no other reason, Sorano is unmissable because it might not be there next time. Landslides have already claimed some streets and houses. Still, it is no ghost town. The core remains inhabited and an energetic community of local craftspeople is fighting to save it.

Florence to Arezzo via Casentino

Ratings

Castles	●●●●○
Food and drink	●●●●○
Monasteries	●●●●○
Nature	●●●●○
Outdoor activities	●●●●○
Scenery	●●●●○
Shopping	●●●●○
Museums	●●○○○

The Casentino is the name given to the wild reaches of the upper Arno. The landscape, formed during the last ice age, oscillates between sharp ridges, dense forest, high pastures and flat valley bottoms (that were once ancient lakes). The Arno river tumbles and loops through the valley. It flows from sources high on the slopes of Mount Falterona beneath the village of Stia and past the towns of Poppi and Bibbiena, before curving just north of Arezzo on its way to Florence. The region was settled by Etruscans and became an all-important north–south passage in the Middle Ages, guarded by numerous castles. The heights of the Casentino have been a place of spiritual retreat for almost a millennium, since St Romuald founded a hermitage at Camáldoli, and St Francis is said to have found peace where the monastery of La Verna now stands.

AREZZO❖❖

ⓘ Informazioni turistiche *Piazza della Repubblica 28, by the train station; tel: 0575 377678, fax: 0575 20839; e-mail: info@arezzo.turismo. toscana.it; www.provincia.arezzo.it & www.comune.arezzo.it. Open Apr–Sept Mon–Sat 0900–1300, 1500–1900, Sun 0900–1300; Oct–Mar Mon–Sat 0900–1300, 1500–1830, first Sun of the month 0900–1300.*

Although Arezzo is not that popular with tourists, Italians recently voted it as one of Italy's best places to live. The Etruscans thought so too – it was part of the League of 12 cities. One of the two most famous Etruscan bronzes was found here – the Chimera (Florence has the original). It became Roman *Arretium* in 294 BC and still has a well-preserved amphitheatre. The poet Petrarch (1304–37) would recognise much of the *Centro Storico* today, and native son and Renaissance man Giorgio Vasari (1511–74) even more, since he designed a lot of it.

The nexus of the old, hilly part of town is the Piazza Grande, framed by Vasari's Palazzo delle Logge, the Palazzo della Fraternità dei Laici and the Romanesque Pieve di Santa Maria. This splendid Romanesque church is a massive, almost geometrical collection of porticos, columns, blind arcades and loggias, all crowned by an ambitious bell tower (1330), known as 'the tower of a hundred holes'. The sombre

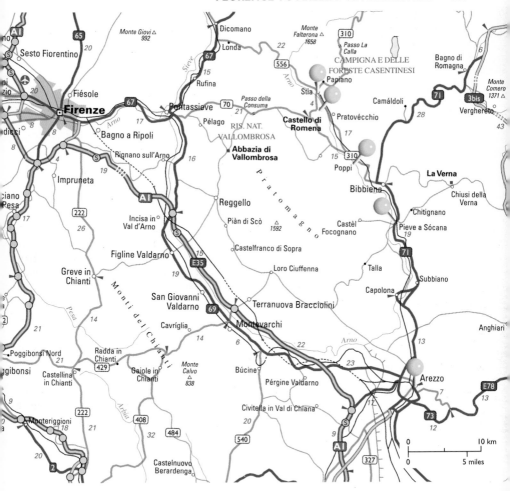

Legend of the True Cross €€ *Piazza San Francesco. Ticket office tel: 0575 352727; fax 0575 302001; www.pierodellafrancesca.it. Open Mon–Fri 0900–1800, Sat 0900–1730, Sun 1300–1730. To see the restored frescos, book into a guided tour.*

Casa di Giorgio Vasari
€ *Via XX Settembre 55; tel: 0575 409040. Open Mon, Wed–Sat 0900–1900, Sun 0900–1300.*

interior feels empty and its big arches are said to be a prelude to Gothic style. The oldest part is the presbytery and five-naved crypt. The star artistic attraction is the *Madonna and Saints* on the main altar, a polyptych by Pietro Lorenzetti (1320).

However, the jewel in Arezzo's art history crown is in the main choir chapel of the church of San Francesco. This fresco cycle – the *Legend of the True Cross*+++ (1452–66) by Piero della Francesca – is one of the most important works of art created in the Renaissance. Part of it is on view again after years of restoration. It has been suggested that the frescos were commissioned to boost interest in the Crusades, which were beginning to lose popularity. One panel, the first night scene in Western painting, depicts the Emperor Constantine's prophetic dream of victory over Maxentius, aided by the cross that he will carry the following day into battle.

Duomo San Donato € *Piazza del Duomo. Open 0630–1230, 1500–1900.*

There is a vast, vast **antique fair** in the *Centro Storico*, around the Piazza Grande, on the first weekend of each month *(information, tel: 0575 377678).*

Pitti *Via San Lorentino 15; tel. 0575 299779.* Handles for doors, drawers, and so on, made from glass, porcelain, steel, wood, bone and stone.

Bussati Tessuti *Corso Italia 48; tel: 0575 355295; www.busattitessuti.it. Open Tue–Sat 0900–1300 and 1600–2000.* Fabrics of great quality at affordable prices in a tradition that goes back many centuries. They are created in a small Tuscan workshop in the town of Anghiari, founded in the 19th century.

Above
Arezzo's Piazza Grande

The **Casa di Giorgio Vasari**◆ was the home of the artist and consultant to the Medici Duke Cosimo I. Vasari decorated the rooms himself with frescos and paintings in Mannerist style. The Camera della Fama (hall of fame) has Vasari assuming a heroic pose in a group of famous artists whose lives he described as a biographer.

Arezzo's cathedral, the **Duomo San Donato**◆, occupies the highest point in the city. Begun in 1277, it was not finished for several hundred years – the 'Gothic' campanile and façade were actually completed in the 19th and 20th centuries. Guillaume de Marcillat, a Domenican monk from Chartres, created the rare 16th-century stained-glass windows, including the *Miracle of Whitsun, Raising of Lazarus* and *Expulsion of Moneychangers from the Temple.* In the left aisle, the tomb of Bishop Guido Tarlati impresses with marble reliefs of miracles and battles; just to the right is a fresco of Maria Maddalena by Piero della Francesca.

Giostra del Saracino

The 'Joust of the Saracen' takes place on the third Sunday in June and the first Sunday in September. Two hundred and fifty participants – soldiers, musicians, valets, flag-jugglers and knights – parade to the Piazza Grande. Eight knights in heavy armour, two from each of Arezzo's four quarters, take turns charging a huge effigy of a Saracen. They score by striking his shield with their lances and avoiding the effigy's counter-attack when it rotates and strikes back with a whip. The winner receives a golden lance.

CASTELLO AND PIEVE SAN PIETRO DI ROMENA❖

Castello di Romena
€ *Via Romena, 12/A;*
tel: 0575 582520; fax:
0575 504526. Open daily
1000–1200, 1500–1800
(The modest Museo
Archeologico e delle Armi € is
open mid-Jun–mid-Sept
Sat–Sun 1000–1200,
1500–1800 or by
appointment).

Pieve di Santo Pietro
Tel: 0575 582060. Open
0900–1200, 1500–1800.

Originally built by the counts of Guidi to defend the upper Arno valley, the Castello was, in its glory days, the most famous castle in the Casentino and mentioned with great respect by Dante. Only one of its original 14 towers has survived but the weed-covered castle ruins are still impressive. The austere 13th-century **Pieve di Santo Pietro di Romena** is an imposing Romanesque church resting squat in a broad field of sunflowers below the castle. (If it is locked, there is a guardian across the road. She will sometimes open it, depending on the time of day; that is, not during the lunch and siesta period.)

PIEVE A SÓCANA❖

Pieve di
Sant'Antonino *Tel:*
0575 592561; Open
summer 0800–1300,
1530–1900; winter
0830–1230, 1500–1730.

The site of the Romanesque parish church of **Sant'Antonio** has seen some form of worship for 2500 years: an Etruscan temple once stood here. Behind the apse of the church, in a cornfield, is an altar used by the Etruscans to perform sacrifices – of what or whom we don't know – but the blood grooves are clearly visible.

Below
Arezzo's Chimera fountain

POPPI⚜

Castello dei Conti Guidi € *Piazza Repubblica 1, Stia; Tel: 0575 529343; www.casentino.it. Open daily mid-Mar–Oct 1000–1800; Nov–mid-Mar Thu–Sun 1000–1800 (daily 21 Dec–6 Jan).*

About 15km from Poppi, La Verna is the spot where St Francis fasted and prayed and, on the night of 16 September 1224, received the stigmata on a *crudo sasso* ('bare rock').

Poppi is visible for miles around thanks to the extraordinary **Castello dei Conti Guidi⚜⚜**, a fairy-tale fortress that leaps out at you from its deep moat. The castle was built in 1260–72 with additions in 1291 by Arnolfo di Cambio (of Palazzo Vecchio fame). The courtyard seems to have gone untouched for some 700-odd years. The balustrade of its free-standing staircase has a hundred miniature stone columns and is decorated with coats of arms from the entire region. The Knight's Hall impresses, as does the bedroom of the counts of Guidi, with remarkable medieval mod cons. The library possesses 20,000 volumes and 600 illuminated manuscripts.

From the ramparts of the castle you can look north up the valley towards Campaldino where Dante fought in a battle between Arezzo Ghibellines and Florentine Guelphs on a hot summer day in 1289; or east across the Apennines towards Camáldoli; or southeast towards La Verna. After the castle, the centre of historic Poppi is well worth a visit – you can stroll through most of it beneath ancient arcades. The central 'piazza' is scarcely bigger than one of the Mercedes Benz that occasionally park there.

Right
Poppi's Castello dei Conti Guidi

STIA ✜

In the immediate vicinity of Stia are two medieval castles built by the counts of Guidi: the **Castello di Palagio Fiorentino**, now a small contemporary art museum, lies in an enchanting garden (€ *Via Vittorio Veneto; tel: 0575 50471; www.comune.stia.ar.it. Open Jun–Sept Sat 1600–1900, Sun 1030–1230, 1600–1900; or during exibitions or by appointment*); the **Castello di Porciano** (€; *Porciano; tel: 0575 583533; open daily mid-May–mid-Oct 1000–1200, 1600–1900; or by appointment, tel: 055 400517*) has the best view, from its imposing tower above the narrow valley of the upper Arno. Today, it contains an agricultural museum.

Right
Stia's Piazza Tanucci

One of the most beautiful villages in the Arno valley, Stia is a starting point for excursions into the area around Monte Falterona. The parish of Santa Maria Assunta dates back to 1150 when it was built on a pre-existing religious building referred to around the year AD 1000. Little remains of the exterior of the 12th-century building. The apse and façade were demolished and given baroque replacements. The interior, with a nave and two aisles separated by monolithic columns in sandstone, preserves the Romanesque forms. The capitals bear distinctive decorations of animals, floral plants and alien-seeming humans. There is an ineffable *Madonna and Child* by Andrea della Robbia on which he used the long-lost secret of his glaze to strikingly radiant effect. .

Cucina in the Casentino

The Casentino makes use of some of Italy's best olive oil and lots of game, *charcuterie*, mushrooms and mountain-stream trout. As a first course, locals relish *maccheroni*, also known as *pappardelle* (broad noodles). *Scottiglia* is a spicy stew of several meats – chicken, rabbit, lamb and sometimes game. Another local speciality is chicken, duck or rabbit *in porchetta* ('stuffed with herbs').

Accommodation and food

Two of the most memorable places to stay in the region are the monasteries of La Verna and Camáldoli. Both have guest rooms with en-suite bathrooms (cold stone cells are not on offer). There are family rooms, too – just don't ask for a double bed. Guests are in no way required to follow the monastic routine. Reserve far in advance.

Foresteria del Santuario della Verna € *Monastery of La Verna; tel: 0575 534210; fax: 0575 599320.* Saint Francis slept here (before the monastery was established) and received the signs of the stigmata.

La Foresteria € *Monastery of Camáldoli; tel: 0507 556013; e-mail: foresteria@camaldoli.it; www.camaldoli.it.* Bunk with the monks here.

Hotel Continentale €€ *Piazza Guido Monaco 7, Arezzo; tel: 0575 20251; fax 0575 350485; www.hotelcontinentale.com.* Excellent mostly for its location and roof terrace.

Buca di San Francesco €€ *Piazza San Francesco 1, Arezzo; tel: 0575 23271. Closed Mon eve and Tue.* One of Arezzo's best. The dining-room is a sumptuously decorated cellar of a medieval palace.

La Lancia d'Oro €€ *Loggie del Vasari, Piazza Grande, Arezzo; tel: 0575 21033. Closed Sun eve and Mon.* Over-priced, but located on one of the most beautiful squares in Italy.

La Torre di Gnicche € *Piaggia San Martino 8, Arezzo; tel: 0575 352035. Closed Wed, and for two weeks in Jan, one week in Aug.* In a 13th-century palace with a view of Piazza Vasari. Excellent soup, pasta and traditional dishes such as *grifi all'aretina* served with local wine.

La Tana degli Orsi €€ *Via Roma 1, Pratovécchio; tel: 0575 583377. Eves only, closed Wed and Apr, Nov.* This *trattoria* renders homage to local ingredients with tremendous flair and enthusiasm, particularly in game dishes such as hare with bilberries and forest mushrooms.

Suggested tour

Total distance: 92km; detours: the loop to Vallombrosa, 14km; La Verna, 46km (return).

Time: It is possible to enjoy the Casentino 'on the way' from Florence to Arezzo and do it in one day of driving. However, that will leave little time for getting out of the car.

Links: The route ends in Arezzo, which is the beginning of the Upper Tiber Valley route (*see page 199*).

Route: Leave **Florence ❶** on the N67 in the direction (east) of **Pontassieve ❷** and continue east on the N70, lurching in abrupt turns above the valley.

Detour: After only 5.5km, you come to a fork and the beginning of a panoramic road (signposted Vallombrosa). The rural scenery and silvery-grey olives give way, after much toing and froing, to a vast forest of spruce and pine as well as elm, maple, chestnut and beech trees; beneath them are ferns, broom and, in spring, alpine violets. The road takes a wide curve through the resort town of Saltino that became fashionable at the turn of the century and still boasts palatial hotels such as the Grand and Croce di Savoia. At the heart of the forest lies the **Abbazia di Vallombrosa ❸** . Giovanni Gualberto Visdomini, having persuaded warring knights to retire from the world and live in solitude, founded the Order in 1051. However, today's fortress-like abbey dates from the 16th to 17th centuries, when Vallombrosans were rich and wallowing in baroque conspicuous consumption. Twenty monks still live there and work the garden. John Milton visited the abbey in 1638 and found the surroundings worthy of mention in *Paradise Lost*. The abbey's Antica Farmacia ('old pharmacy') offers all kinds of interesting souvenirs including an elixir that 'makes life healthier, more delicious and desirable'. Right in front of the abbey grounds is an old stone bridge that leads back to the N70 (signposted San Miniato in Alpe) via a narrow, leafy tunnel of a road. In the autumn, chestnuts rain down on the pavement and the forest is full of mushroom-hunters in rubber boots poking in the ground and ignoring the rusty signs telling them to leave the *funghi* alone.

Continue to the highest point in the range, **Passo della Consuma ❹** . The road gently descends through the magnificent countryside of the Casentino along a ridge reaching a fork after 10km. Drive left (north) in the direction of Stia/Pratovécchio. Three kilometres further downhill, a narrow lane on the right leads off to **CASTELLO DI ROMENA ❺** . The main road executes a few delightful turns through lush scenery and levels out just in time for an old stone bridge over the Arno. **STIA ❻** is at the opposite end.

Getting out of the car: From Stia, take the road towards the Passo La

Calla for 2km and make a left turn in the village of Papiano to reach
the tiny church of Madonna di Montalto (856m). From here, a trail
leads to Lago degli Idoli through a forest of ancient chestnuts and fir
trees. It is advisable to take a detailed topographic map (*available in
Stia and Pratovécchio*).

Paolo Uccello, the artist whose obsession with perspective virtually
drove him mad, was born in **Pratovécchio ❼** though he didn't leave
any work there. It is a pleasant town with arcaded squares – a typical
feature in this region. The most interesting town in the whole valley is
POPPI ❽, living like many Tuscan towns on two levels – uphill is
history and downhill is work.

Further down the valley is **Bibbiena ❾**. One of the oldest cities in the
region, it was on the frontline of the medieval struggle between
Arezzo and Florence for domination of the Casentino. Today it is the
industrial centre of the valley. In the town centre, the Pieve di Sant
Hippolito e Donato (12th century) has some beautiful Sienese school
paintings and an altar by Bicci di Lorenzo (1373–1452). From
Bibbiena's Piazza Tarlati, you can see far up the valley to Poppi and
beyond.

Detour: Turn off at Bibbiena to take the road to the monastery of La
Verna ❿, which is at 1 129m in a forest of pine and beech. During the
tourist/pilgrim season, La Verna offers more people-watching than
solitude.

A few kilometres south of Bibbiena, **PIEVE A SÓCANA ⓫** is clearly
marked. However, if you drive too fast, you might blow through the
little town where it is located. After looking at the church and the
Etruscan altar in the cornfield behind it, get back on the route by
returning to the entrance of the village and cruising the peaceful
country road that wanders south along the Arno for 10km (avoid the
turn towards Tulliano) as far as **Subbiano ⓬**, *Sub Janum* to the

Above
Poppi

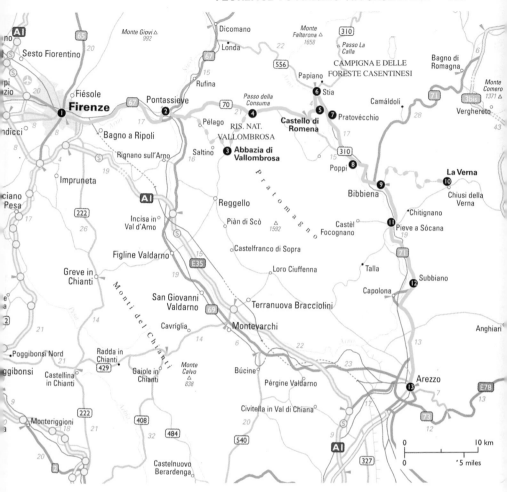

Romans, a riverside village built on the remains of an ancient castle. Carry on another kilometre and you will find yourself on the main road again with a fleeting left look at the Castelnuovo, a massive 15th-century tower. Crossing back over the Arno, the road shoots past a couple of modest suburbs and then, suddenly, the splendid cathedral of **AREZZO** ⓭ appears on a hilltop. The N71 deposits you at the gates of its historic centre.

Also worth exploring

St Romuald established the monastery at **Camáldoli** in 1024 and set in motion a movement of reform within Benedictine monasticism, which left important traces in Umbria and the Marches. St Romuald lived to be 120 years old (like Moses), having spent 20 years in the world, three years in the monastery and 97 as a hermit.

Upper Tiber Valley

Ratings

Architecture	●●●●○
Art	●●●●○
Food and drink	●●●●○
Shopping	●●●●○
Children	●●●○○
Nature	●●●○○
Scenery	●●●○○
Museums	●●○○○

The Upper Tiber Valley, or Valtiberina, begins in Tuscany at its easternmost edge and continues deep into Umbria, alternating between narrow ridges, hilly farmland and canals used to drain swampland. In ancient times, the Tiber river formed the line between the Umbrians (east) and the Etruscans (west). It remained a borderland through the centuries, divided between Byzantines and Lombards and fought over by the bishops of Arezzo, Roman popes and Florence. Culturally, it is an eccentric place. Wealthy Romans such as Pliny erected villas here, feudal lords built castles and abbots constructed monasteries. There is a strong local craft tradition, based on lacemaking. It is also an important agricultural centre, particularly for tobacco. The spirit of Piero della Francesca, the most enigmatic Renaissance artist, pervades this itinerary. His greatest masterpieces are found in his birthplace Sansepolcro, in Arezzo, and the village of Monterchi.

BADIA DI SAN SALVATORE DI MONTE CORONA✢

At the foot of the hill of Monte Corona stands this beautiful abbey (*open daily*) with one of the finest crypts in Umbria. It was founded shortly after the year 1000, perhaps by St Romuald (*see page 193*). In the elevated presbytery there is an ancient (8th-century) *ciborium*. On the top of the hill is a hermitage where a reformed Camaldolese community called 'montecoronese' was founded in the 16th century by the Venetian Paolo Giustiniani, the author of the authoritative *Rules of the Hermitic Life*. The abbey is linked to the hermitage (700m) by an idyllic path.

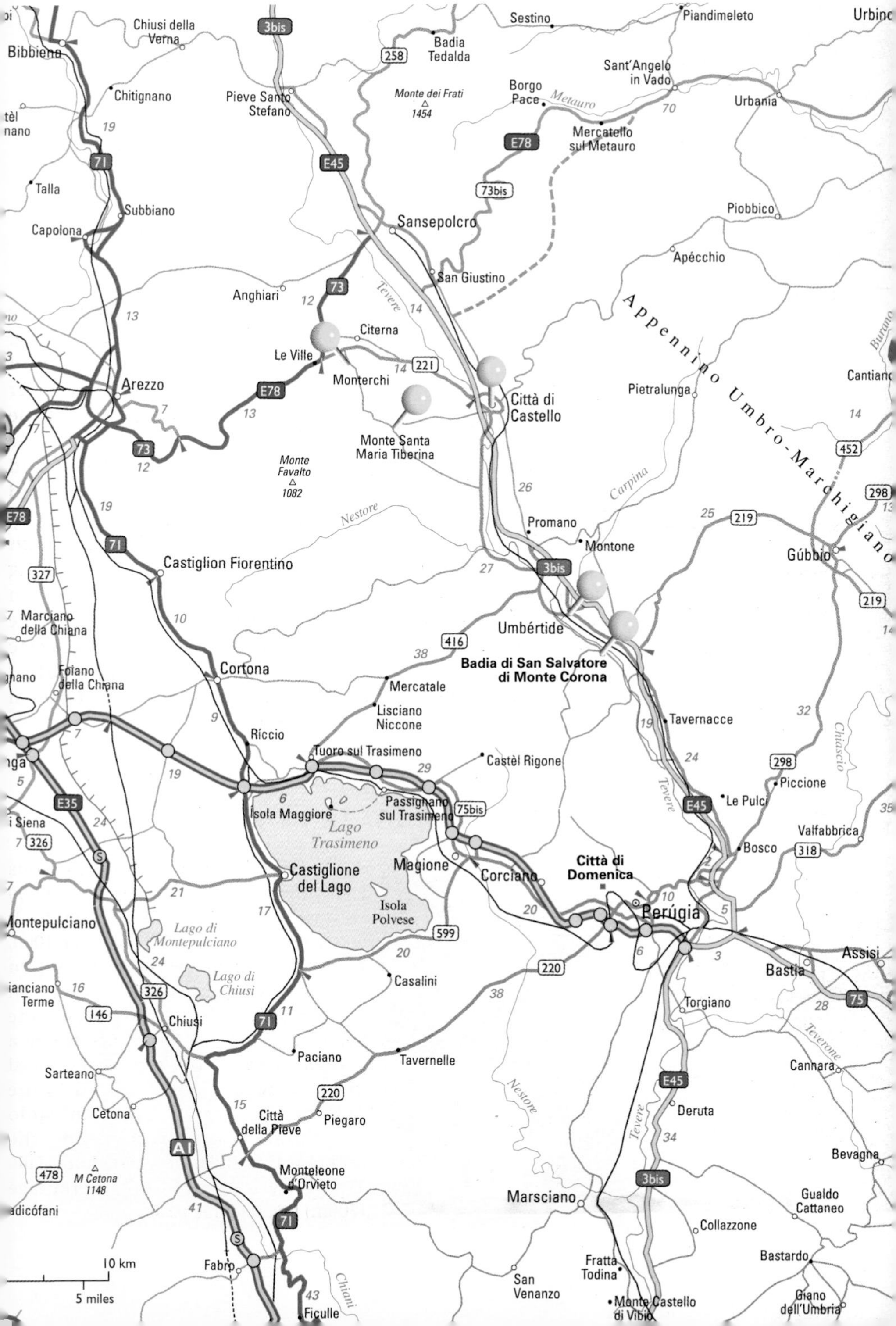

Urbino

Piandimeleto

Sestino

Chiusi della
Verna

3bis

258

Badia
Tedalda

Bibbiena

Chitignano

Pieve Santo
Stefano

Monte dei Frati
△
1454

Sant'Angelo
in Vado

Borgo
Pace

Metauro

70

Urbania

tèl
nano

19

Mercatello
sul Metauro

E78

Piobbico

71

Talla

E45

Apécchio

Subbiano

73bis

Sansepolcro

Cantiano

Capolona

13

San Giustino

Appennino Umbro-Marchigiano

Burano

73

12

Anghiari

Tevere

14

Citerna

Le Ville

221

Città di
Castello

452

298

Pietralunga

Arezzo

E78

13

Monterchi

14

26

Carpina

Monte Santa
Maria Tiberina

Promano

219

Gúbbio

Monte
Favalto
△
1082

Nestore

Montone

25

73

12

27

3bis

219

327

71

Castiglion Fiorentino

Umbértide

416

298

Marciano
della Chiana

10

38

Badia di San Salvatore
di Monte Corona

32

Chiascio

Cortona

Mercatale

19

Tavernacce

E35

24

Folano
della Chiana

9

Riccio

Lisciano
Niccone

24

298

Piccione

5

326

Tuoro sul Trasimeno

29

Castèl Rigone

Valfabbrica

7

19

6

Isola Maggiore

Passignano
sul Trasimeno

75bis

Le Pulci

Bosco

318

Lago
Trasimeno

Tevere

E45

Castiglione
del Lago

Magione

Città di
Domenica

Montepulciano

Lago di
Montepulciano

17

21

Isola
Polvese

Corciano

20

10

Perúgia

5

Assisi

i Siena

Lago di
Chiusi

599

6

3

Bastia

75

ianciano
Terme

16

326

146

Chiusi

20

220

Torgiano

28

71

11

Casalini

38

Sarteano

Paciano

Tavernelle

Cannara

15

Città
della Pieve

Piegaro

Nestore

E45

Deruta

Cetona

220

34

Bevagna

478

M Cetona
1148

Monteleone
d'Orvieto

Tevere

3bis

Gualdo
Cattaneo

adicófani

71

Marsciano

Collazzone

Bastardo

10 km

Fabro

Chiani

San
Venanzo

Fratta
Todina

Monte Castello
di Vibio

Giano
dell'Umbria

5 miles

Ficulle

CITTÀ DI CASTELLO*

ⓘ Informazioni turistiche *Via Sant'Antonio 1; tel: 075 8554817; fax: 075 8552100; e-mail: info@ iat.citta-di-castello.pg.it; www.cdcnet.net & www.cittadicastello.com.*

🔔 Torre Civico € *Open Tue–Sun 1000–1230 and 1500–1830.*

Pinacoteca Comunale €€ *Via della Pendinella, 22/a; tel: 0758 554202. Open Tue–Sun Apr–Oct 1000–1300, 1430–1830; Nov–Mar 1000–1230, 1500–1730.*

Palazzo Albizzini (Collezione Burri) €€ *VIa Albizzini 1; tel: 0758 554649; e-mail: burriart@tiscalinet.it. and* the former **Seccatoi del Tabacchi** € *1.5km on the old Perugia road. Both open Tue–Sat 0900–1230, 1430–1800; Sun 1030–1230, 1500–1700.*

Centro Tradizioni Popolari € *Villa Cappelletti; tel: 0758 552119 (2km in the direction of Umbértide). Open Tue–Sun 0830–1230, 1400–1800.*

🛍 There is a clothing and shoe market on **Piazza Gabriotti** every Thursday and Saturday.

In the Middle Ages, the valley was as famous for lace as Flanders. **Bussati Telerie**, *Via del Popolo*, sells traditional textiles, curtains and lace.

Right
Città di Castello's
Palazzo Comunale

In Roman times, Città di Castello was known alliteratively as *Tifernum Tiberinum* and residents still refer to themselves as Tiferni. The Lombards dubbed it *Castrum Felicitatis* ('Castle of Happiness'). Cesare Borgia seized it for the Church in 1500. It is a working town that doesn't attract too many tourists within its 16th-century walls. Growing and curing tobacco are more important to the local economy than souvenirs.

Architecturally, the influence of early Renaissance Florence is ubiquitous in its *Centro Storico*, from the Palazzo Comunale to the **Duomo Florido e Amanzio*** (minus the unfinished baroque façade) on the triangular Piazza Gabriotti. The most remarkable work of art in the Duomo (*open daily*) is a Mannerist painting by the Florentine artist Rosso Fiorentino in which Christ appears as an afterthought while pride of place is given to peddlers and a Moor. From the **Torre Civico***, you can see as far north as Monte La Verna in Tuscany.

In the Via della Pendinella, you will pass the Palazzo Vitelli alla Cannoniera (1521–32) designed by Antonio da Sangallo the younger with a sgraffito façade by Giorgio Vasari and Cristoforo Gherardi. Inside is the **Pinacoteca Comunale***, the second most important art gallery in Umbria (after the one in Perugia). Its highlights include works by Raphael and Luca Signorelli.

The work of modern conceptual artist Alberto Burri can be admired in two places – the Renaissance palace of **Albizzini***, and the **Seccatoi del Tabacchi*** (a former drying hall for tobacco) just outside the city walls in the direction of Umbértide. Also outside town, the **Centro Tradizioni Popolari*** offers a break from monuments and churches, providing a glimpse into the vastly humbler world of Umbrian farmers and artisans.

MONTERCHI (MUSEO DELLA MADONNA)**

Museo della Madonna € *Via della Reglia. Open Tue–Sun 1000–1300, 1400–1900; (Nov–Apr until 1700).*

The high hill of Monterchi was dedicated to the cult of Hercules in Etrusco-Roman times. Today, visitors come here to pay homage to a woman: a heavily pregnant Madonna painted by Piero della Francesca. She is as rare as she is beautiful – there are very few representations of pregnant women in Western art. The Madonna del Parto is located in a climatically controlled chamber behind glass, in a school building next to a cemetery. She appears to be an ordinary middle-class woman of her time getting over a bout of morning sickness. But symmetrical angels flank her, a reminder that it is the Saviour moving in her womb. The banal and divine are serenely juxtaposed here. Pregnant women from the region used to come to pray in her presence until the local authorities decided to turn her into a one-woman museum (moving her from the cemetery chapel), and to charge admission.

MONTE SANTA MARIA TIBERINA*

This extraordinary hill-town (population 150), Etruscan in origin, has sweeping views as far as the eye can see of golden fields interrupted by dark-green copses, and the humid Tiber valley.

The town actually became the capital of an independent mini-state in 1355 with a little help from the Holy Roman Emperor, Charles IV. The rulers, the Del Monte family, proudly called themselves 'Bourbons' from then on. They minted their own money and built an official duelling ground next to the church of Sant'Agostino, where citizens were allowed to fight to the death in public. Somehow the family held its own for many centuries while the rest of Umbria was swallowed up through force or strong-armed persuasion by the Papal State. Ironically, it was the arrival of Napoleon's troops in 1798 that brought down these hilltop 'Bourbons'.

The Del Monte castle, a weathered medieval-Renaissance amalgam, is worth a look. The parish church of Santa Maria has a very early Romanesque altar (to the right in the choir) with a St George and the Dragon that look like they were carved by aliens.

Alberto Burri (1915–95)

A native of Città di Castello, Alberto Burri began his artistic career as a prisoner of war in Texas, USA, after serving as a military doctor in Tunisia. His first works of art were executed on burlap potato sacks (the only form of canvas he could get as a POW). After the war, he spent his entire artistic career exploring the properties of simple materials in works such as *Sacchi* ('Sacks'), *Legni* ('Wood') and *Ferri* ('Iron'). He also experimented with fire to 'transform' his works in a series entitled *Combustioni*. Burri was a major influence on American pop artists Robert Rauschenberg and Jasper Johns. By the 1970s, he had entered a phase of extreme minimalism, creating simple geometric forms with *cellotex*.

UMBÉRTIDE✢

ℹ️ **Informazioni turistiche** *Piazza Caduti del Lavoro; tel: 075 9417099; www.comune.umbertide.it.*

The square tower of the Rocca (1374–90) is the town landmark. The *condottiere* Braccio Fortebraccio was captured and shut up in the fortress in 1393. His ransom was his own castle in Montone. Twenty years later he returned to sack the town. The city suffered under heavy bombing during the Second World War when Allied forces were fighting for the Tiber valley. King George VI reviewed the Allied troops here in July 1944.

Piazza Matteotti is a perfect little square framed by *palazzi* and the 13th-century church of San Francesco. The city's artistic pride and joy is the magnificent (and beautifully restored) *Deposition* (1516) by Luca Signorelli in the 17th-century church of Santa Croce.

Accommodation and food

Cucina in the Valtiberina

Porchetta, oven-roasted pig stuffed with herbs, is especially popular. Other local ingredients that contribute to the good life are the precious white truffle, well-aged *pecorino* cheese and local watermelon.

La Locanda del Capitano €€ *Via Roma 7, Montone; tel: 075 9306521; fax: 075 9306455; www.ilcapitano.com.* A castle conversion in the home town of Fortebraccio.

Tiferno €€ *Piazza R Sanzio 13, Città di Castello; tel: 075 8550331; fax: 075 8521196 .* Well-appointed rooms in a 17th-century *palazzo.*

Valuberti € *Postal address: Valuberti 16.17.18.19 Montanina 52043 Castiglion Fiorentino; tel: 0575 650234; e-mail: aldafa@tin.it.* Alda Fantina is originally from Padua but moved in the 1960s to this remote spot in Tuscany near the Umbrian border (25 minutes from Città di Castello). She and her companion Claudio rent out rustic stone cottages furnished with antiques. For the gourmand, they supply vegetables (in season), olive oil, wine, eggs, cheese, rabbit, *prosciutto* – you name it.

Il Postale di Mario e Barbara €€€ *Via de Raffaele Cesare 8, Città di Castello; tel: 075 8521356.* Savour truffle-enhanced dishes here. Prices are very reasonable for the quality.

Trattoria il Cacciatore € *Via della Braccina 3, Città di Castello; tel: 075 8520882.* A mamma and son team serve their own cheese and garden vegetables, and traditional Umbrian specialities.

Oscari € *Via Roma 25, Monte Santa Maria Tiberina; tel: 075 8571023.* This place functions as the village-everything: bar, café, *trattoria* and grocery shop. There is a small patio for an alfresco meal of pasta with *funghi* and truffles.

Suggested tour

Total distance: 116km; detour add 20km.

Time: One to two days.

Links: The Upper Tiber Valley meets the Arno Valley and Casentino region at Arezzo (*see pages 184–6*). It is traversed in its entire length by the N3bis and the *Superstrada* E45, which connects Rome with northern Italy.

Route: From **Arezzo ❶**, drive southeast (from the Piazza San Giusto) along Via Mino da Poppi, which soon enters Via Trento e Trieste and Via Anconetana. Keep right at the first T-intersection and stay on the main road as it passes through a village called La Pace (ignoring the right to Loce de Stoppe). You now wind through olive groves and umbrella pines up to the village of San Firenze. Idyllic scenery – you would hardly believe you just left the city. A reminder is at the top of the road where prostitutes in miniskirts and hot pants loiter by the roadside in the middle of the fragrant pine forest. Turn left here to get on the N73 and follow the signs for Sansepolcro. The curvy road moves in sync with a tributary of the Tiber, the Cerfone. The scenery is lovely but new roads are being cut through the valley and the construction has created some desolation. After 17km, take the right fork in the direction of Città di Castello. **MONTERCHI ❷** is signposted after just a couple of kilometres.

Leave Monterchi on the road going south to **MONTE SANTA MARIA TIBERINA ❸**. This is a country road, the worse for wear but idyllic and solitary. Keep to the left (ignoring roads to Ripoli and Fonaco). After visiting the town, retrace the route 100m. The road to Città di Castello is just below the town. Follow the bends of a plunging road that drops into the Tiber valley and forces the occasional sharp turn between the oaks and shrub. It finally lands you in the rich vegetation of the river valley floor brushing past tobacco and sunflowers. The road crosses the Tiber and hugs the old city walls. There is a dusty, free car park along the Tiber outside the walls of **CITTÀ DI CASTELLO ❹**.

Continue down the east side of the Tiber, on the country road rather than the *autostrada*.

Detour: Just after the village of Promano, the road leads under the *autostrada*. At the next fork, turn left (east) and drive up to **Montone ❺**. The fortified village once belonged to one of Italy's most famous medieval *condottieri*, Andrea Braccio, nicknamed 'Fortebraccio' ('strong arm'). From the remains of his fortress you can see yet another old castle, the Rocca d'Aria – 'Rock of Air'. The former convent of San Francesco has a serene cloister and a terrace with amazing views of the Tiber valley. Inside is the **Museo Comunale e Museo Etnografico** (€ *Via San Francesco 4; tel: 075 9306139; www.sistemamuseo.it. Open Apr–Sept Fri–Sun 1030–1300, 1530–1800; Oct–Mar Sat–Sun 1030–1300,*

1500–1730) with original frescos and paintings by Bartolomeo Caporali.

Leaving the town, follow the signs for Corlo. UMBÉRTIDE ❻ spreads out in the flat part of the Tiber valley below. Upon leaving, return the way you came, curving past a round church and the castle and crossing the Tiber over the same rusty iron bridge. Take the first left under a trestle, signposted **BADIA DI SAN SALVATORE DI MONTE CORONA ❼**. You will all but collide with its polygonal tower that stands on the roadside, at the end of a lane of cypresses. A mysterious, five-naved crypt leads into the chapel (*due to reopen in 2000 after extensive restoration*).

Getting out of the car: From the Badia di Monte Corona, there is a path, flanked by old beeches and chestnut trees, leading up to the Éremo di Monte Corona. The path is now officially a 'nature trail'. The Éremo is an ancient hermitage built by the Camaldolensians during the 16th century.

Leave the abbey, following the Tiber further south along a shelf-like road that squeezes between fields of tobacco and corn on one side and oaks on the other. Eventually, it hits a T-crossing at Pieve San Quirico. Turn left to cross over to the east side of the Tiber and carry on south. Continue through the villages of **Le Pulci** and **Bosco**. From there, drive into **Perugia ❽**, following the bull's-eye symbol for the *Centro Storico*.

Museo Civico € *Via Aggiunti 65, Sansepolcro; tel: 0575 732218; www.sansepolcro.net. Open Jun–Sept 0900–1330, 1430–1930; Oct–May 0930–1300, 1430–1800.*

Also worth exploring

Situated 39km northeast of Arezzo, at the foot of the last tract of the Tuscan Apennines, is the birthplace of Piero della Francesca. **Borgo Sansepolcro** dominates the Upper Tiber Valley as it opens out in a vast amphitheatre of hills. The heart of the town forms a quadrangle of medieval walls, four towers and a Medici fortress. The cathedral and the Loggia delle Laudi are certainly of interest and, on the second Sunday in September, a *Palio della Balestra* (crossbow tournament) takes place. But the main reason to come is a painting in the **Museo Civico** – *Resurrezione* (1459), regarded in Piero's lifetime as his greatest work. In modern times, it rendered Kenneth Clark speechless though he later wrote an entire book about it, observing apologetically that the painting expresses 'values for which no rational statement is adequate'. Aldous Huxley went the tourist brochure one better and called it 'the greatest painting in the world'.

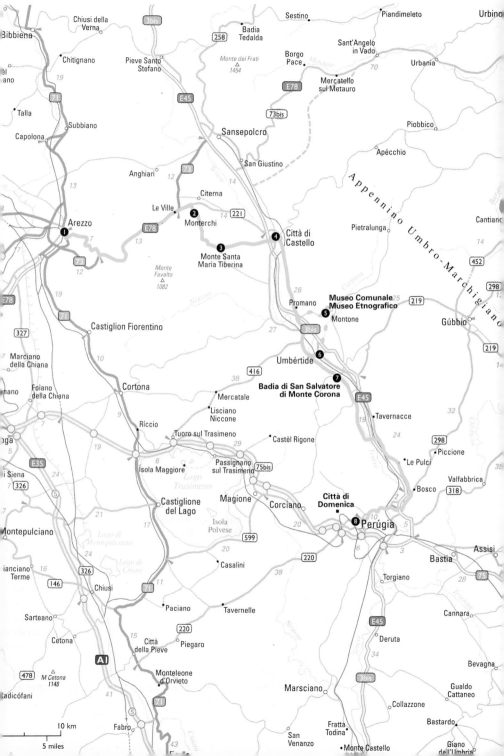

Perugia

Ratings

Architecture	●●●●●
Art	●●●●●
Entertainment	●●●●○
Museums	●●●●○
Shopping	●●●●○
Children	●●●○○
Food and drink	●●●○○
Nature	●●○○○

Time travel is easy in Perugia. All it takes is an escalator ride from the underground car park, which sweeps you past the foundations of an entire medieval district. The city sits on a mountaintop that has been inhabited for at least 3000 years and still bears traces of an Etruscan Golden Age (3rd–1st centuries BC). There is much to see here: Umbria's most important art gallery with masterpieces by Fra Angelico, Piero della Francesca and Perugino; a palace, square and fountain that rival any in Italy; and a monumental Etruscan arch. And if that is not enough, the cathedral claims to have the Virgin's wedding ring. In the Middle Ages, Perugia had a reputation for blood feuds and the practice of self-flagellation. Today, it is better known for *baci* – 'kisses' (chocolates with nougat cream), its university and one of Europe's best jazz festivals.

Sights

APT office *Via Mazzini 21; tel: 075 5728937; e-mail: info@apt.umbria.it; www.umbria2000.it.*

Informazioni turistiche *Piazza IV Novembre 3 (Palazzo dei Priori); tel: 075 5736458, fax: 075 5739386; e-mail:info@iat.umbria.it.*

P Cars are virtually excluded from the city centre and parking spaces around the periphery are full by 0900.

Arco Etrusco*

Perugia's best surviving city gate is indeed 'Etruscan' in its lower reaches. The massive blocks of stone forming the two towers belonged to 3rd-century BC Etruscan defences. This was the main gate of seven that pierced a vast wall encircling the city for nearly three kilometres. The upper level of the gate, with its Ionic columns, arches and frieze of shields, was added to by the Romans. Crowning the whole structure is a 16th-century loggia, its delicacy forming a lyrical contrast with the Cyclopean foundation beneath.

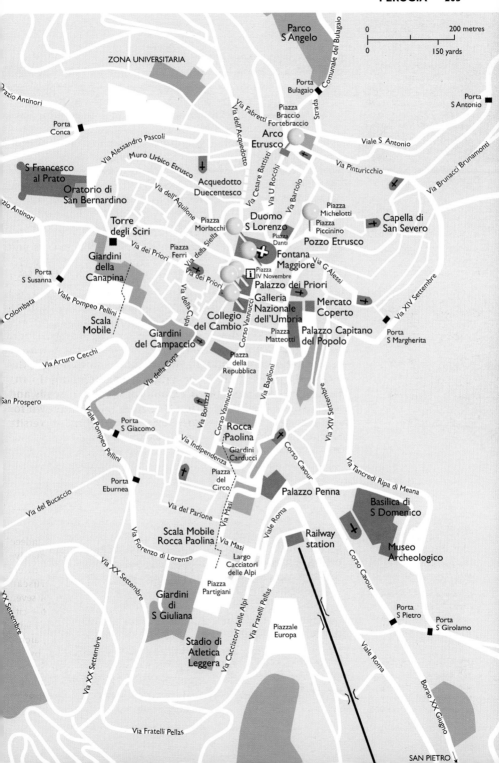

ZONA UNIVERSITARIA

Parco
S Angelo

Porta
Bulagaio

Strada Comunale del Bulagaio

Porta
S Antonio

Piazza
Braccio
Fortebraccio

Arco
Etrusco

Viale S Antonio

Via Pinturicchio

Via Brunacci Brunamonti

Orazio Antinori

Porta
Conca

Via Alessandro Pascoli

Muro Urbico Etrusco

Via Fabretti

Via dell'Acquedotto

Via Cesare Battisti

Via U Rocchi

Via Bartolo

S Francesco
al Prato

Oratorio di
San Bernardino

Via dell'Aquilone

Acquedotto
Duecentesco

Piazza
Morlacchi

Duomo
S Lorenzo

Piazza
Michelotti

Piazza
Piccinino

Capella di
San Severo

Torre
degli Sciri

Via dei Priori

Piazza
Ferri

Via della Stella

Piazza
Danti

Pozzo Etrusco

azio Antinori

Giardini
della
Canapina

Via dei Priori

Via della Cupa

Fontana
Maggiore

Via G Alessi

Porta
S Susanna

Piazza
IV Novembre

Palazzo dei Priori

Via XIV Settembre

Viale Pompeo Pellini

Colombata

Scala
Mobile

Collegio
del Cambio

Corso Vannucci

Galleria
Nazionale
dell'Umbria

Mercato
Coperto

Palazzo Capitano
del Popolo

Porta
S Margherita

Via XIV Settembre

Giardini
del Campaccio

Piazza
Matteotti

Via Arturo Cecchi

Via della Cupa

Piazza
della
Repubblica

Via Baglioni

San Prospero

Viale Pompeo Pellini

Porta
S Giacomo

Via Bonazzi

Via Indipendenza

Corso Vannucci

Rocca
Paolina

Giardini
Carducci

Via XIV Settembre

Corso Cavour

Porta
Eburnea

Piazza
del
Circo

Palazzo Penna

Via Tancredi Ripa di Meana

Via del Bucaccio

Via del Parione

Via Masi

Viale Roma

Railway
station

Basilica di
S Domenico

Scala Mobile
Rocca Paolina

Via Masi

Largo
Cacciatori
delle Alpi

Corso Cavour

Museo
Archeologico

Via Fiorenzo di Lorenzo

Via XX Settembre

Piazza
Partigiani

Giardini
di
S Giuliana

Via Cacciatori delle Alpi

Via Fratelli Pellas

Piazzale
Europa

Porta
S Pietro

Porta
S Girolamo

Stadio di
Atletica
Leggera

XX SETTEMBRE

Via XX Settembre

Viale Roma

Borgo XX Giugno

Via Fratelli Pellas

SAN PIETRO

0   200 metres

0   150 yards

Collegio del Cambio € *Corso Vannucci 25; tel: 075 5728599. Open Mar–Oct, Dec Mon–Sat 0900–1230, 1430–1730, Sun 0900–1230; Nov, Jan–Feb Tue–Sat 0800–1400, Sun 0900–1230.*

Duomo San Lorenzo € *Piazza Danti. Open daily.*

Collegio del Cambio**

The rooms of the medieval Exchange Guild are one of Perugia's unmissable sights. In 1496 the members of the Guild commissioned the local artist Pietro Vannucci – known to posterity as Perugino – to paint the walls. The result is one of the masterpieces of the Italian Renaissance.

In the spirit of Renaissance humanism, the frescos unite pagan and Christian imagery. On the left wall are the allegorical figures of *Prudence* and *Justice* above the historical figures whose life and works were filled with such qualities – Socrates and the *Emperor Trajan*; then *Strength* and *Temperance* exemplified by *Pericles* and *Leonidas*, amongst others. Between the two, Perugino painted his own unflattering self-portrait. The great artist is ... a fat man with a double chin. One of his lyrical landscapes, suffused with the dawn sunlight, forms the background to the Nativity scene on the end wall. Perugino was a master of three-dimensional perspective, and the Nativity demonstrates that particular gift. We glimpse the landscape of wooded hills and winding streams through a series of arches, under which shepherds kneel. The arches are supported on classical columns – another reference to a fusion of classical and Christian values.

Duomo San Lorenzo*

The main façade (unfinished) of the cathedral is in the Piazza Danti. The stone pulpit outside was built for San Bernardino, a medieval preacher who attracted crowds too large for the cathedral. The baroque portal was added in 1729. From the 15th to the 18th centuries many important artists contributed their works of art to San Lorenzo; among them Agostino di Duccio, Perugino, Luca Signorelli and Federico Barocci (his magnificent Deposition of 1569 is to the right of the entrance). The Cappella del Sant'Anello contains what is said to be the Virgin's wedding ring.

The fountain was a hydraulic as well as artistic achievement: it was completed in 1277 with the help of Friar Bevignate, a hydraulic genius who pumped water into Perugia from Monte Pacciano nearly 3km away.

Fontana Maggiore**

The great medieval sculptors Nicola Pisano and son Giovanni seem to have had a head start on the Renaissance with this fountain, such is its realism and balance. The themes are an eclectic mixture of Christian and pagan, secular and religious, fabulous and mythical subjects – an encyclopaedic hodgepodge that made perfect sense to the medieval mind. The labours of the months, signs of the zodiac, the Garden of Eden, Samson and Delilah and Aesop's Fables are all here, and a Vestal Virgin for good measure. Twenty-four statues personify Perugia, nearby Lake Trasimeno (the woman with the fish), saints, monks, evangelists, prophets and a long since forgotten governor of Perugia, sceptre in hand. The three bronze water-carriers are the Three Graces or the Three Theological Virtues, depending on whom you ask.

Right
The Fontana Maggiore

Galleria Nazionale dell'Umbria €€
Palazzo dei Priori, Corso Vannucci 19; tel: 075 741247. Open daily 0830–1730 (Sat mid-Jun–mid-Sept until 2300). Closed 1st Mon of each month.

Galleria Nazionale dell'Umbria✦✦✦

This is the richest artistic collection in Umbria, filling 33 rooms with state-of-the-art lighting and multimedia exhibits in English and Italian. Unsurprisingly, Umbrians are well represented. The former palace chapel is still decorated with magnificent frescos by Benedetto Bonfigli (1450), some of which are damaged. There are a dozen works by Umbria's greatest painter, Perugino, including his early masterpiece the *Adoration of the Magi* (1475–7), his *Madonna della Consolazione* (1496–8) and a mature work, *Christ Entombed*, a stark and expressive painting of the dead Christ. Major works by Perugino's followers, Lo Spagna and L'Alunno, are given pride of place as well as Fiorenzo di Lorenzo's lovely *Adoration of the Shepherds* (1490). However, there is only one huge painting by Pinturicchio, the *Pala di Santa Maria dei Fossi*; otherwise, his best work is to be seen in Spello and Siena (*see pages 240 and 76–87*). There are many masterpieces from beyond Umbria's borders, including two of the gallery's most sublime works of art: Fra Angelico's luminous *Madonna and Child with Angels and Saints* and a legendary polyptych by Piero della Francesca painted at about the same time as the cycle of frescos in Arezzo (*see page 185*).

Pozzo Etrusco €
Piazza Piccinino 1; tel:
075 5733669. Open daily
Apr–Sept 1000–1330,
1430–1830.

Palazzo dei Priori*

Perugians call their palace, which has been polished by 600 years of
sunshine and rain, the most beautiful public building in Italy. Since
the Middle Ages, the palace has been the heart of political life in town.
It was built intermittently between the 13th and 15th centuries but a
sense of unity somehow prevails, provided in part by the two tiers of
14th-century windows that traverse the walls of pink and white stone.
The windows of the lower tier have Gothic lancets contained within
rectangles, while those above are surmounted by triangular frames.
The battlement on top was a 19th-century addition.

Right
The Palazzo dei Priori

Pozzo Etrusco**

The Etruscan Well is located beneath the Palazzo Ranieri di Sorbello.
One of the most important and well-preserved Etruscan hydraulic
works, it dates back to the second half of the 3rd century BC. The well,
35m deep, has a diameter of 5.6m at the top and decreases to 3m at
the bottom. A small passageway leads down the shaft to a gangway
suspended above the water. The top of the well is in the middle of
Piazza Piccinino (to the right when you exit).

Entertainment and festivals

Perugia is full of students, Italian and foreign, who come to study at its ancient University, the Academy of Fine Arts or the University for Foreigners. Nightlife in Perugia is never dull, especially during Rockin' Umbria (first half of June), Umbria Jazz Festival (first half of July) and *Sagra Musicale Umbra* (second half of September).

Accommodation and food

Perugia is by far the liveliest city in Umbria and well worth a stopover. However, because of the traffic and modern suburbs, it makes no sense to use Perugia as a base for touring the surrounding region.

Locanda della Posta €€€ *Corso Vannucci 97; tel: 075 5728925; fax: 075 5732562.* Ornate façade outside, period interiors and mod cons inside; and parking.

Hotel La Rosetta €€ *Piazza Italia 19; tel and fax: 075 5720841; www.perugiaonline.com/larosetta. Facing Piazza Matteotti.* The *camera da letto matrimoniale* (No 55) has vaulted, *trompe-l'oeil* ceilings and Venetian glass chandeliers. There is parking, too.

Hotel Fortuna €€ *Via Luigi Bonazzi 19; tel: 075 5722845; fax: 075 5735040.* Central, with a garage.

Castello dell'Oscano €€€ *Strada della Forcella 37, Cenerente, 5km north of Perugia; tel: 075 690125; fax: 075 690244; e-mail: info@oscano.com; www.oscano.com.* A castle fit for a king, cardinal, aristocrat or anyone with a bit of plastic. All the history and luxury still costs less than the top hotels in Perugia. Suite 402 has the best view.

Aladino €€ *Via della Prome 11; tel: 075 5720938.* Owner Marco Loredana has an Umbrian wife and Sardinian mother. Regional Umbrian cuisine still rules the kitchen but with a lot of creative variations and the occasional seafood dish. There are two *degustazione* menus accompanied by wines from the local hills – the Colli Perugini.

Cesarino € *Piazza IV Novembre 5; tel: 075 5728974. Closed Wed.* Excellent *trattoria-pizzeria* set in a 13th-century palace with a view of the Fontana Maggiore. It serves delicious pizza and homemade *tagliatelle*. Main courses might be *agnello a scottadito* ('lamb chops') or roast *piccione* ('pigeon'). It is often very crowded.

Shopping

La Salumeria dei Fratelli Temperini *Corso Cavour 30; tel: 075 5721606.* Umbrian salami comes in many forms here, some unpronounceable, and all delicious: *coppa, mazzafegati, salsicce* and, of course, *prosciutto*.

La Panetteria Ceccarini *Piazza Matteoti 16; tel: 075 5721960.* The best baker in Perugia – 30 kinds of bread, festive and seasonal sweets, and pastries such as *torciglioni* and *torte al formaggio e biscotti*.

Pasticceria Sandri *Corso Pietro Vannucci 32; tel: 075 5724112.* Pastry heaven behind a turn-of-the-century façade.

Casa del Parmigiano *Via Sant'Ercolano 36; tel: 075 5731233.* Owner

Majolica

The town of Deruta, 17km south of Perugia off the N3, is given over almost entirely to majolica. Its long main street is lined with workshops and showrooms. You can choose between reproductions (*reproduzione* or *tradizione*) and contemporary designs (*artistiche* or *moderne*). Many shops will offer a discount of 20 per cent for payment in cash.

If you want to see the complete range of ceramics under one roof, visit the **Museo Regionale della Ceramica** in the former Convento di San Francesco (€ tel: and fax: 075 9711000; www.sistemamuseo.it. Open Jul–Sept 1000–1300, 1530–1900; Apr–Jun 1030–1300, 1500–1800; Oct–Mar 1030–1300, 1430–1700). The earliest records of pottery production here date to 1387 and the earliest surviving pieces, from the end of the 15th century, show the influence of Faenza in their colours and designs. The Derutans came to specialise in monumental plates and vases with heavy relief moulding. Grotesque ornament, fruit and foliage scrolls are typical and the predominant colours are rich yellow and midnight blue.

Mario Corradi sells cheese and salami from all over Umbria. Ask for *pecorino di botte* – sheep cheese packed in a bottle in such a way that it continues to age; or the rare *il roccaccio*, a cheese made near Todi, that is aged for 10 to 18 months.

Guiditta Brozzetti *Via T Berardi 5–6; tel: 075 40236; www.brozzetti.com. Open 0900–1300 and 1400–1800; weekends by appointment only.* Fabrics are woven on 18th- and 19th-century looms in a converted Franciscan convent.

Suggested tour

Total distance: 2km.

Time: Two days should be the minimum for Perugia.

Links: The tour of the Upper Tiber Valley ends here (*see page 199*), and Perugia is the starting point for the Umbrian Apennines (*see page 225*). Lake Trasimeno (*see page 212*) and Assisi (*see page 228*) are a just few kilometres away.

Route: From the car park at Piazza Partigiani, the escalators that lead up to Perugia pass through an eerie underground city, the remains of 25 towers and 3 churches that were used as a foundation for the Rocca Paolina, a papal fortress that stood here for 300 years. It was torn down in the 19th century after Perugia regained its independence. At the top are the 19th-century Piazza Italia and the **Giardini Carducci** ❶, a terrace with a sheer drop of 300m and a view that takes in Assisi and the Umbria valley.

The **Corso Vannucci** ❷ is the main street of Perugia (named after the famous painter, better known to the world as Perugino) and perhaps the best place in all of Umbria for people-watching. The *passeggiata* here is endlessly fascinating. There are hundreds of young men and women strolling, gossiping, flirting, pairing off – Botticelli or Raphael could easily have recruited nymphs and pageboys here – as well as couples with children, schoolchildren and grandparents. After just 200m, the Corso ends in the Piazza IV Novembre, an extraordinary medieval ensemble, framed by the **PALAZZO DEI PRIORI** ❸ and the **DUOMO SAN LORENZO** ❹, with the **FONTANA MAGGIORE** ❺ in the middle (*note: the tourist office in the Palazzo dei Priori has excellent city maps*).

After walking in a circle around the fountain, turn right into Via Maestà delle Volte and pass under the strange medley of arches into Piazza Cavalotti, bear right into Via Baldeschi then duck under the first arch to the left – this is Via Appia, really just a set of stairs. The steps deposit you on the **Via dell'Acquedotto** ❻. A 13th-century aqueduct that brought water to the Fontana Maggiore, it is now a

🏛 Museo
Archeologico
Nazionale dell'Umbria
€ Former Convento di San
Domenico; Piazza G. Bruno
10; tel: 075 5727141; fax
075/ 5728200;
www.archeopg.arti.benicultur
ali.it. Open Mon
1430–1930; Tue–Sun
0830–1930. Houses a rich
collection of Etruscan
finds.

street and surely one of the most original in Umbria. This improbable byway practically leads through the living rooms of several Perugian residents and affords a bird's-eye view of lush, secret gardens. At the bottom, make a sharp right into Via Fabretti and continue to the end of the street and round the corner. Stepping into Piazza Braccio Fortebraccio, you will come face to face with the monumental **ARCO ETRUSCO ❼**.

Detour: The street that leads under the arch – Via Ulisses Rocchi – has a vaulted wine bar, **Bocca Mia**, at No 32 and the city's best wine shop, **Enoteca Provinciale**, at No 16.

Facing the arch, walk left up a series of steps (the Via Bartolo) past the city wall (the lower stones are also Etruscan). Keep hugging the stone parapet and you will soon find yourself marching up a zig-zag of steps, the Via delle Prome. Catch your breath at the narrow square at the top, the Piazza delle Prome, while studying the city rooftops and the surrounding hills. There are usually young Italian couples here, snogging passionately and oblivious to tourists.

Walk to the end of the square and turn right at the university building into Piazza Michelotti, technically the highest part of town, where you have a choice of two lefts. Take the second one into the murky Via dell'Aquila. After a few metres, a couple of curves and some steps, an arch appears to the right. Duck underneath it, climbing up to the Piazza Raffaello. The small church to the left, the **Capella di San Severo ❽**, contains the city's only painting by Raphael (1505), which depicts the Holy Trinity and a brace of saints. The saints were actually painted by Perugino in 1521 when he was 70 and no doubt he thought of his former pupil Raphael – already dead at 37 – whose fame had so greatly surpassed his own. You can spy on it through the crevice in the wooden door or pay (negligible) to enter and see it.

Cross the square and veer under the arch to your left, walking up another set of stairs through a no-name piazza and descending through a narrow passage between the Chiesa della Compagnia della Morte and a wall. In the middle of the Piazza Piccinino is the well-head of the **POZZO ETRUSCO ❾**. A staircase follows the shaft of the well some distance underground. The entrance is at the end of the square on the left. Continue on to Piazza Danti (in front of the cathedral) and walk up the steps into the Duomo. On exiting, walk into the now familiar Piazza IV Novembre.

Detour: Walk back through the throng of people on the Corso Vannucci and duck under the archway – the Priori Arch – below the bell tower that interrupts the Palazzo dei Priori, and let gravity do the rest. The steep Via dei Priori is one of the most remarkable streets in Umbria. The name of the first cross street, the Via della Gabbia ('cage'), recalls the days when prisoners were hung out for the public to abuse in an open-air cage. To the left is Sant'Agata church.

Downhill a bit further is the Piazza Ferri. The only city tower that
survives in its original state, **Torre degli Sciri** ⓾, is just beyond the
escalator. The baroque San Filippo Neri (1626–34) is near the end of
the street. Beyond it is the green and the salmon-pink façade of the
church of San Francesco al Prato, which has been threatening to
collapse for 500 years and nearly did during the 1997 earthquake (*not
presently open to the public*); right next to it is the **Oratorio di San
Bernardino** ⓫ with a striking façade of dancing girls, cherubs and
musicians playing viols, sackbuts and trumpets in an orgy of
celebration. It's an odd way to honour the pulpit-thumping St
Bernard, one of the greatest orators of the Middle Ages, who
specialised in sermons on vanity, usury and greed. Ironically, he has
been declared the patron saint of advertising. It is hard to imagine
him plugging *haute couture*. The dresses of 14th-century rich women
were, in his words, ' … the fruit of robbery and usury, of peasants'
sweat and widows' blood, of the very marrow of unprotected orphans.
If you were to take one of these gowns and press it and wring it out,
you would see, gushing out of it, a human being's blood'.

Turn right into Via Calderini to reach **Piazza Matteotti** ⓬ and right
again along Via Baglioni past **Palazzo Capitano del Popolo** ⓭, a
15th-century Renaissance palace. Just to the left, is the entrance to a
market, the **Mercato Coperto** ⓮ with stunning views from its terrace.

Also worth exploring

The most interesting church in Perugia is one of the least visited. Built
in the second half of the 10th century over an Etruscan-Roman
graveyard, **San Pietro** received a Mannerist facelift in the 16th century
that only partly covered its primitive medieval design. There are no
less than three cloisters. A 17th-century porch leads to the first one
(1614) which hides the old façade:
here a 16th-century portal gives
access to the church. Worth noting
are the ceiling by Benedetto da
Montepulciano (1553) and the
superb choir (1525–35) carved and
engraved by Stefano Zambelli di
Bergamo. Outside the church, a
corridor leads to a second cloister
(also early 16th century) and yet
another corridor leads to the
'Cloister of the Stars' designed by
Perugian architect Galeazzo Alessi in
1571. Across the street, the 18th-
century Giardini del Frontone
(Frontone Gardens) have a fine view
of the plain of Assisi.

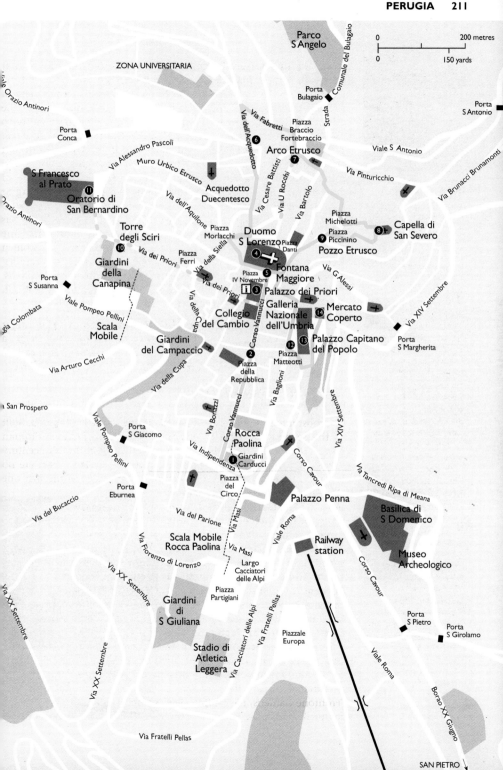

Parco
S Angelo

Strada Comunale del Bulagaio

0   200 metres

0   150 yards

ZONA UNIVERSITARIA

Porta
Bulagaio

Porta
S Antonio

Viale Orazio Antinori

Via dell'Acquedotto

Via Fabretti

Piazza
Braccio
Fortebraccio

6

Arco Etrusco

7

Viale S Antonio

Via Pinturicchio

Via Brunacci Brunamonti

Porta
Conca

Via Alessandro Pascoli

Muro Urbico Etrusco

Acquedotto
Duecentesco

Via U Rocchi

Via Cesare Battisti

Via Bartolo

S Francesco
al Prato 11

Oratorio di
San Bernardino

Orazio Antinori

Via dell'Aquilone

Torre
degli Sciri

Piazza
Morlacchi

Duomo
S Lorenzo

Piazza
Danti

Piazza
Michelotti

Piazza
Piccinino 9

Piazza
Ferri

Via della Stella

4

8

Capella di
San Severo

Pozzo Etrusco

10

Giardini
della
Canapina

Via dei Priori

Piazza
IV Novembre

5

Fontana
Maggiore

Via G Alessi

Porta
S Susanna

Via della Cupa

Via dei Priori

i 3

Palazzo dei Priori

Via XIV Settembre

Viale Pompeo Pellini

Scala
Mobile

Galleria
Nazionale
dell'Umbria

Mercato
Coperto

Loggia Colomba

Collegio
del Cambio

14

Via Arturo Cecchi

Giardini
del Campaccio

Corso Vannucci

2

12

13

Palazzo Capitano
del Popolo

Porta
S Margherita

Piazza
della
Repubblica

Piazza
Matteotti

Via Baglioni

a San Prospero

Viale Pompeo Pellini

Via Bonazzi

Corso Vannucci

Via XIV Settembre

Porta
S Giacomo

Via Indipendenza

Rocca
Paolina

1

Giardini
Carducci

Corso Cavour

Via Tancredi Ripa di Meana

Via del Bucaccio

Porta
Eburnea

Piazza
del
Circo

Palazzo Penna

Basilica di
S Domenico

Via del Parione

Via Masi

Scala Mobile
Rocca Paolina

Via Fiorenzo di Lorenzo

Via Masi

Largo
Cacciatori
delle Alpi

Railway
station

Corso Cavour

Museo
Archeologico

Via XX Settembre

Piazza
Partigiani

Giardini
di
S Giuliana

Via Cacciatori delle Alpi

Via Fratelli Pellas

Piazzale
Europa

Porta
S Pietro

Porta
S Girolamo

Via XX Settembre

Via XX Settembre

Stadio di
Atletica
Leggera

Viale Roma

Borgo XX Giugno

Via Fratelli Pellas

SAN PIETRO

Lake Trasimeno

Ratings

Scenery	●●●●●
Art	●●●●○
Children	●●●●○
Food and drink	●●●●○
Nature	●●●●○
Architecture	●●●○○
Museums	●●○○○
Shopping	●●○○○

Lago Trasimeno is the largest lake on the peninsula of Italy. A vast sheet of blue-green water with 45km of shoreline, it is shut in by gentle hills on three sides covered in oak and olive trees. The lake and its shore have been all things to men: Etruscan gardens and graveyards; the stage for Hannibal's greatest victory over Rome; the region's most important source of protein (fish) in the Middle Ages; an underwater Duchy for Napoleon (he meant to have it drained); and, today, a rare natural reserve attracting migratory birds. For the painter Perugino, the lake was a prelude to infinite space, a golden, tranquil landscape that shimmers behind his saints and virgins.

CASTIGLIONE DEL LAGO✧

ⓘ APT office *Piazza Mazzini 10; tel: 075 9652484; fax 075 9652763; e-mail: urat@lagotrasimeno.net; www.lagotrasimeno.net.*

ⓘ Palazzo della Corgna *€ Tel: 075 9658210. Open mid-Mar–Apr 0930–1300, 1530–1900; May–Jun 1000–1330, 1600–1930; Jul–Aug 1000–1330, 1630–2000; Sept–Oct 1000–1330, 1530–1900; Nov–mid-Mar 0930–1630.*

The Etruscans living in Chiusi used the territory of Castiglione for farming. The headland was a formidable defence of the Byzantine Duchy of Perugia in the 7th century against the neighbouring territories of Lombardic Tuscany. Castiglione was then fought over by Arezzo, Cortona and Perugia; the latter emerged the victor. In 1247 Frederick II of Swabia conquered and destroyed the town and rebuilt it in the form it is today, with the help of Elias, a monk with a knack for fortification from Cortona. His symmetrical plan – three roads, three squares and three city gates – is still in place. The monk's masterpiece was the nearly impregnable Rocca del Leone (1247) – a pentagon with four towers; it remains one of the finest examples of medieval military architecture in Umbria and still dominates the lake from the tip of its promontory.

By the 16th century, the town was in Perugian hands again. It became a part of the Papal State in 1648. The **Palazzo della Corgna**✧

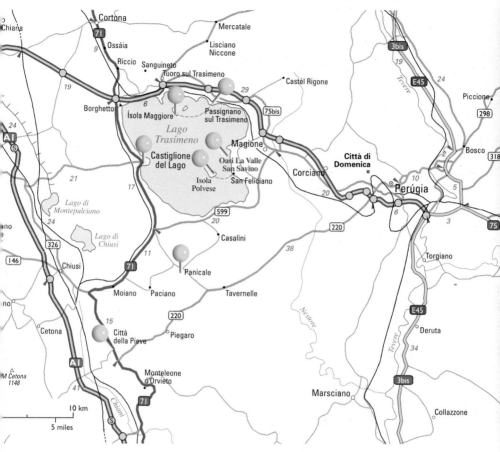

may not look like much but behind the unfinished façade are lifelike frescos begun by Niccolò Circignani (known as Il Pomarancio) in 1574. The best are in the Room of the Exploits of Asciano della Corgna with scenes from the battle of Lepanto. A 300-m corridor through the city wall joins the *palazzo* to the castle.

Città della Pieve*

ℹ Informazioni turistiche *Piazza Matteotti 4; tel: 0578 298031.*

The dramatic hill-town above Lake Trasimeno was Perugino's birthplace and possesses several interesting works by him. In pre-Christian times, it was called Monte di Apollo, and successively Castelforte di Chiuscio and Salpio or Castrum Salapinum. With the coming of Christianity and the parish worship of San Gervasio, it assumed the name *Castrum Plebis*, which has been perfected in today's Città della Pieve. One of the striking things about the town is that it is made almost entirely of deep red brick. Città was a major producer of

**Oratorio di Santa
Maria dei Bianchi €**
*Via Pietro Vannucci; tel:
0578 299375. Open
May–Sept 0930–1300,
1600–1930; Oct–Apr
1000–1230, 1530–1800.* If
the door is locked during
these hours, ask for the
custodian at No 42 or
inquire at the tourist
office.

Right
Fishing nets, Lake Trasimeno

brick in the Middle Ages.
Chief among Perugino's
works here is the
Adoration of the Magi in
the **Oratorio di Santa
Maria dei Bianchi***. If
you have nothing better
to do, seek out the
evocatively named Via
della Baciadonna ('of the
woman's kiss') and
decide for yourself if it
is, as the townspeople
claim, the narrowest
street in Italy.

Isola Maggiore*

**For sailing times of
ferries to the island,**
*tel: 075 50 67 81 or view
the website
www.apmperugia.it.*

Second in size of the three Trasimeno islands, Isola Maggiore is said to
have been visited by St Francis one stormy night in 1211. The hamlet
on the shore has not changed that much since it was a 15th-century
fishing village. Even native son and medieval Umbrian poet Matteo
dell'Isola might recognise it. On the south side of the island is an
18th-century villa (residence of the Marquesses Guglielmi), built on
the former site of the Franciscan convent founded in 1328.

A trail from the village leads up through olive groves to San
Michelle Arangelo (309m), the highest point on the island with
sweeping views in all directions. From there, you descend to the
opposite (east) side of the island to the Cappella di San Francesco and
a second chapel, where St Francis is said to have disembarked. The
trail continues around the island and passes the Romanesque church
of San Salvatore. Isola Maggiore has a centuries-old tradition of
lacemaking and exquisite pieces are still produced by hand using a
simple crochet hook.

Isola Polvese*

Isola Polvese € The
island is open to
visitors from Easter to end
Sept, and year round to
groups (*tel: 075 9659547;
fax: 075 9659546; www.
polvese.provincia.perugia.it*).

Ten minutes by boat from the village of San Feliciano, Polvese is a
heavily forested and uninhabited island. There is a ruined Franciscan
monastery to explore, with thousands of olive trees planted by its
former residents, as well as alleys of oleander and a good beach for
swimming.

Oasi La Valle San Savino[*]

Oasi La Valle San Savino € *tel: 075 8476007; e-mail: oasilavalle@libero.it; www.provincia.perugia.it/oasil avalle/home.htm. Open Jun–Sept daily 0900–1300, 1600–2000; Oct–May Tue–Sun 0900–1300, 1500–1800.*

Lake Trasimeno is on an important route used by birds migrating to the tropics. This part of the lake is strictly protected and far and away the best for bird watching. Red herons arrive from Africa to breed here in spring. Cormorants come in winter. There are watchtowers to view them from and, on weekends, visitors are allowed to circle noiselessly in electric boats.

Panicale[*]

Pro Loco *Piazza Umberto I; tel: 075 837581.*

San Sebastiano € *Tel: 075 837183. Frescos on view May–Sept 1030–1230, 1600–1900; Oct 1000–1230, 1500–1800; Nov–Apr 0930–1230, 1500–1700.*

Below
Lake Trasimeno fisherman

This town has a helical plan – fairly typical in medieval Umbria. The name has multiple meanings: 'holy hill', 'everything is beautiful', 'Pan got angry' and 'millet is cultivated here'. Although its origins are probably Etruscan, Panicale came into its own as a Roman fortress. In the Middle Ages, it was witness to countless sieges and wars, particularly between Perugia and Chiusi. Its officially impregnable castle was surrendered in 1643 to Mathias, leader of the Florentine army.

The walled town has two legendary frescos – the *Coronation of the Virgin* and the *Martyrdom of St Sebastian*, both by Perugino, in the church of **San Sebastiano**[*].

Passignano sul Trasimeno[*]

Pro Loco *Via Roma 36; tel: 075 827635.*

Historically, Passignano, built on the shores of the lake with houses rising above one another, was the easiest way to get from point 'A' (Umbria) to points 'B' (Florence and Siena), without going across or around the lake. Thanks to this strategic position, it was constantly attacked throughout its history. That explains the two medieval towers with ogival gates. The town was once home to Società Aeronautica Italiana, a company that manufactured seaplanes in the 1920s and 1930s. As a result, it was heavily bombed during the Second World War. They still train pilots here. However, the lakeshore is given over to cafés, bars and souvenir shops. Passignano has regular ferry services to the other lakeside towns and the Isola Polvese and Isola Maggiore.

Accommodation and food

Azienda Agraria F.lli Palombaro *Via della Strage 8, Monte del Lago; tel: 075 8400122. Open 0700–0900 and 1600–1800.* You can buy excellent local olive oil here (some of it is classified *denominazione d'origine Umbria*), for example, Il Castel di Zocco.

The tourist office in Castiglione del Lago has printed the wild boast that, from Lake Trasimeno '20% of the world's artistic heritage' is 'at hand'. Rome is only a couple of hours' drive on the A1 *autostrada* and much of Tuscany and Umbria is within easy driving range.

Relais La Fattoria €€ *Via Rigone, Castèl Rigone 1; tel: 075 845322; fax: 075 845197.* A medieval building in an idyllic hilltop location with a kidney-shaped swimming pool and managed with a friendly, personal touch.

Locanda del Galluzzo € *Trecine, 2km west of Castèl Rigone; tel/fax: 075 845352; www.perugiaonline.com/locandadelgalluzzo.* Welcoming *agriturismo* that accepts overnight guests.

Sauro € *Via Guglielmi 1, on Isola Maggiore in Lake Trasimeno; tel: 075 826168.* The only place to stay overnight on the lake islands, run by a fisherman and his family. Their restaurant serves outstanding starters such as *linguine alla tinca* or *risotto al pesce di lago*.

L'Acquario €€ *Via Vittorio Emanuele II 69, Castiglione del Lago; tel: 075 9652432; www.castiglionedellago.it/acquario. Closed Fri; in winter Tue and 15 Jan–15 Feb.* Elegant hole in the wall restaurant on the main street with a terrific *menu degustazione*. The house speciality is *filetti di anguilla* – skewers of lightly smoked eel. They also serve other typical Trasimeno fish dishes such as *carpa regiona in porchetta* ('stuffed carp'). Homemade desserts.

Rosso di Sera € *Via Fratelli Papini 81, Magione; tel: 075 8476277. Dinner only. Closed Tue and half Nov.* Earthy lakeside *trattoria* with an emphasis on regional cuisine as well as fish – stuffed pigeon and veal tongue, for example.

The landscape of Perugino

During Perugino's lifetime (1450–1523), central Italy experienced over 30 years of bloodshed, beginning with the invasion of Charles VIII in 1494. Every available army in Europe made its way to Italy to get its share of plunder. The countryside was burnt and devastated; there was hunger, disease and despair. There is, however, no famine, rape or murder in the artistic universe of Perugino. 'He had a feeling for beauty in women, charm in young men and dignity in the old, seldom surpassed before or since', observed art critic Bernard Berenson. His beautiful people inhabit a fantastic topography almost as enigmatic as the scenery in the *Mona Lisa*. The background of many paintings is the same: a rarefied ring of low hills hovers around a misty lake that is and isn't Lake Trasimeno. While driving around Lake Trasimeno, you can contemplate its mystic counterpart in Perugino frescos and paintings in Città della Pieve and Panicale. He died of the plague while at work in the hamlet of Fontignano, in view of the lake.

Suggested tour

Total distance: 160km; detour add 4km.

Time: One long day.

Links: This route begins 31km from Perugia (*see page 202*); it is just an 11-km downhill drive from Città di Castello to Chiusi, which is on the Crete and Val d'Órcia tour (*see page 105*).

Route: The best way to begin a tour of Lake Trasimeno is with a boat ride. Boats leave from **PASSIGNANO SUL TRASIMENO** ❶ several times a day. On your way, look left (southeast) at the abstract sculpture of a jet plane. After a visit to **ISOLA MAGGIORE** ❷, retrieve the car and follow the lakeside road towards Tuoro. An international team of artists created the Campo del Sole ('Field of the Sun') at Punta Navaccia on the Lido di Tuoro (another point of embarkation for island ferries). The works form a large spiral (comet-shaped) marked by 27 sculpted columns leading to a central table surmounted by a symbol of the sun.

Detour: Turn north to drive to **Tuoro** ❸. A natural amphitheatre of low hills surrounds it with farmland in between. Not much at first glance but this was the scene of one of the greatest battles in European history. Sixteen thousand Romans lost their lives, massacred by Hannibal's Carthaginian army in 217 BC. The names of villages in the neighbourhood record the battle's aftermath: Sanguineto ('bloody') and Ossáia ('bones').

In the hilly part of Tuoro (it was on the lakeshore during the Middle Ages), the Centro di Documentazione sulla Battaglia del Trasimeno has an exhibition that looks at the various theories about what happened. You can then follow a history trail, the Percorso Storico-Archeologico della Battaglia, on the actual site of the battle. There is also a pit where Hannibal burned the Roman bodies. It takes imagination to visualise the battle, something the Roman historian Livy had no shortage of: 'So great was the fury of the struggle', according to him, 'so totally absorbed was every man in its grim immediacy, that no one even noticed the earthquake which ruined large parts of many Italian towns, altered the course of rivers, brought the sea flooding into estuaries and started avalanches in the mountains'.

Follow the signs for Castigliano del Lago. Be sure to take the left fork into Borghetto or you will be sucked on to the *autostrada* and deported to Tuscany. A blind turn through the village leads past the cemetery and alongside the lakeshore. The fortified peninsula of **CASTIGLIONE DEL LAGO** ❹ rises up in the distance looking very much like an island in the lake. There is usually free parking outside the walls. From

Above
Lake Trasimeno carp

there, it is more or less a straight shot to Moiano, following the N71. On the way, the landscape in the rear view window widens to include all of Lake Trasimeno, framed by the gentle hills of Paciano and Chiusi. The glowing redbrick city of CITTÀ DELLA PIEVE ❺ has paid parking just outside the walls.

Upon leaving, drive back to the north entrance to town and steer west around the city along a smart belvedere that ends beneath a row of parasol pines. The road now cruises through a dreamy piece of 'mystic Umbria'. The visibility is breathtaking and the smooth curves down to Tavernelle will make even a cheap rental car feel like a Porsche. The hills are covered with pines, spruce, oak and orderly rows of cypresses.

You must leave the road and veer steeply left to reach PANICALE ❻, constructed of the same red brick as Città della Pieve. Here are spectacular views of Lake Trasimeno that take in most of the places described in this chapter: the shoreline that seems to come and go like an optical illusion, the peninsula of Castiglione del Lago to the left, Polvese island on the right, and the Maggiore and Minore islands in the lake's centre. The scene is encircled by an undulating crown of hills that gently roll away into the flats of Valdichiana. On the way down, the lake approaches slowly, as the road wheels around olive groves and sloping fields of wheat. Carry on through the village of Casalini and keep right (in the direction of Perugia).

Turn right again on the lakeside road and follow the shore, then go uphill away from the lake as it rounds a swampy point. Watch for signs to the left leading to **San Feliciano ❼**. You will pass the Castello San Savino before actually reaching this small fishing village. Its **Museo della Pesca** ('Museum of Fishing', *€ Lungolago Alicata 1; tel: 075 8479261; www.museodellapesca.it. Open Jul–Aug daily 1000–1300, 1600–1900; Apr–May, Jun–Sept Tue–Sun 1000–1230, shorter winter hours*) has much to tell about the daily lives of lake fisher folk through the centuries. Twenty types of lake fish swim in aquariums and wooden models show traditional boats and palisades used to catch them. This is also the point where you can catch a ferry to the ISOLA POLVESE ❽, the largest island on the lake and the best one for walking and bird watching.

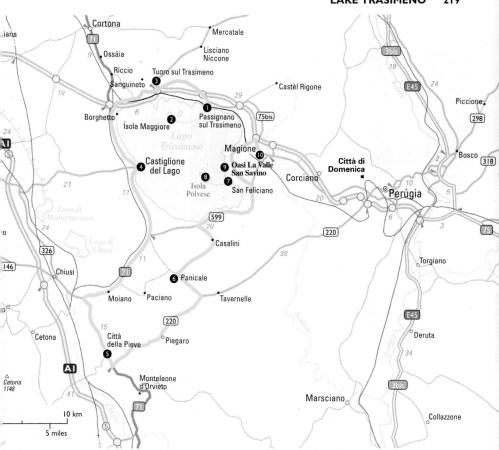

The road now follows the shore closely, along the **OASI LA VALLE SAN SAVINO** ❾ and past the ruined Castello di Zocco before narrowing in on **Magione** ❿, a town of Etruscan origin at a strategic point between Perugia and Chiusi. To assist medieval pilgrims, the Jerusalem Knights Hospitallers founded a hospice here. From Magione, either return to Passignano sul Trasimeno or take the *autostrada* to Perugia.

Also worth exploring

Castèl Rigone is one of Umbria's most charming villages in an area of almost empty hills northeast of Lake Trasimeno. You can see half of Tuscany from it – Montepulciano, Monte Cetona and the extinct volcano of Monte Amiata – before you even begin to look at Umbria. On a clear day, even Monte Vettore (2476m) and the Apennines reveal themselves. Its church, the Santuario della Madonna dei Miracoli, is a Renaissance masterpiece. The solitary road that leads from here to Umbértide offers pastoral, off-the-beaten-track bliss.

Gúbbio and the Umbrian Apennines

Ratings

Mountains	●●●●●
Outdoor activities	●●●●●
Architecture	●●●●○
Nature	●●●●○
Scenery	●●●●○
Walking	●●●●○
Shopping	●●●○○
Museums	●●○○○

Gúbbio claims to have been one of the first five towns founded after the biblical Flood. That would at least explain why it is built so high up a mountain. To the southeast, the stretch of Apennines beneath Monte Cucco (1566m) is sometimes called the 'womb of the Apennines' because of its vast system of caves. The springs from these mountains provide much of the water that makes Umbria 'the green heart of Italy'; some of the best mountain hiking in the region is to be had here. The Parco Regionale del Subásio could be called the park of St Francis. In it lies the mountain where he felt moved to compose his great spiritual poem, *The Canticle of Creatures*.

GUALDO TADINO❖

ⓘ Pro Loco *Via Calai 39; tel: 075 912172; www.gualdo.tadino.it.*

☂ Gualdo Tadino is famous for a type of ceramic with red and gold glazing; there are workshops along the Via Flaminia. The small town is the centre for a lot of *caccia* ('hunting') with many shops selling guns and accessories that no self-respecting Italian huntsman would be seen without.

Time has been cruel to the people living here: invaders pushed them to build their houses ever higher up a steep hill and earthquakes brought them tumbling down. It is still recovering from the effects of the 1997 quake that hit Umbria. The Roman *Tadinum*, a city on the plain and a staging post along the *Via Flaminia*, survived the depredations of Hannibal and an attack by Caesar during the Roman civil war but Totila the Goth annihilated it when his forces swept down through Italy towards Rome. The Byzantine commander Narses avenged the town in AD 442 by killing Totila beneath its ruined walls. The new city – Gualdo Tadino, meaning 'wooded Tadino', from the Lombardic *wald* ('wood') – was built in relative safety higher up the side of Monte Penna.

The modest main square, the Piazza dei Martiri della Libertà, recalls the partisans who fought the Nazis during the Second World War. The Duomo, closing the eastern side of the square, has a delicate rose

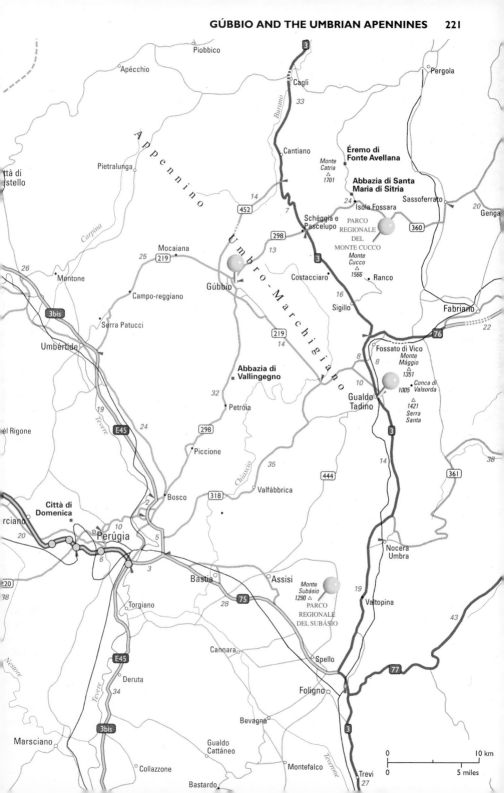

window and Romanesque portal (1256). Unfortunately, the Pinacoteca Comunale with works by Alunno and native son Matteo da Gualdo is closed. The former church of San Francesco, however, is also an art space, devoted to temporary exhibitions. It has frescos by Matteo da Gualdo as well as a Roman sarcophagus. It is a stiff but rewarding climb from the car park outside the city walls up to the Rocca Flea, the 13th-century fortress built under the rule of the Holy Roman Emperor Frederick II.

GÚBBIO**

APT office *Piazza Oderisi 6; tel: 075 9220693, fax: 075 9273409; e-mail: info@iat.gubbio.pg.it; www.comune.gubbio.pg.it. Open Mon–Fri 0830–1345, 1530–1830; Sat 0900–1300, 1530–1830; Sun 0930–1230.*

Pinacoteca e Museo Archeologico Comunale € *Palazzo dei Console, Piazza della Signoria; tel: 075 9274298. Open Apr–Sept 1000–1300, 1500–1800; Oct–Mar 1000–1300, 1400–1700.*

Palazzo Ducale € *Via Federico da Montefeltro; tel: 075 9275872; Open Thu–Tue 0830–1930.*

Local Gúbbio craftspeople make black burnished *bucchera* vases, modelled on graceful Etruscan prototypes.

In many respects, Gúbbio is the perfect medieval hill-town. The population in the Middle Ages was actually twice what it is today. The tall austere buildings seem as ancient as time. Many have been rebuilt so many times that they are now a patchwork of centuries. The Roman part of the town is mostly in the plain, with remnants of a rectilinear street pattern, walls, town gates and the well-preserved 1st-century Roman theatre (off the Viale dei Teatro Romano); it is still used for summer theatrical performances.

When Gúbbio was partly destroyed by Totila the Goth, the Gubbians shifted higher up the side of Monte Ingino. They constructed two narrow terraces shored up by cliff-like walls over 20m high. The scale of this achievement can best be appreciated from the Giardini Pensili, a small garden in front of the Palazzo Ducale, which offers dizzying views down over the cascading rooftops of the medieval town.

The town's focal point, the Piazza dei Consoli, has a similar view and the **Palazzo dei Consoli**, one of the most magnificent town halls in Umbria with tripartite windows, battlements and a finger-like campanile. High on the buttress to the right of the façade is an iron cage in which the civil authorities used to dangle criminals, exposing them to the sun and the ridicule of all Gúbbio. Inside, the barrel-vaulted 14th-century hall seems untouched since it functioned as council chamber. The **Pinacoteca e Museo Archeologico Comunale** occupies the upper floors and is worth seeing for its medieval interiors alone and the extraordinary loggia that overlooks the rooftops of Gúbbio. The star exhibits are the seven massive bronze Eugubine Tablets (*see box on page 225*). Otherwise, the art collection is modest (the best work, Fiorentino's *Madonna of the Pomegranate*, was stolen in 1979).

The Duomo is just a few streets uphill from the Piazza dei Consoli. The interior has fine and rare stained-glass windows and an unusual vaulted ceiling. However, the 15th-century **Palazzo Ducale**, just opposite, is more interesting for its period Renaissance interiors. It was built for the Duke of Urbino, probably by the same architect who designed the Duke's palace in Urbino. From here, it is a steep 2km

Funicular € *Porta Romana, Via San Girolamo; tel: 075 9273881. Open daily Mar 1000–1315, 1430–1730, Apr, May 1000–1315, 1430–1830; Jun 0930–1315, 1430–1900; Jul–Aug 0830–1930; Sept 0930–1900; Oct 1000–1315, 1430–1800; Jan–Feb, Nov–Dec Thu–Sun 1000–1315, 1430–1700.*

walk to the Basilica Sant'Ubaldo (827), the church dedicated to the city's patron saint – 300m higher than the city (note: there is an old **funicular** from the Porta Romana). The most interesting thing in the church is the *ceri*, or candles, that are carried in the annual, uphill race from the cathedral to commemorate the saint's feast day (his 'incorrupt' body is sealed inside a glass coffin on display). The view from the top is superb – you see the peaks of the Apennines, the Scheggia and, of course, the profile of medieval Gúbbio.

Back in the town centre, the 13th-century Palazzo del Bargello in the Via dei Consoli is also worth seeking out. It was a 13th-century prison. The Fontana dei Matti ('Fountain of the Mad') stands in front of the Bargello and is so named because it was once believed that you would go mad if you waded round the basin three times. Today, on holidays, young men wade around the fountain to qualify as 'honorary madmen of Gúbbio'. South of the Bargello, the River Camignano flows down the side of the street of the same name, and emerges in the wide, oval-shaped Piazza Quaranta Martiri ('Square of the Forty Martyrs'). On 22 June 1944, retreating Nazis shot 40 Gubbian women and children here in 'retaliation' for an attack by the Italian resistance on local German troops.

PARCO REGIONALE DEL MONTE CUCCO✤✤

Centro Nazionale di Speleologia *Corso Mazzini 9, Costacciaro; tel: 075 917271; fax: 075 9170647; www.parks.it & www.parchi.provincia.perugia .it.* This centre organises excursions into the region's cave system. It also sells detailed maps for walking and rents out hang-gliding equipment.

The stretch of Apennines on which the Monte Cucco (1 566m) rises up has a vast system of caves and its mineral springs fill up the region's aqueducts with water before flowing into the Sentino river. It is heavily wooded and abundant in fossils. Hiking, cross-country skiing, hang-gliding and spelunking are popular (the Parco Regionale has some 30-odd trails). There are even wolves here, though you are not likely to see one; you might see deer, wild boar and porcupine as well as hawks, golden eagles, eagle owls and kingfishers.

On the more northern part of the territory there are several Benedictine and Camaldolensian abbeys of which the most important are Sant'Emiliano at Isola Fossara and the hermitage of San Girolamo at Pascelupo.

PARCO REGIONALE DEL SUBÁSIO✤✤

Maps and guides to the park are available from the Tourist Information Centre in Assisi (see page 228), or contact the Ente Parco tel: 075 815181; www.parks.it & www.parchi.provincia.perugia. it. Open daily 0900–1300.

The park of Subásio takes its name from the most famous mountain in Umbria. Monte Subásio (1 290m) rises at the southern end of the chain, looking out over a landscape of valleys and hills that includes the Umbria valley. The mountain provided the pink stone for the churches of the town of Assisi. Indeed, the historic centre of Assisi is included in the park.

Right
Gúbbio roof tops of Siena-brown tiles

Accommodation and food

Hotel Bosone Palace €€ *Via XX Settembre 22, Gúbbio; tel: 075 9220688; fax: 075 9220552. Closed Jan–Feb.* Near the cathedral with great views. It even has parking.

Dei Consoli € *Via dei Consoli 59, Gúbbio; tel: 075 9273335.* The best budget option in the best possible location but no parking. Ask for a room off the street.

Valsorda € *in Valsorda, 8km northeast of Gualdo Tadino; tel: 075 913261. Open May–Sept.* Camping in the Apennines and a point of departure for walkers.

Taverna del Lupo €€€ *Via Ansidei 21, Gúbbio; tel: 075 9274368; www.mencarelligroup.com.* Creative variations on Umbrian tradition.

Shopping

Medio Evo (Acacia Giuseppe) *Zona Industriale Ponte D'Assi, Gúbbio; tel: 075 9272596; fax: 075 9228455; www.medioevo.com.* 'Middle Ages' is a company specialising in the reproduction of ancient weapons. This is the place to get value for money if your idea of a souvenir is a crossbow, pike or double hatchet. Mallets come with 1–3 spiked balls and there are iron chastity belts for both sexes. The delivery of a suit of armour or full-size guillotine takes two months. Owner Giuseppe Acacia insists that an ancient weapons fetish doesn't reflect a love of war and violence but simply an appreciation of the region's history (he is certainly right about the history bit).

Suggested tour

Who were the first Umbrians?

Total distance: 140km; add 6km for the detour to Abbazia di Santa Maria di Sitria, 18km for Monte Cucco and 16km for Conca di Valsorda (all return).

Although the Umbri gave their name to the Umbria, we know next to nothing about them. This mysterious people lived a thousand years before Christ. They did not leave much behind except for the foundations of some massive walls and seven bronze tablets, which were discovered in Gúbbio. These Eugubine Tablets were found in 1444 in a field close to Gúbbio's Roman amphitheatre and the text, written in a mixture of Etruscan and Latin characters, describes religious rites, forms of prayer and liturgical regulations practised by the Atiedii, a local college of priests. There is a list of enemies and precise instructions on how to sacrifice them ritually if captured.

Time: Gúbbio is the highlight on this itinerary for the culture vulture (not counting Perugia or Assisi) and it can be explored in half a day. For nature lovers, with or without a spiritual bent, or spelunkers, this stretch of Apennines is almost too good to be true and could absorb many days.

Links: This route departs from Perugia (*see page 202*) and ends in Assisi (*page 228*); it is readily combined with the route through the Upper Tiber Valley (*page 199*).

Route: Leaving **Perugia** ❶ on the N298, take the road to Gúbbio, one of the most beautiful in Umbria. After passing through a zone of creeping industrialisation and a town called Piccione, it begins a long climb, bringing into view the steeples of Perugia, the rounded summit of Monte Subásio and, on a clear day, Lake Trasimeno. The road follows a ridge for some distance. On the right, the Castello di Petróia appears and, a little further uphill, the Abbazia di Vallingegno. The first sight of **GÚBBIO** ❷, stranded so high up on the side of Monte Ingino, is memorable. To get there you have to drive across the wide plain below and past some light industry. There is a large, free car park between the Roman theatre and the *Centro Storico*. Upon leaving Gúbbio, take the N298 northwest through the gorge of the Camignano river that seems to slice through Monte Ingino. Turn south on the N3 at **Schéggia** ❸, which still has a tower from the time when it was *Shisa*, a Roman city.

Detour: The N360, at Schéggia, climbs up the Sentino valley to Isola Fossara. From this village, a winding byroad leads through beautiful wooded countryside until, after about 3km, you reach the semi-ruinous **Abbazia di Santa Maria di Sitria**, with its restored 11th-century church sitting on the top of a 6th-century crypt. St Romuald built the small monastery in 1014. He stayed in one of the cells, maintaining a seven-year vow of silence (1014–21), in which he nevertheless converted many men to Christianity.

Continue on for another 10km and you will reach an even more remote abbey just across the Umbrian border – **Éremo di Fonte Avellana**. This hermitage, surrounded by oak woods and mountain pasture, was founded in AD 980. Off the graceful Romanesque cloister, you can visit the original monastic cells. Dante stayed in one in 1310 while in exile from his native Florence. Perhaps it was here that he had his vision of Hell, wrote out the list of the damned (including many of his enemies), assigned them to seven levels and refined their

Via Flaminia

The *Via Flaminia* is
named after the ill-fated
Gaius Flaminius who
lost a brilliant political
career and an entire
army, to say nothing of
his life, in the Battle of
Lake Trasimeno (see
page 217). The road
crossed Umbria from
Narni, passing through
the towns of Terni,
Spoleto, Foligno, Spello
and Gualdo Tadino, and
on up the Chiascio
valley through the
coloniae (towns built by
retired Roman army
veterans) such as Sigillo,
Scirca, and Costacciaro
and finally to Scheggia.
From there, it linked
Rome to the town of
Arminium (now Ravenna)
on the Adriatic Sea. As
the Roman empire
grew, the road carried
goods from all over the
Mediterranean. In later
centuries, the road
traffic included invading
armies of Goths and
Lombards heading for
Rome.

eternal tortures in *terza rima*. The hermitage was an important medieval centre of learning: the Dante Alighieri library, named in honour of the poet's visit, occupies the former scriptorium where manuscripts were laboriously copied by hand. It is one of the very few examples in Europe to have survived in perfect condition.

Continue through a fertile plain with the flat-topped mountains rising in a row on the left. Just a couple of hundred metres before **Sigillo ❹**, there are impressive remains of a Roman bridge to the right. Beyond it, fields and meadows spread out to the west in the direction of Chiascio. You are now in the middle of the **PARCO REGIONALE DEL MONTE CUCCO ❺**.

Detour: The mountains can be explored by taking the left turn in Sigillo. After 9km this scenic road comes out near the summit of Umbria's highest peak, **Monte Cucco ❻** (1 566m). The mountain meadows here make a popular picnic spot for local people in the summer. A short walk back down the same track, at Ranco di Sigillo, gains the entrance to a vast cave system that penetrates deep into the mountain reaching to a depth of almost 1km. During the summer one of the more accessible caves, the **Grotta del Monte Cucco**, is open to the public (*for a more extensive tour, enquire at the Centre for Speleology: see page 223*). Ranco is also the starting point for numerous hikes.

GUALDO TADINO ❼ seems to hang from the edge of Serra Santa mountain. It suffered major damage in the earthquake and the town is still struggling. Huge metal braces buttress many buildings and no one knows when they will come down.

Detour: The road up to Conca di Valsorda (1 000m) leads to a vast mountain meadow between the peaks of Monte Mággio and Serra Santa. Depending on the time of year, it is bright with the sky-blue of chicory, the yellow of broom, the pink of perennial sweet peas and campion and the white of ox-eye daisies. An easy-to-follow track leads to the summit of the Serra Santa (1 421m) with a tiny pilgrim church and sweeping views of the Apennines.

From Gualdo, follows the signs west for the N444. The road leads directly into the **PARCO REGIONALE DEL SUBÁSIO ❽** and a 34-km roller-coaster ride through scenery so dear to the heart of St Francis. The road slips into **Assisi ❾** through the Porta Perlici.

Also worth exploring

The N219, which follows the Assino river from Gúbbio to Umbértide in the Tiber valley (*see page 198*), could easily be nicknamed 'castle row'. There is the Castello di Carbonara, near Mocaiana, followed by the ruins of Castello di Monte Cavallo looming above the abbey of Campo-reggiano. Further down the road are the Castello di Serra Partucci and the Castello di Poggio at the junction of N219 and N3bis.

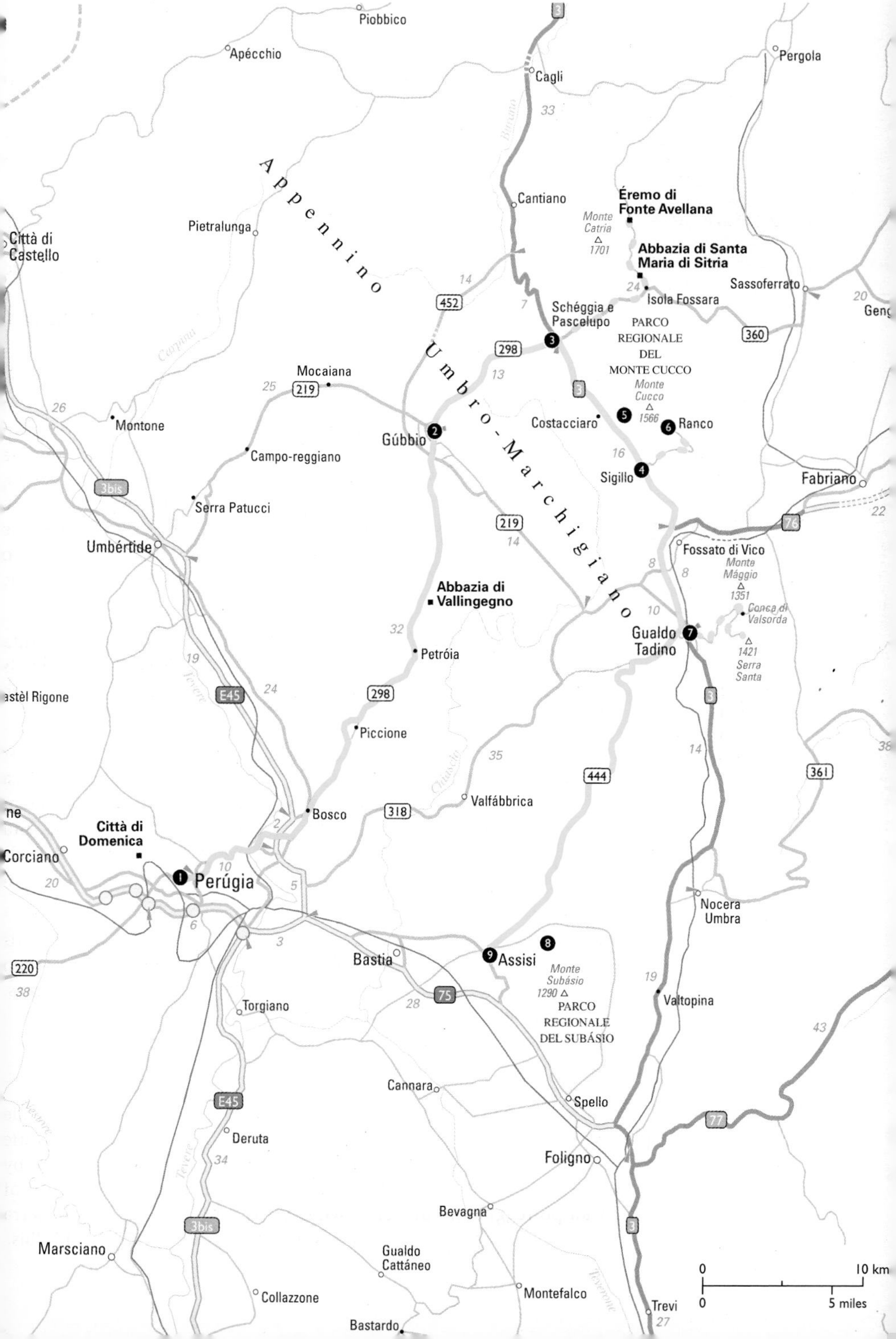

Piobbico

Apécchio

Cagli

Pergola

33

Città di
Castello

Pietralunga

Cantiano

**Éremo di
Fonte Avellana**

Monte
Catria
△
1701

**Abbazia di Santa
Maria di Sitria**

Sassoferrato

20

Geng

A p p e n n i n o

14

452

7

Schéggia e
Pascelupo

Isola Fossara

PARCO
REGIONALE
DEL
MONTE CUCCO

360

Mocaiana

25

219

298

13

❸

Monte
Cucco
△
1566

❺

Ranco

❻

26

Montone

Campo-reggiano

Gúbbio

❷

U m b r o - M a r c h i g i a n o

Costacciaro

Sigillo

❹

16

Fabriano

3bis

Serra Patucci

219

14

76

22

Umbértide

Fossato di Vico

Monte
Mággio
△
1351

Conca di
Valsorda

8

8

**Abbazia di
Vallingegno**

32

Petróia

298

Piccione

Gualdo
Tadino

❼

10

△
1421
Serra
Santa

astèl Rigone

E45

24

35

Chiascio

Valfábbrica

444

3

14

38

361

ne

**Città di
Domenica**

318

Bosco

2

Corciano

20

❶ Perúgia

5

10

❻

3

Nocera
Umbra

220

38

Bastia

Torgiano

28

75

❾ Assisi

❽

Monte
Subásio
1290 △

PARCO
REGIONALE
DEL SUBÁSIO

19

Valtopina

43

E45

Cannara

Spello

77

Deruta

34

Foligno

Marsciano

Bevagna

3bis

Gualdo
Cattáneo

Montefalco

Trevi

Collazzone

27

Bastardo

| 0 | | | 10 km |
| 0 | | 5 miles | |

Assisi

Ratings

Architecture	●●●●●
Art	●●●●●
Scenery	●●●●○
Food and drink	●●●○○
Children	●●○○○
Museums	●●○○○
Nature	●●○○○
Shopping	●○○○○

Assisi, the birthplace of St Francis, is one of the world's most important pilgrimage destinations – as sacred in the minds and hearts of Christians as St Peter's in Rome. The two-storeyed Basilica where St Francis is buried attracts tourists in almost equal numbers (in other words, millions), eager to gaze on frescos by Giotto, Cimabue, Simone Martini and Pietro Lorenzetti. The entire city is of pinkish travertine hewn from Monte Subásio, the mountain it rests on, and its 'stones speak infinitely of virtue and sanctity', according to Pope John Paul II. They also change colour at sunset, glowing several shades redder. The town's position on a spur above the valleys of the Topino and Chiascio rivers attracted Umbrian and Etruscan inhabitants and the Romans left an impressive temple of Minerva. However, the Assisi that survives is almost entirely medieval.

Sights

ℹ **Informazioni turistiche** *Piazza del Comune 12; tel: 075 812534, fax: 075 812450; e-mail: info@iat.assisi.pg.it; www.comune.assisi.pg.it & www.assisiaccessibile.it. Open in summer Mon–Fri 0800–1400, 1530–1830, Sat 0900–1300, 1530–1830, Sun 0900–1300; in winter Mon–Fri 0800–1400, 1500–1800, Sat 0900–1300, 1500–1800.*

Basilica di San Francesco✦✦✦

The saint who led a life of absolute simplicity and poverty is buried in one of the most monumental churches in Christendom. The two-storeyed edifice, combining earthy Romanesque features with limitless engineering ambition, rests on a series of arcaded buttresses that looks like an aqueduct. The German poet Goethe called it a 'dreary pile' and compared it to the tower of Babel – two centuries before the installation of multilingual tourist tapes. The first stone was laid the day after Francis's canonisation only two years after his death in 1226. The saint was buried in secret in 1230 by Brother Elias, one of his original disciples, to prevent someone (namely, the Perugians) from stealing the body. His remains were discovered in 1818 and re-interred in the crypt. It is best to begin here and make your way up, symbolically, from darkness to light.

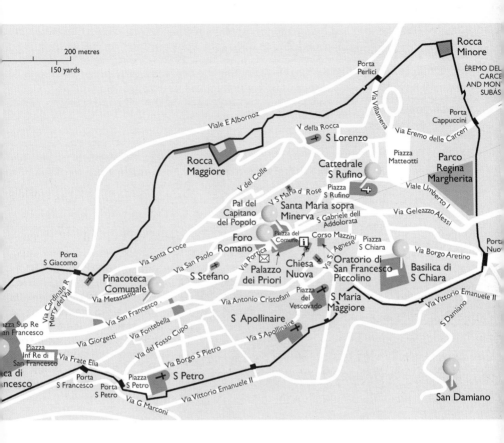

Basilica di San Francesco € *Piazza San Francesco; tel: 075 819001; e-mail: sconvento@sanfrancescoassisi.org; www.sanfrancescoassisi.org. Upper and lower churches open Easter–Nov 0630–1900; Nov–Easter 0630–1800 (upper church 0830–1800) Closed depending on the services, usually Sun morning and holidays.*

The ceilings and walls of the lower basilica are covered in some of the most important medieval frescos in Europe (bring a powerful hand torch or a pocket full of change to feed the coin-operated spotlights). The *Scenes from the Life of St Martin* in the Cappella di San Martino, the last of the frescos to be executed in the lower basilica, are arguably the best. The artist, Simone Martini, worked on the chapel from 1322 to 1326 and was responsible for all the decorations, including the stained-glass windows depicting 18 saints and the marble decoration of the floor.

The earthquake of September 1997 caused considerable damage to some of the frescos in the upper basilica. However, it has been painstakingly restored. Modern technology played an important role: restorers recorded 120,000 fragments of a Cimabue fresco in a database and reassembled it with the help of a virtual model.

The luminous upper basilica is still the artistic highlight of a visit to Assisi. The plan of the basilica is simple and has remained untouched since completion in 1253: just a nave, choir, transepts and apse. The

San Damiano *Tel:*
075 812273. Open
1000–1200, 1400–1800
(1630 in winter)

Palazzo dei Priori *Piazza*
del Comune; reception office
open Mon–Sat 0800–1400.
See local events calendar for
exhibitions.

apse and transepts, which you enter first, are covered in frescos by Cimabue and his assistants. Look hard at Cimabue's *Crucifixion*, considered to be his finest work. However, the glory of the basilica is the fresco cycle illustrating the *Life of St Francis* on the lower walls of the nave, a work that transformed the emphasis of Western art. Giotto 'was always going to nature itself for new ideas' according to Vasari. He found inspiration in the life of St Francis.

Palazzo dei Priori

Still a Town Hall after all these centuries, this palace is not one but four linked buildings, pierced by tunnels, one of which is painted with colourful grotesque ornament. This haphazard group is not exactly beautiful but the 14th-century façades are decorated with massive wrought-iron lamps. After the 1997 earthquake it was completely restored and continues to function as a municipal seat, with space for public exhibitions and concerts.

Below
The cloister of San Damiano

San Damiano*

A humble building of rough, unadorned stone, San Damiano could be mistaken for a farmhouse were it not for the simple arcade in front of the church and the cloisters, added in the 16th century. Inside the church, on the right, 14th-century frescos recall the decisive incident in the life of St Francis when Christ spoke to him from the cross saying 'Go, Francis, and repair my house'. Another scene shows St Francis offering money for the restoration of San Damiano and then being pursued by his angry father. The church contains a remarkable crucifix. It is said that the artist Innocenzo carved the body and left the work unfinished overnight. When he returned the next day, he found the head miraculously completed. Moreover, the head of Christ has three different expressions – anguish, death and tranquillity – depending on whether you view if from the left, right or centre.

San Rufino € *Tel: 075 816016. Open in summer 0800–1300, 1400–1800; in winter 0700–1900.*

Below
Romanesque Madonna and Child on the façade of San Rufino

San Rufino*

San Rufino has perhaps the most outstanding Romanesque façade in Umbria, a sculptural masterpiece, partnered by the massive and stately Romanesque campanile. This site was chosen for the cathedral because, before the canonisation of St Francis, the town's principal saint was the early Christian martyr, San Rufino (d AD 238).

The façade is divided into three parts, both vertically and horizontally, with a rare symmetry to the whole. The middle tier, horizontally, is separated from the lower one by a running arcade carved with eccentric humans, animals and birds. Above, three caryatids – comical figures straining under the supposed weight of the structure – support the central rose window. Symbols of the evangelists are carved at the corners of an imaginary square frame enclosing the whole window. Christ is seated between the sun and the moon below the lunette of the central portal.

The crypt is entered through the door on the right side of the piazza (signposted *Accesso al sotteraneo*) and San Rufino's 3rd-century sarcophagus tomb lies there. However, his bones are now beneath the cathedral's main altar not far from the ironbound marble font used to baptise three future saints – Francis, Clare and Agnes – and the future Holy Roman Emperor, Frederick II (born in 1194). The Museo Capitolare, entered from the right of the apse, contains a fine triptych by Nicolò Alunno, one of the best of the early Umbrian painters, depicting the martyrdom of San Rufino.

On leaving the cathedral look for the small door in the right-hand aisle near the exit; this leads down to the 1st-century BC Roman water storage cistern that now forms the foundation for the campanile.

Santa Chiara *Piazza Santa Chiara; tel: 075 812282. Open 0630–1200, 1400–1900 (1800 in winter)*

Foro Romano e Collezione Archeologica € *Via Portica 2; tel: 075 813053; www.sistemamuseo.it. Open 1000–1300, 1400–1800 (1700 mid-Oct–mid-Mar)*

Santa Chiara**

Huge flying buttresses anchor this church to the ground making it look like some great pink and white insect – the buttresses were added in the late 14th century to prevent the whole structure from collapsing. In plan, the basilica is a copy of the upper church of the Basilica di San Francesco. Begun in 1257, it was built alongside the little 12th-century church of San Giorgio – the place in which St Clare first set eyes on St Francis at the age of 18. The speed with which the basilica was built might explain its penchant for falling over. As for its plainness, the church was once covered in colourful frescos, but these were whitewashed over by a disapproving mother superior because they were attracting too many admiring visitors who were distracting the nuns from their prayers. The decorative bands of alternating rose and white limestone and the delicate rose window form the principal elements of the west front next to the campanile – all essentially Romanesque in style.

Inside, the great aisle-less, groin-vaulted nave is Gothic. The best of the surviving frescos are found in the transepts. On the end of the wall on the left (north) transept there is a touching Nativity scene painted in the 14th century and a 13th-century Virgin and Child, a pure and powerful work in Byzantine style. The remains of St Clare herself are displayed in the crypt beneath a rather ugly neo-classical high altar. Clare's body was rediscovered in 1850 and, as you would expect of a saint's body, it was perfectly preserved inside the coffin. She did not long survive exposure to the open air and deteriorated rapidly until human hands intervened to produce the saintly sleeping figure that lies in the crypt today.

Santa Maria sopra Minerva (Temple of Minerva)**

The former temple still possesses six elegant fluted Corinthian columns that form the classical porch (*pronaos*). The garden-variety baroque interior was added in 1634 when the church was dedicated to San Filippo Neri.

The lower steps of the Temple are underground in the **Foro Romano***. This is located in the crypt (all that survives) of the 11th-century church San Nicolo – now full of Roman coffins and Etruscan funerary urns. A passage from the crypt leads beneath the Piazza del Comune to the subterranean remains of what was once regarded as the city's *Foro Romano* (Roman forum). However, some scholars now believe they belonged to the sanctuary of the Minerva Temple and that the forum was located beneath San Rufino. In any case, walking down the chilly lane of the former Roman town of *Assisium* under the medieval piazza of Assisi is an eerie experience. The massive blocks of travertine are worn by chariot wheels and equipped with gutters that collected rain almost 2 000 years ago.

Accommodation and food

The tourist office keeps a list of 20 monasteries in the region that accept guests. Many convents in Assisi board guests; they are a homely alternative to budget hotels, albeit one with a curfew.

Hotel Subásio €€€ *Via Frate Elia 2; tel: 075 812206; fax: 075 816691; e-mail: s.elisei.hotelsubasio@interbusiness.it.* Right next to the Basilica , with wonderful views from many rooms. A hotel with a lot of tradition – Marlene Dietrich lounged on a bed here – that still sets itself high standards.

Hotel Umbra €€ *Via degli Archi 6; tel: 075 812240; fax: 075 813653; e-mail: humbra@mail.caribusiness.it. Closed mid-Jan to mid-Mar.* A well-equipped hotel just off the main square. Room 34 has a view of the Umbria valley.

Castel San Gregorio € *Via San Gregorio 16, Frazione San Gregorio di Assisi – 10km north of Assisi off the N318; tel: 075 8038009; fax: 075 8038904. Closed three weeks Jan.* Atmospheric castle complex that goes back 700 years. There are only 12 rooms with views of the plain below Assisi or the beautiful Italian-style garden.

Buca di San Francesco €€ *Via Brizi 1; tel: 075 812204; www.assisi.com/ buca-san-francesco.* Perhaps the best in Assisi for regional cuisine and wines though it is a little self-conscious about it and usually full of well-heeled tourists. Choose between the medieval cellars and the well-planted garden.

La Piazzetta dell'Erba € *Via San Gabriele dell'Addolorata 15b; tel: 075 815352. Closed Mon and two weeks Jan.* A dedicated young couple runs this small *trattoria* (their parents work the kitchen). Choices are few but all good. Choose one course or many, starting with Umbrian soup or a sandwich made with a traditional bread called *torta al testo*.

Umbra €€ *Via degli Archi 6; tel: 075 812240.* Family-run restaurant attached to hotel of the same name.

Suggested tour

Total distance: 2km.

Time: There is a great deal to see in Assisi and it is convenient for visiting other towns in Umbria but the atmosphere is often monopolised by the relentless flow of tourists and pilgrims. Two days is enough.

Links: Assisi is the destination of the Umbrian Apennines tour (*see page 225*) and the beginning of the route to Todi (*see page 244*). It is only 20km from Perugia (*see page 202*).

Route: The best time of day to begin a tour of Assisi is when it opens at 0630. You can be sure of a parking space and serenity in the **BASILICA DI SAN FRANCESCO ❶** before tour groups storm the place (if early is not an option, try late in the afternoon). After the Basilica, walk down Via San Francesco, lined with shops selling overpriced majolica plates, made-in-China embroidered blouses, wooden crucifixes and leather sandals. You can also buy a plastic friar in an Inter Milan T-shirt.

Cars can be left in one of the car parks at Porta San Pietro (tel: 075 813311), Porta Moiano (tel: 075 813707), Piazza Matteotti (tel: 075 815164), Porta San Giacomo, Piazzale Ufficio or Piazza del Mercato.

Pinacoteca Comunale €€ *Via San Francesco 10; tel: 075 812033; www.sistemamuseo.it. Open daily mid-Mar–mid-Oct 1000–1300, 1400–1800; mid-Oct–mid-Mar 1000–1300, 1400–1700. It contains a number of works by Umbrian painters from the 14th to the 17th century, including Puccio Capanna and Andrea Assisi.*

Rocca Maggiore € *Tel: 075 815292; www.sistemamuseo.it. Open daily 1000–sunset (Aug 0900–sunset)*

Look up on the way at the Renaissance façades above the shop windows, often framed by the Umbrian arch using a keystone shaped like an inverted teardrop. Nos 14–16, on the left, are the stumpy remains of a 13th-century defensive tower, and alongside is a 15th-century *palazzo* with Renaissance torch-holders and animal-head finials. Once the headquarters of the Guild of Masons, it still bears their insignia – a flower and pair of compasses – as well as the date, 1477. No 10 is the newly restored Palazzo Vallemani, and the site of the **Pinacoteca Comunale ❷**. Next door, No 12, is a fine 17th-century *palazzo* with an ornate balcony (it is now the Municipal Library). Opposite, at No 7, the Oratorio dei Pellegrini (Pilgrims' Chapel) was converted to a hostel for pilgrims in 1431. A 16th-century inscription on the fountain you pass to the right warns you not to use the water for laundry on pain of having your underwear confiscated. Via del Seminario, Via A Fortini and Via Portica link Via San Francesco to the **Piazza del Comune ❸**. Just before the piazza, at Via Portica 2, there is an entrance to the **Foro Romano ❹**.

The Temple of Minerva, or **SANTA MARIA SOPRA MINERVA ❺**, stands on the Piazza del Comune. The civic buildings of Assisi are diagonally opposite. The 13th-century Romanesque Torre del Comune ('Municipal Tower') recalls the feuding Guelph and Ghibelline factions. Another reminder of those ancient conflicts is found in the battlements of the tower and the **Palazzo del Capitano del Popolo ❻** ('Palace of the People's Captain') next door. The tower has fishtail Ghibelline crenellations, the palace has square Guelph ones (the latter added in 1927, long after the two sides had stopped murdering each other). Further up the square, on the opposite side, is the **PALAZZO DEI PRIORI ❼**.

The left-hand passageway that passes beneath the Palazzo descends to a small piazza dominated by the domed **Chiesa Nuova ❽**. This was built in 1615 on the supposed site of the birthplace of St Francis. Inside is the cell in which St Francis was imprisoned for stealing his father's cloth and selling it to pay for the rebuilding of San Damiano. The saint's birthplace is said to have been in the Via San Antonio, east of the church. Although St Francis was the son of a wealthy cloth merchant, a Latin inscription in the **Oratorio di San Francesco Piccolino ❾** informs us that 'the light of the world, St Francis, was born in the stable of an ox and an ass'.

From the Piazza del Comune, veer into the leftmost street out of the square, Via San Rufino. This steep and narrow lane climbs to the upper part of the town and levels out at the Piazza San Rufino, in front of **SAN RUFINO ❿**. Many visitors are not even aware that this cathedral exists at all, tucked away as it is some distance from the central square.

Detour: Walk up Via Porta Perlici and then climb the steep stone

Above
The Rocca Maggiore

staircase called Vicolo San Lorenzo. It leads to the **Rocca Maggiore** ❶ ('great rock' or 'fortress'), which was once the mightiest castle in Umbria. The first castle was built in 1174 at the order of Frederick Hohestaufen known to Italians as Barbarossa – 'Redbeard' who invaded Italy in 1155 to reassert the territorial claims of the Holy Roman Emperor against those of the Pope. Barbarossa's grandson, Frederick II, spent some time living in the castle under the care of Duke Conrad of Urslingen but, in 1198, the people of Assisi destroyed the castle in an uprising against the Duke's tyrannical rule. The present castle therefore dates to the rebuilding, this time under papal control, of 1367, with modifications carried out up to 1535. In later centuries, the people of Assisi used it as a source of building material. It was massively restored in the 19th century. The panoramic view from the central tower sweeps from the orange-brown rooftops of Assisi, the town's churches and campanile, down to the Vale of Spoleto.

Most of the narrow lanes that lead south from the Piazza San Rufino eventually descend to the Piazza and church of **SANTA CHIARA** ❷, the burial place of St Clare, founder of the Poor Clares. In Assisi, the countryside that St Francis loved seems ever present. When you step out through the **Porta Nuova** ❸, it is like stepping from a tame garden into a slightly wilder countryside (after you have crossed the busy road, Viale Vittorio Emanuele II, that encircles Assisi). The steep pedestrian road that leads to **SAN DAMIANO** ❹, just over 1km in length, passes through tranquil olive groves where ancient and gnarled trees rise from a carpet of wildflowers and tall dark cypresses sign the direction to the little sanctuary.

St Francis (1181–1226)

It is not the least of St Francis's qualifications for sainthood that he appeared hopelessly mad to many of his contemporaries. The son of an Assisi cloth merchant took to kissing lepers and wearing hair shirts – nothing exceptional in the Middle Ages. But he went a step further and declared his love, with seeming promiscuity, to the sun, the moon, the elements and all God's creatures. He referred to his body as an 'ass', poverty as his 'bride' and death as his 'sister'. Francis has been seen as a medieval animal rights activist, social worker and Christianity's first environmentalist (Greenpeace International made him their patron saint). However, nothing that Francis did was more revolutionary than living in imitation of Christ and it was by personal example as much as ideas that he influenced the Christian Church.

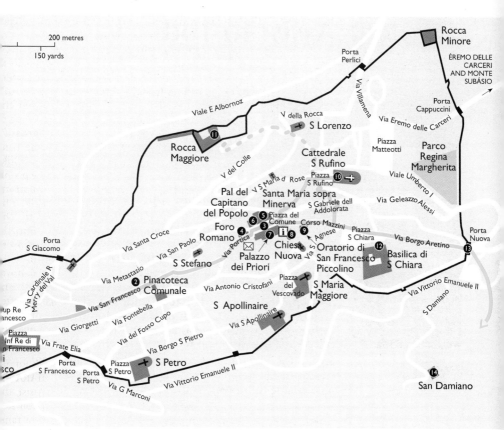

Also worth exploring

The Éremo delle Carceri is set in the woods half way up Monte Subásio (4km east of Assisi). This is the site of several miracles attributed to St Francis. Despite the number of visitors, the hermitage does still have the feeling of remoteness, isolated as it is in a sea of evergreen holm oak. The cave, the Grotta di San Francesco, survives at the core of the modern complex, reached through a tiny narrow passageway and staircase off the diminutive chapel of Santa Maria. At the southern end of the hermitage, a path leads to a stone bridge, which crosses a precipitous ravine. By the side of the bridge, hanging over the brink of the ravine, is a broken and weathered oak – the one, so they say, where birds gathered to listen to St Francis preaching. From this spot, several pathways penetrate the dense woodland that surrounds the hermitage, skirting caves once occupied by St Francis and his followers.

Assisi to Todi

Ratings

Scenery	●●●●●
Architecture	●●●●○
Art	●●●●○
History	●●●●○
Nature	●●●●○
Vineyards	●●●●○
Children	●●●○○
Shopping	●○○○○

The best way to commune with the spirit of nature-loving St Francis while driving a car is to leave Assisi through the back door of Porta Perlici, where few tourists ever venture, and drive to Spello on the ancient carriage road that curves around Monte Subásio. There are sweeping views across the Vale di Umbra, an ancient lake settled by Roman veterans who planted wheat, vines and olive trees – all still an important part of the local industry. This route then crosses the valley flats (skipping the *autostrada*) and the hills around Monte Martana. On the way, it links some of the most charming sights in Umbria: the Roman gates of Spello, the Romanesque square of Bevagna, the Renaissance frescos in Montefalco, and one of Umbria's oldest and most charismatic hill-towns, Todi.

BEVAGNA*

Pro Loco *Piazza Filippo Silvestri 1; tel: and fax: 0742 361667; www.bevagna.it.* Open 0930–1230, 1530–1900; shorter hours in winter.

Bevagna was much bigger in the 1st and 2nd centuries AD when it was Roman and called *Mevania*. Native son and poet Propertius called it 'cloudy Mevania, standing among rain-soaked fields'. The tree-lined **Piazza Garibaldi*** lies just within the town walls. To the right, in the basement of Via Porta Guelfa 2, is a Roman bathhouse that still seems ready for business. Triton sports on its mosaic floor flanked by dolphins, octopuses, sea horses and lobsters. The scant remains of a Roman temple are still visible in Via Crescimbeni. The Romans used to breed sacred bulls in Bevagna, whose whiteness and deer-like expressions qualified them for sacrifice on an altar to Juno or Jupiter.

The sleepy main street of today's town, the Corso Matteotti, leads (right) into the Piazza F Silvestri with scarcely any buildings later than the 13th century. It shows the pride medieval citizens took in their status as an independent commune. The most elegant building, the Palazzo dei Consoli, was built in 1270 and now houses the Teatro

Above
Montefalco

Torti. The church of San Silvestro was built of Roman masonry. Almost windowless, the interior has a set of columns in the nave with mysterious motifs on them that might have been copied from an ancient Roman temple devoted to Isis. The church of San Michele also recycles material with Roman egg-and-dart mouldings. Strange beasts and angels adorn the portal.

MONTEFALCO✢✢

Montefalco produces a strong candidate for the 'best red' in Umbria – the full-bodied Sagrantino, as well as Sagrantino Passito, a heady dessert wine that tastes a little like port.

Because of the stupendous panoramic position, dominating the Topino and Clitunno plains, Montefalco likes to call itself the balcony (*ringhiera*) of Umbria. On a clear day, you can see almost everything – Perugia, Spello, Foligno, Bevagna and the Apennines. In the church of Sant'Agostino, on the main street, Corso G Mameli, there is a fresco which shows the view from Montefalco to Foligno as it was in the 15th century – much the same as today except for a lake (since drained). No less than eight saints were born here though it now prides itself on wine more than sanctity.

Museo Civico di San Francesco

Ringhiera Umbra 6; tel: 0742 379598; www.comunemontefalco.it & www.sistemamuseo.it. Open daily Jun–Jul 1030–1300, 1500–1900; Aug 1030–1300, 1500–1930; Mar–May, Sept–Oct 1030–1300, 1400–1800; Nov–Feb Tue–Sun 1030–1300, 1430–1700.

The **Museo Civico** in the former church of San Francesco✠ is one of the finest art museums in Umbria with a glorious fresco cycle in the apse (1450–52) by Florentine artist Benozzo Gozzoli. Twelve scenes from the life of St Francis reflect the formidable range of Renaissance painting technique and the influence of Fra Angelico. Montefalco itself features in the best scene of all, to the right of the window, in which St Francis preaches to the birds. In the nave of the former church is a potpourri of Umbrian painting that includes a very fine *Nativity* by Perugino and works by Mezzastris, Tiberio d'Assisi and Francesco Melanzio.

Spello✠

Pro Loco *Piazza Matteotti 2; tel 0742 301009; www.comune.spello.pg.it.*

An ancient Umbrian settlement chosen by Augustus as a place of retirement for veterans of his military campaigns, Roman *Hispellum* was demarcated by a wall some 2km around, and modern Spello, a town of just over 1000 inhabitants, has scarcely grown beyond this boundary. The walls still stand to an impressive height, defining the shape of the town as it climbs up the narrow shoulder of a hill beneath Monte Subásio. Polygonal 12th-century towers flank the massive Roman Porta Venere.

Spello's artistic highlight is a lavish set of frescos by Pinturicchio in the Cappella Baglioni of Santa Maria Maggiore (Piazza Matteotti). He never created anything more sensual, exotic or colourful. Pinturicchio left a self-portrait hanging on the wall of the house in the scene where the Archangel Gabriel appears to the Virgin. The floor of the chapel also contributes to the rich effect. The 16th-century majolica tiles, made in Deruta (on the opposite side of the valley, *see p 208 and map on page 239*), are painted with dragons and griffins.

Below
Hilltop Spello

Todi✶✶

ℹ️ **APT office** *Piazza Umberto I, 6; tel: 075 943395; fax: 075 942406; e-mail: ifo@iat.todi.pg.it; www.comune.todi.pg.it & www.todi.net. Open 900–1300, 1500–1900; horter hours in winter.*

Pro Loco *Via dei Condotti ; tel: 075 8943933.*

ℹ️ **San Fortunato €** *Open daily 0930–1230 nd 1500–1700.*

Museo-Pinacoteca € *alazzi Comunali, Piazza del opolo; tel:075 8944148; www.sistemamuseo.it. Open aily Apr–Aug 1030–1300, 400–1800 (Mar, Sept until 700); Oct–Feb Tue–Sun 030–1300, 1400–1630.*

Lo Studiolo *Corso Cavour 48; tel: 075 8944585. Charming ollection of prints, books nd antiques.*

The **Piazza del Popolo** has changed little in appearance since the end of the 14th century. The sense of being surrounded by medieval buildings, still used for their original purpose, is remarkable.

A town of great beauty, blessed with views over unspoiled countryside. Thanks to its strategic position on a hill between the valleys of the Tiber and the Naia, Todi was settled early by the Umbrians. Its original name, *Tuderte*, meant border, because the Etruscans were just next door. The town's coat of arms shows an eagle with a napkin in its talons. A legend says that Todi was founded on the spot where the eagle let the napkin drop, after seizing it from an Etruscan banqueting table. The people of the town – nicknamed Marzia after the Roman god of war – have a reputation for defending their liberty with great ferocity. They repulsed Hannibal and turned away Totila the Goth. Three sets of walls – Etruscan, Roman and medieval – still encircle the city. Inside, many medieval houses have been restored as weekend and holiday homes for Rome's jet set.

From the car park near the Piazza Oberdan (close to Santa Maria della Consolazione) it is a short climb to **San Fortunato**✶, the highest point in the town. The church has a magnificent Gothic portal, set into the half-finished façade that is bursting with biblical figures. The interior also feels buoyant thanks to the slender composite columns, encircled by clusters of shafts, rising up to massive Corinthian columns from which the roof vaults spring. The best fresco, in the fourth chapel on the right, is Masòlino da Panicale's delicate and dreamy *Madonna and Child* (1432).

To the left of the church, a path leads down to Via San Fortunato and the Porta Marzia, the town's one surviving Etruscan gate. This straddles the Corso Cavour, the main street, which leads to the broad **Piazza del Popolo**✶✶. The Duomo, at the far end of the square, incorporates Romanesque, Gothic and Renaissance features. Inside, a dark crypt lurks beneath the cathedral – it was built on the site of an Etruscan temple. Upstairs, the entire west wall is painted with a familiar fresco, a 17th-century copy of Michelangelo's *Last Judgement* in the Sistine Chapel. From the cathedral steps, a left turn leads down the Via del Duomo for a look at the external detail of the Romanesque apse and for the views from the little belvedere. This stands on the site of one of four gates at the corners of the Piazza del Popolo that allowed the whole square to be sealed off and defended in the event of an attack.

Also on the square is the **Museo-Pinacoteca**✶, the town's picture gallery and archaeological museum, in the Palazzi Comunali. After 20 years of 'restoration', it has reopened. Aside from a modest collection of pictures, one of which is by Lo Spagna, there are historical odds and ends from Todi's long history – ceramics, coins and Etruscan and Roman finds. On the way back to the car park, look at the Renaissance church of Santa Maria della Consolazione. It has been attributed to Bramante, the architect of St Peter's, though it was more likely built by a succession of wannabe Bramantes.

Accommodation and food

Palazzo Bocci €€ *Via Cavour 17, Spello; tel: 0742 301021; fax: 0742 230772.* Old *palazzo* near Santa Maria Maggiore.

Villa Pambuffetti €€€ *Via della Vittoria 20, Montefalco; tel: 0742 379417, fax: 0742 379245; e-mail: villabianca@interbusiness.it.* A 19th-century brick villa in its own park surrounded by cypresses.

Palazzo Brunamonti €€ *Corso Matteotti 79, Bevagna; tel: 0742 361932; fax: 0742 361948; www.brunamonti.com.* Sixteen elegant rooms in a recently restored palace full of *trompe-l'œil* fantasy.

La Cantina €€ *Via Cavour 2, Spello; tel: 0742 651775. Closed Wed.* A *trattoria* made in heaven (so come early) whose medieval dining-room fills up with locals and visitors keen to devour hearty Umbrian dishes at low prices. Try the *coniglio in porchetta* ('herb-stuffed rabbit'), the grilled meats or *maccheroni dolci*, a pasta dessert.

Opposite
Todi in the early morning mist
Below
Fresco in Todi's San
Fortunato church

Rifugio San Gaspare € *Strada Statale Flaminia, Giano; tel: 0742 90189. Closed Mon in winter and at end of Sept.* You can indulge a passion for grilled meat, watching it sizzle on a vast fire inside, or waiting on the terrace outside with views of the Martano mountains.

Da Nina € *Piazza Garibaldi 6, Bevagna; tel: 0742 360161. Closed Tue and 15–31 July.* No-nonsense *trattoria* frequented mostly by locals.

Perbacco € *Via Umberto I, 14, Cannara; tel: 0742 720492. Evening only. Closed Mon and 20 July–20 Aug. No credit cards.* This is the onion capital of Umbria so you have to have onion soup, followed perhaps by *polenta con sputature di maiale* or *piccione in casseruola* ('pigeon casserole') and the excellent local *pecorino* cheese.

La Mulinella € *Ponte Naia 29; tel: 075 8944779. Closed Tue and Nov.* An earthy *trattoria* on the Tiber river just outside Todi. Everything on the menu is homemade and based on seasonal ingredients, from *tagliatelle al sugo d'oca* ('in goose sauce') to the house speciality, a lamb dish called *agnello alla Mulinella*.

Suggested tour

There are three roads to Spello: the one taken by this route and two others: the *autostrada*, obviously the fastest; and a dirt road that climbs right over Monte Subásio but is only recommended for four-wheel drive vehicles.

Total distance: 65km; detour add 14km (return).

Time: Two to three days.

Links: The route begins in Assisi (*see page 228*), which marks the end of the tour of the Umbrian Apennines (*see page 225*). It crosses the Umbria valley, which leads to Spoleto (*see page 250*). There are two roads to Orvieto (*see page 276*) from Todi: the N79 over the hills, or the faster N448 along Lago di Corbara.

Route: Leave **Assisi ❶** through the northern gate of Porta Perlici and watch for a right turn after a few hundred metres. This leafy lane of a road takes you to the hamlet of Armenzano (759m) and then the village of Collepino (600m) snug within its medieval ring of walls. On the way, you will probably meet cyclists, walkers and people picnicking by the side of the road. You might be tempted to join them. **SPELLO ❷** is a pink and white city of travertine stone, of Roman gates and Renaissance frescos. It suffered in the earthquake but most of the damage has been repaired. A steep descent drops to the plain by the gates of the city (where there is large dusty car park). To cross the valley, drive beneath the busy N75 (avoiding, at all costs, the maze of traffic around Foligno) and follow the signs for Cannara. You are now crossing an extinct lake. Drainage began under the Romans and, by 1600, it had virtually dried up. Crossing the Topino river, you'll find yourself in **Cannara ❸**, a city founded among the reeds in the Middle Ages. Today, it is the purple onion capital of Umbria and known for an unusual red wine called Vernaccia di Cannara. Take the first left after passing through town under the shadows of a magnificent walled cemetery. Continue south, cruising fields of tobacco, maize and sunflowers, to reach **BEVAGNA ❹**. A straight road leads out of town beneath an alley of plane trees and after just 6.5km climbs up to **MONTEFALCO ❺** (park outside the walls). A tranquil road leads from there through vineyards and olive groves to the evocatively named town of **Bastardo ❻**.

Detour: Follow the signs for **Giano dell'Umbria ❼**, founded by Norman invaders in the 11th century. It's a slow, twisty 7km up to the Rifugio San Gaspare and its panoramic viewpoint.

The road out of town skirts the Puglia river, then crosses it and climbs up to a broad ridge. There are no villages or towns, just green Umbrian hills and an occasional villa. In a strange outburst of road-building ambition, the road widens and resembles a traffic-free *autostrada* for a couple of kilometres before narrowing suddenly at a tiny place called Petroro. Carry on down to the Tiber river, cross under the Perugia *autostrada* and follow the curves up to **TODI** ❽ .

Also worth exploring

At **Trevi**, the modern world is left behind as you step within the walls. Streets too narrow and steep for cars have been turned into minor works of art, paved with pebbles set in frames of stone or brick to divide the surfaces into patterns of squares, diamonds or herringbone. You never know what to expect around the next turning: ancient buildings pierced by medieval archways that offer glimpses of shady, flower-filled courtyards, oversailing buttresses and massive corbels holding up the jettied upper storeys of sombre *palazzi.*

Below
Trevi's narrow cobbled streets

Nera Valley and Spoleto

Ratings

Architecture	●●●●●
Monasteries	●●●●●
Nature	●●●●●
Scenery	●●●●●
Children	●●●●○
Food and drink	●●●●○
Walking	●●●●○
Museums	●●○○○

The upper valley of the River Nera – the Valnerina – is wild, dramatic and uncrowded, with the exception of the famous Marmore Falls. The heights of the surrounding hills are covered by beech forest and meadows that bloom in spring with violets, lilies and gentian. Willows, poplars and black alders line the riverbank, and trout and crayfish live in the streams. Crumbling fortresses and ancient towers are ubiquitous – a legacy of the time when papal and imperial forces fought each other for territorial power in Umbria. Just north of the valley, separated by a mountain and a tunnel is Spoleto, a Romanesque hill-town with modern flair. Percy Bysshe Shelley was not the first or last traveller to call it 'the most romantic city I ever saw'.

ABBAZIA DI SAN PIETRO IN VALLE✤✤

ⓘ Abbazia di San Pietro in Valle €
Open daily 1000–1200, 1400–1700 (see page 252 for contact information). If closed, stop at the friendly custodian's house on the left side of the road to the abbey.

It would be hard to exaggerate the beauty of this abbey, which is deeply secluded on a shelf of Monte Fionchi. It is the oldest monastery in Umbria and built, according to legend, on the site of the first Umbrian city. Its founder was the Lombard Duke of Spoleto, Faroaldo II. The Lombards invaded Italy in the wake of the Goths in the early 6th century AD and remained a powerful force in the region for several centuries. They arrived as Teutonic pagans but settled and adopted Christianity – inspired by the example of St Benedict, born a mere 24km from here in Nórcia, and his Benedictine order of monks. When his son, Trasamondo II, deposed him in AD 720, Faroaldo II joined the Benedictines and founded this monastery.

Much of the abbey complex, including the noble campanile, dates from the 12th century, but there are some earlier remains. The peaceful small cloister, to the right of the abbey church, fuses sculptural fragments from Faroaldo's original building. The apse of the

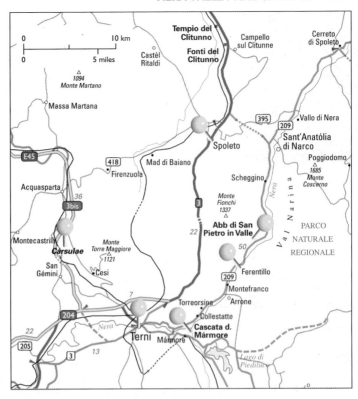

8th-century church still stands and the extraordinary altar, carved with totemic figures and crude foliage, is inscribed with the names 'Ursus', the sculptor, and 'Iderico', who became Duke of Spoleto in AD 739. Several very fine 3rd-century Roman sarcophagi are displayed here; one of them, carved with Bacchic scenes, was supposedly used as Faroaldo II's tomb. Frescos of the nave, dating from the 1190s, illustrate the Creation, and Adam and Eve in the Garden of Eden (left), the Nativity and the Crucifixion (right). Few frescos of this date survive in such good condition. Art historians regard them as the first examples of an emerging Italian – as distinct from Byzantine – artistic style. Across the valley is the ruined hulk of the *castello* of Umbriano.

CÁRSULAE❖

Founded around 220 BC, and built on either side of the *Via Flaminia*, *Cársulae* blossomed briefly but was hit by an earthquake towards the end of the 1st century AD. Never rebuilt, the masonry was stolen and weeds gradually hid the remains. The ancient town was rediscovered again in the 16th century and excavations have continued sporadically ever since.

Tacitus and Pliny visited *Cársulae* and described it as beautiful. The delicate pink colour of the stone remains hints at the lost splendour.

The only intact building is the 11th-century chapel of San Damiano, built of brick and stone taken from the Roman forum. Just in front of the church, the original *Via Flaminia* climbs up through the centre of the town, its stone-paved surface rutted with wheel grooves. Following the road northwards, you pass two ruined temples on the left. Their walls retain some original marble cladding. The forum comes next, then the law courts, followed by an expanse of unexcavated sheep pasture. To the right, in the distance, you can see the little village of Portaria clinging to a steep spur of the Naia valley. Finally you reach the northern gate of the town and the cemetery with two large intact funerary monuments, one a circular sepulchre.

On the left-hand side of the *Via Flaminia*, as you return, are the baths and cisterns. The amphitheatre, built into the sides of a large natural hollow, is the most complete structure on the site and stands side by side with the theatre. From here you can look back across a grassy plain littered with the fallen columns and marble fragments of this once impressive Roman town.

CASCATA DELLE MÁRMORE (THE MARMORE FALLS)**

Cascata delle Mármore € Tel: 0744 62982; fax: 0744 362231; www.marmore.it. The park is open daily Jun–Sept 1000–2200; mid-Mar–May Mon–Fri 1000–1900, Sat–Sun 1000–2200; Oct Mon–Fri 1000–1800, Sat (Sun until 1800). However, the waters are released according to a more complicated time schedule: Jul–Aug Mon–Fri 1200–1300, 1700–1800, 2100–2200; Sat 1100–1300, 1500–2200; Sun 1000–1300; 1500–2200. Off-peak it ranges from once to three times a day.

This stupendous waterfall – 162m in height – is actually man-made. The fall was engineered under the rule of the Roman consul Curius Denatatus in 271 BC. Surrounded by rivers, the plains around Terni were constantly subject to flooding, and always marshy. The Romans diverted the Velino river away from the plain in order to drain it and cut a channel to carry it northwards. The slight waterfall that already existed, where the Nera spills over the side of Monte Mármore, became a powerful cascade with the combined force of two rivers.

In 1938, the Velino was dammed at Lake Piediluco and the waters used to drive hydroelectric turbines. Consequently, the Marmore Falls flow at a trickle much of the time. At certain times, the sluice gates are opened and the pent-up torrent crashes thunderously down the rocks and creates a cloud of spray and multiple rainbows. If your first encounter with the falls whets your appetite to see them again, go at night when they are illuminated. You also have a choice of two viewpoints. The N209 out of Terni takes you to the base of the falls whereas the N79 takes you to the top.

FERENTILLO*

Museo delle Mummie € San Stefano crypt; tel 0743 54395. Open Apr–Sept 0900–1230, 1430–1930; shorter hours in winter.

Ferentillo lies at the foot of a wild and narrow valley. Its decaying walls climb both sides of the gorge, punctuated by ruined lookout towers. No army or lone traveller could pass this way without being funnelled through the village and challenged. It is not surprising that this region remained a last stronghold of the emperor, so well was the gorge defended.

The village has a truly bizarre museum, the **Museo delle Mummie***. On display are bodies thrown into the crypt of San Stefano that were unintentionally desiccated and preserved by the biting winds that cut through the valley in winter. The cast of characters includes two soldiers from Napoleon's army who were lynched; an unwed mother who died in childbirth on a roadside along with her child; a farmer and lawyer – they killed each other in a quarrel over land – and a Chinese couple that succumbed to cholera on their honeymoon in the 1880s.

The rugged Salto del Cieco valley, around Ferentillo, is home to peregrine and lanner falcons, porcupine, wild boar and lynxes.

Below
San Pietro in Valle

SPOLETO❖❖

ⓘ APT office *Piazza della Libertà 7; tel: 0743 49890; fax: 0743 46241; e-mail: info@iat.spoleto.pg.it; www.comune.spoleto.pg.it.*

🏛 Pinacoteca Comunale € *Palazzo Rosari Spada, Corso Mazzini; tel: 0743 45940. Open daily mid-Mar–mid-Oct 1030–1300, 1500–1830; mid-Oct–mid-Mar Wed–Mon 1030–1300, 1430–1700. In 2004–5, the collection will take its final place in two locations: works dating from the late 15th century will be relocated to the renovated Museo Nazionale del Ducato di Spoleto in the Rocca while 16th–19th-century works will share the Palazzo Collicola with the Galleria Civica d'Arte Moderna. The Palazzo Spada will house the Museo del Tessile e dei Costume Antichi ('textiles and ancient costumes').*

◍ Since the 1950s, Spoleto has become internationally famous for its Festival dei Due Mondi ('Two Worlds Festival'), founded by the Italian-American composer Giancarlo Menotti and held at the end of June and beginning of July.

Umbrian in the 7th–6th centuries BC, Spoleto became Roman in 241 BC. It played a major role in the Gothic wars and became the capital of the Lombard duchy of Spoleto in AD 570. The Umbrians, Romans and Lombards who built Spoleto appreciated its prime hill-top location and it showed its military value when the city successfully repulsed Hannibal in 217 BC, fresh from his victory at Lake Trasimeno. In the 9th century Spoleto was one of the most important cities in central Italy and at its apogee as an independent duchy ruled by the Lombards. Architecturally speaking, the Lombards picked up where the late Romans left off and its architectural development displays rare continuity from late antiquity to the beginning of the 13th century.

From the Piazza della Libertà, you can see a Roman theatre (*access through the Archaeological Museum*) to the south. From there the Corso Mazzini leads you past the newly renovated Palazzo Rosari Spada, temporary home to the city's **Pinacoteca❖** ('picture gallery'). Here, among many anonymous and unlabelled paintings, you will find two works by Lo Spagna: one showing the virtues (1512) and a *Madonna and Child* (1516). Few other works of this accomplished artist survive in Umbria even though he spent much of his life in the region. The Via dello Sdrucciolo links the Palazzo to the perfect medieval Piazza del Mercato, with a splendid 18th-century fountain by Roman architect Costantino Fiaschetti. Veer into the Via di Visiale and look out for the Palazzo Comunale in the Piazza del Municipio; its ancient vaults contain the remains of a 1st-century AD Roman house, once claimed to be the home of Vespasia Polla, the mother of the Emperor Vespasian.

The Piazza del Duomo (across the Via Fontesecca) is one of Umbria's most striking. To appreciate the full grace of the cathedral façade (1190), walk to the opposite end of the wide piazza and sit on the long stone bench at the foot of the wall. Of the exquisite rose windows, the central one is framed by two caryatids with symbols of the evangelists carved in the corners. Inside, the best things are the floors of inlaid marble and the frescos by Filippo Lippi (in the sanctuary), the last he ever did. He was at the height of his powers and filled them with lyrical and tender figures, painted in vibrant colours. His tomb is in the right-hand transept.

The monumental fortress, the **Rocca❖**, towers above the town. Much of it was built with stone looted from the Roman amphitheatre. It was converted into a luxurious palace for Lucrezia and Cesare Borgia. More recently, the Rocca served as a maximum-security prison, holding the Pope's would-be assassin and Red Brigades terrorists. It has been undergoing conversion to a museum for a number of years and is occasionally used for exhibitions. An even better reason for climbing to the top of town is the **Ponte delle Torri❖❖**, the extraordinary aqueduct built in 1345 that spans the gorge between Monte Sant'Elia, on which the Rocca is built, and Monteluco, opposite. Water no longer flows along it (though it can be turned on if necessary) and it is possible to walk across the massive structure, 230m long and 80m high, to the wooded slopes of Monteluco, enjoying the views up and down the Tessino gorge.

Below
Spoleto's Duomo

TERNI✣

ⓘ **APT office** *Viale C Battisti 5; tel: 0744 423047, fax: 0744 427259; e-mail: info@iat.terni.it; www.comune.terni.it & www.umbria2000.it.* Open Mon–Fri 0900–1300, also Tue, Thu 1500–1800.

🎨 **Pinacoteca Comunale** € *Via Teatro Romano 13; tel: 0744 434210.* Open Tue–Sun 1000–1300, 1600–1900.

Terni claims to be the burial place of St Valentine (the Basilica of San Valentino is in the suburb of San Valentino, 2km south of the city centre). The head of the mummified saint was stolen in 1986 but his body remains and the town honours him with a festival on St Valentine's Day, 14 February.

The Industrial Revolution in peninsular Italy began in Terni – the 'Italian Manchester'– in the late 19th century. Terni built Italy's first steelworks, tapped the fast-flowing Velino river to generate hydroelectric power and began producing plastics as early as the 1920s. Unsurprisingly, the city was hit by Allied air raids during the Second World War. It is still the centre of the Italian armaments industry: the rifle used to assassinate President Kennedy was manufactured here; and rumours linked Terni to pieces of a supercannon bound for Iraq that were impounded in England before the Gulf War.

The part of the city that escaped destruction is concentrated around the cathedral (*park in the Corso del Popolo*), including a stretch of Roman wall. Close by is the recently renovated Palazzo Gazzoli which now houses the **Pinacoteca***, dedicated to both ancient and contemporary art. The collection includes Benozzo Gozzoli's *Marriage of St Catherine*; works by Miró, Kandinsky, Chagall and Leger; and industrial landscapes by naïf artist and shoemaker, Orneore Metelli (1872–1938). The nearby church of San Salvatore, almost opposite the Palazzo Spada, is a circular sanctuary resembling a beehive from the inside. It might have been built as a temple to the sun, perhaps by the Umbrians as early as the 3rd century BC. The nave was added in the 12th century and the little Cappella Manessei in the 14th century.

Accommodation and food

If you want to stay in Spoleto during its famous summer event, the Festival of Two Worlds, book months, even a year, ahead. Hotel prices will be double.

Hotel Gattapone €€ *Via del Ponte 6, Spoleto; tel: 0743 223447; fax: 0743 223448; e-mail: hgattapone@libero.it.* Each of 15 comfortable rooms is decorated individually with antiques and Italian designer furniture. There are dramatic views of the Ponte delle Torri aqueduct and Tessino gorge. Reserve early.

Abbazia di San Pietro in Valle €€ *SS 209 Valnerina, Macenano, Ferentillo; tel: 0744 780129; fax 0744 435522; www.sanpietroinvalle.com.* This guesthouse has a dream setting in the green and mystic Nera valley, next to the secluded abbey of San Pietro.

Palazzo Dragoni €€ *Via del Duomo 13, Spoleto; tel: 0743 222220; fax: 0743 222225.* Its 15 bedrooms are divided between three floors in this *palazzo* filled with antiques, oriental carpets and Venetian glass chandeliers. Breakfast is served in a loggia with a view of the cathedral.

Above
Spoleto's Ponte delle Torri

Sportellino €€ *Via Cerquiglia 1, Spoleto; tel: 0743 45230. Closed Thu and in July.* Come here for great starters such as *gnocchi*, the chewy pasta called *stringozzi* and, in season – of course – truffle dishes. If you don't like truffles, try the savoury *coniglio alla cacciatora* or *cacciagione*, or *ossobuco con i piselli* ('oxtail with peas').

Pecchiarda € *Vicolo San Giovanni 1, Spoleto; tel: 0743 221009. Closed Thu except in summer.* Spoleto's best culinary bargain. The gnocchi filled with ricotta are perfect, and so is the house speciality, *pollo alla Pecchiarda*, a chicken de-boned and stuffed with ground meat and artichokes. The owner serves his own wine from the hills around Spoleto.

Albergo-Trattoria del Ponte €€ *Via del Borgo 15, Scheggino; tel: 0743 61253.* Foodies will love this hotel because its restaurant is one of the best in the region and specialises in truffle-enhanced cooking. Speciality of the house is local crayfish with truffles.

Caffè da Vincenzo € *Corso Mazzini 43, Spoleto; tel: 0743 49654. Closed Mon.* The number one address for the ritual consumption of Umbrian pastries and sweets, which are baked on the premises. It will also do for a light lunch, saving room for the homemade ice cream.

Suggested tour

Total distance: 87km; add 10km (return) for the detour by Lake Piediluco and another rugged 20km (return) to Monte Torre Maggiore.

Time: Two to three days.

Links: This route overlaps at *Cársulae* in the Middle Tiber and Nera Valley itinerary (*see page 274*). Spoleto is also the beginning of the Nera Valley and Monti Sibillini tour (*see page 264*).

Route: Drive north from **SPOLETO** ❶ and follow the signs for Nórcia. After passing through a long tunnel, turn right (south). The first town is **Scheggino** ❷, rising on a slant around its triangular castle. Parts of the 12th-century walls are still standing. The town withstood a brutal siege by Picozzo Brancaleoni in 1522; part of it is built over an enchanting spring (to the left of the Nera). It is the home of the Urbani family and headquarters of their truffle empire. By some estimates, they control the collection and processing of 80 per cent of the truffles consumed in Italy and 40 per cent of the world market.

There are two roads up to **SAN PIETRO IN VALLE** ❸. Avoid the first one (with the rusty yellow signpost) and take the second that begins the climb up to the serene abbey on a cypress-lined avenue. A clearing below the church serves as the monastery car park. Back on the N209,

Below
Romanesque friezes from the façade of San Pietro church showing (left) Jesus appearing to the Apostles by Lake Tiberias and (right) the Parable of the Sower

it is just a couple of short kilometres to **FERENTILLO** ❹, which straddles the road. The most interesting part of town (and the one with the mummies) is to the left (southeast).

Arrone ❺ is a couple of hundred metres off the N209. The town was founded by a family from Rome in the 9th century. The upper part of the village (called La Terra, 'The Land') is yet another fortified piece of the Valnerina's medieval war zone.

Detour: Take the road south from Arrone. It climbs then drops steeply and climbs again through endless olive groves on its way to **Lake Piediluco** ❻. As the road gets higher, fir trees take over and you enter a Parco Naturale Regionale, an area of protected highland that is still home to wild boar, not to mention a complex system of caves and potholes, mountain torrents, impenetrable forests of holm oak and flower-filled sheep pastures. After the Forca dell'Arrone pass, you have the first look at the lake. Steer northwest along the shore (on the N79). At a height of 365km, Lake Piediluco has a perimeter of about 17km and is the second largest lake in Umbria. It is irregular in shape with a depth of 19 metres. To rejoin the route, follow the signs for Cascata delle Mármore. The 'Belvedere Cascata' is in the village of Mármore. From here you can walk alongside the river channel and past the sluice that controls the water flow, down to the belvedere itself, a lookout point with a bird's-eye view of the falls.

Continue up the valley of Nera past the fortified town of Casteldilago and past the towns of Torreorsina and Collestatte (both were an ancient fief of the Orsini family), to the car park below the **CASCATA DELLE MÁRMORE** ❼. From there, several footpaths lead to the base of the falls. After the waterfall, drive on past Papigno, a medieval village with a moat that Lord Byron sketched while staying in the nearby Villa Graziani. The roofs are a strange shade of grey caused by an air-borne residue from a carbide and calcium cyanide factory that is, mercifully, no longer in use. After the junction for Papigno is the sprawling Galleto power plant.

Driving through **TERNI** ❽, or getting out of it, poses a challenge. You can cross the town by following signs for Perugia but, later, you will want to take the road for San Gemini/Campitello (also signposted for Cesi and *Cársulae*). It rises above Terni through acres of olive groves before cresting at **Cesi** ❾, a town squeezed on to a narrow ledge of Monte Torre Maggiore. Its medieval builders nicked some of their stone from Roman *Cársulae*.

Detour: Brave the road that leads right (west) up to **Monte Torre Maggiore** ❿ and prepare for a vertical challenge. The 12th-century church of Sant'Erasmo is 790m up the mountainside, near an astronomical observatory and the fortified remains of an ancient Umbrian town. An unpaved dead end leads to a point near the summit (1 121m).

The road to *CÁRSULAE* ⓫ is unmissable thanks to a series of chocolate-brown signs with fallen Roman columns on them. Another 14km down into the valley floor, a pass under the *autostrada* and you arrive in **Acquasparta** ⓬. The thermal springs here were already in use in Roman times. Its most beautiful building is the 17th-century

Palazzo Cesi where Galileo was a guest in 1624. From the entrance to town, turn right (east) under the *autostrada* and prepare for a series of curves that become tighter as the road heads up to **Firenzuola** (480m) where the Lago di Arezzo reservoir comes into view cradled by the surrounding hills. A few more kilometres and you pass the *castello* of Baiano. Peaceful, wooded hills gradually give way to a wide valley on the way to Spoleto.

Also worth exploring

Most visitors to Umbria will, sooner or later, end up driving on the N3 between Spoleto and Perugia. They should all take a break from endemic road rage to honour the mythic **Fonti del Clitunno**. The sacred spring waters burst from the rock into a willow-fringed pool. Sadly, the nymphs have long since been driven away and the river god Clitunnus no longer issues oracles. Its fascination has survived though it doesn't attract the same class of visitor as in the days of Virgil and Lord Byron. Just a few metres up the road, the **Tempio del Clitunno** is one of Umbria's earliest churches, a mini Parthenon built in the 4th or 5th century for an early Christian martyr beside the crystal waters. Frescos inside (Christ with SS Peter and Paul), now indistinct, date from the 7th or 8th century and are among the earliest to have survived in Italy.

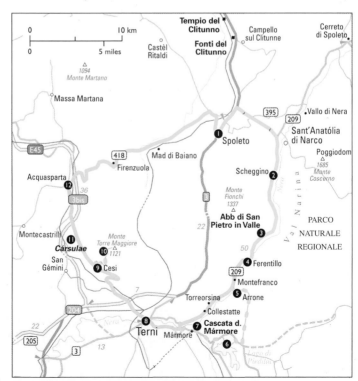

Nera Valley and Monti Sibillini

Ratings

Food	●●●●●
Mountains	●●●●●
Nature	●●●●●
Outdoor activities	●●●●●
Scenery	●●●●●
Walking	●●●●●
Wildlife	●●●●○
Architecture	●●●○○

This remote region offers some of the most scenic landscapes in central Italy. The national park of Monti Sibillini lies at the foot of the mountain range of the same name which rises above 2400m. The park has pockets of true wilderness, alternating with solitary monasteries, churches, towers and castles. Wild orchids cover the vast highland plain of the Piano Grande in the spring. Nórcia, the birthplace of St Benedict, lies at its edge. For all the saints that were born there, it was the sort of place you would go to talk to the Devil in the Middle Ages, a realm of necromancers, fairies and evil spirits. The local people had a reputation for the black arts – and a way with knives. They invented salami, sent a man to perform eye surgery on the Queen of England and castrated boys for the opera.

ABBAZIA DI SANT'EUTIZIO✧✧

Abbazia di Sant'Eutizio € *Open daily 0830–1145 and 1515–1800.*

The main attraction of this famous Benedictine abbey is its setting. It still seems as ideal for solitude and meditation as it must have been in the late 5th century when a Syrian monk laid the first stone. However, during much of the Middle Ages, the abbey was a point of power as well as light, ruling over the neighbouring region. Its wealth supported a major manuscript centre in the 10th–12th centuries (the library is now in the Vallicelliana in Rome). Its monks also played a role in medieval medicine, treating diseases with herbs from the Sibillini mountains.

The abbey has a façade with a rose window much like the one in Spoleto. It also has an 8th-century, sculpted fountain that belonged to an earlier church. The church's evocative interior has a single nave and a raised presbytery above a double-naved crypt. Frescos from the 15th and 17th centuries decorate the sepulchre of St Eutizio.

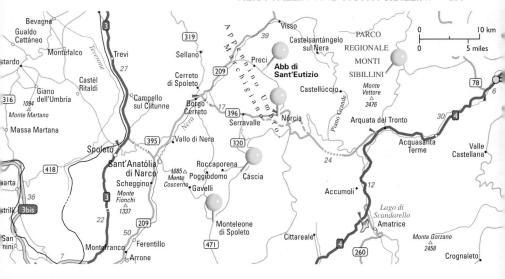

CÁSCIA*

APT office *Via G. Da Chiavano 2; tel: 074 371401; fax: 074 376630; e-mail: info@iat.cascia.pg.it. This is a tourist office for all of eastern Umbria with information about the Valnerina, Nórcia and Piano Grande.*

Phenomenally popular in Italy, St Rita is the patron saint of impossibilities. The town where she was born is now completely monopolised by mass religious tourism focused on the Mussolini-era Basilica di Santa Rita, where the saint's mummified body is on display in a glass coffin. The vast neo-Romanesque and neo-Byzantine structure looks vaguely like a power plant. Local souvenirs include St Rita walking sticks topped by a bicycle bell and hung with a flask of potent green liqueur. The pilgrims, mainly women, are not architecture critics but would-be mothers and grandmothers, the elderly and infirm, and generally, people with a problem and faith in Rita. The rest of Cáscia is interesting for its ensemble of medieval buildings and the Chiesa di San Francesco, adorned by wall frescos by Bartolomeo di Tommaso and paintings by Pomarancio and Cesarei.

MONTELEONE DI SPOLETO*

Biga Museum € *Open daily 1000–1300 and 1400–1900: ring at No 4 if it is closed.*

This prosperous high mountain village (978m) was the site of important Bronze and Iron Age settlements (with mines on Monte Birbone). Ancient stone fragments of its past are scattered across the green in front of the church of San Francesco. The church's Gothic portal is carved with lions, the symbol of the town, and the solitary figure of St Francis. The interior has pleasing 15th-century frescos.

A most extraordinary Etruscan chariot – the Biga – was found here in the 19th century. Made of hazelnut and covered in beaten bronze, it shows Thetis in the act of handing Achilles the armour that Hephaestus has made for him. The **Biga Museum*** must make do with a copy: the original is in New York's Metropolitan Museum.

NÓRCIA✣

Castellina € *Piazza San Benedetto; tel: 0743 817209. Open irregular hours.*

Salumeria Fratelli Ansuini *Via Anicia 105.* The brothers are passionate hunters and make excellent salami of *cinghiale.*

Boutique del Pecoraro *Piazza San Benedetto 7.* Specialists in *pecorino* (sheep's cheese).

Truffles from Nórcia are among the best in the world. The city holds a truffle festival in October.

St Benedict, the founder of Western monasticism, was born in Nórcia (*Nursia* in Roman times) in AD 480. Benedict wrote the book on monastic life exercising a practical and spiritual influence for some 1500-odd years. No wonder the Pope declared him 'patron saint of Europe' in 1964. Today, however, the little town of Nórcia is far more preoccupied with pork than asceticism.

The Piazza San Benedetto is ringed by *norcineria*, butchers' shops selling locally produced *prosciutto* and endless varieties of salami ranging from tiny sausages to great meat-stuffed balloons. The Norcians claim to have invented salami and it may be true since sausage-makers in Italy are often called *norcini*. In the Middle Ages, they branched into other uses of knives – such as eye surgery and the castration of pubescent boys to qualify them for an operatic career.

The centre of Nórcia has a certain rough charm. The best thing about the Basilica di San Benedetto is its elegant Gothic portal. The point of interest in the gloomy interior is the crypt, which was built against the foundations of the main temple of the Roman forum, supposedly on the spot where St Benedict was born. The altarpiece in the church (1621), painted by Filippo Napoletano, portrays St Benedict and Totila the Goth. They met in AD 542 towards the end of the lives of both men. Next to the church is the pinkish Palazzo Comunale, raised above a four-arched loggia. Opposite, the squat **Castellina✣**, built in 1554 as a papal stronghold, contains a small but intriguing museum with some rare 13th-century wooden figures of saints.

The Edicola (also known as the Tempietto, or 'little temple') is on the corner of Via Umberto in the north of the town. This low tower, built in the mid 14th century, is covered in inscriptions and tiny, detailed bas-reliefs of Masonic tools, the sun, Christ the Lamb, the instruments of the Passion, as well as very complex geometrical patterns and animal heads. No one quite knows what purpose this building served, but it may have been associated with a trade guild.

Parco Regionale Monti Sibillini✛✛

ⓘ Casa del Parco *Via Solferino 22, Nórcia; tel and fax: 0743 817090; e-mail: cdpnorcia@tin.it; www.parks.it. Open daily Jul–Aug and weekends all year 0930–1230, 1530–1830.*

Opposite
The Monti Sibillini range, above Nórcia

Below
Statue of St Benedict in Nórcia's Piazza San Benedetto

Located between Umbria and Le Marche, the park is a realm of woods, meadows, high altitude lakes, perennial springs and glacial cirques. It is home to eagles and wolves, the rare marten and an almost extinct species of otter. There are a few ski lifts sharing the park with scattered traditional farms. The Sibillini mountains form the watershed between the Adriatic and Tyrrhenian seas. Among the ten peaks that are above 2000m one can distinguish Monte Vettore (2476m), Monte Sibilla (2175m), Monte Redentore (2448m), Monte Priora (2332m) and Monte Argentella (2201m). Eighteen hundred types of flowers bloom in the park such as edelweiss, Alpine anemone, *Silene acaulis* and countless orchards.

Accommodation and food

Nórcia is an excellent base from which to explore the surrounding region. Castellúccio, however, is best for hikers.

Hotel Grotta Azzurra €€ *Via Alfieri 12, Nórcia; tel: 0743 816513; fax: 0743 828076.* Just off the central square, this is a bustling place run by a friendly and attentive family. An open fireplace and rusty suit of armour decorate the dining-room of its excellent restaurant, the Granaro del Monte – formerly the city's granary.

Sibilla € *Via della Fontana 69, Castellúccio; tel: 0743 870113.* A simple *pensione* with a restaurant specialising in dishes made from the sweet, locally grown lentils. Ask for a room with a view of the Piano Grande.

Taverna Castellúccio € *Via dietro la Torre 8, Castellúccio; tel: 0743 821100. Closed Wed except in summer.* A brother-sister team run this very rustic and *simpatica trattoria.* The best starters are homemade pasta such as *stringozzi* followed by anything with lentils.

Bruscacamelle € *Via della Stazione 2/c, Sant'Anatólia di Narco; tel: 0743 613144. Closed Tue except in Nov and summer.* A simple country *trattoria* serving homemade *pasta ravioli di ricotta, trote arrosto* ('grilled trout') and *agnello allo spiedo* ('lamb on skewers').

Above
Nórcia is renowned for mountain hams and wild-boar salami

Suggested tour

Total distance: 113km; detours add 60km (return to Castellúccio) and 11km (return to Roccaporena).

Time: The route involves strenuous mountain driving. Unless you are in a hurry, allow for two to three days.

Links: As in the previous chapter, this route begins and ends in Spoleto.

Route: Begin as in the previous chapter (*see page 254*), driving north on the N3 from **Spoleto** ❶. Follow the signs for Nórcia. After you pass through the tunnel, turn left (north) on the N209. You soon pass the **Vallo di Nera** ❷ on the right. If it looks like a *castello* it is because it was one. You can still recognise some of the original fortified structure incorporated into village houses. The interior of the church of Santa Maria delle Grazie is covered in frescos with works by Lo Spagna in the apse; ask for the key at No 4 if it is closed. Thermal springs and a 19th-century bathhouse are the roadside attractions at **Borgo Cerreto** ❸.

Getting out of the car: A mountain railway once linked Spoleto to Nórcia. Sadly, it was dismantled, beginning in 1968, but a few bits remain. From the centre of Borgo Cerreto, you can walk down a stretch of the track along the Nera river in the shade of alders and elms as far as a mineral water factory and, after crossing a bridge, the hamlet of Piedipaterno.

Further upstream, Triponzo (from *tre ponti* – 'three bridges') is where the Corno river meets the Nera. You have the option of heading straight for Nórcia from here (and passing a string of ruined castles –

Nortosce, Argentigli and Biselli) but this route carries on further north to the town of **Preci** ❹, which dominates the Castoriana valley at the junction of the Nórcia and Visso roads. In the Middle Ages, there was a school of surgeons in Preci with a hospital and medical library. Here, the skills acquired over the centuries in butchering pigs were refined and local surgeons performed eye operations and extracted gallstones. It still has a 13th-century castle. Carry on and watch for a yellow sign saying **ABBAZIA DI SANT'EUTIZIO** ❺ and turn left uphill a few hundred metres to reach the abbey.

Once you are back on the main road, drive through the hamlet of Piedivalle; Castoriana valley is a road where you will want to potter, downshift and daydream. The woods and pastures eventually give way to Forca d'Ancarano pass (1 008m). After cresting it, you have a first view of **NÓRCIA** ❻. The fertile plains south of Nórcia are spread out to the right, irrigated by warm water springs that enable crops to be grown despite the cold. Next, down on the left, Nórcia itself is revealed far away below, nestling into the side of a natural amphitheatre at the foot of the Sibillini mountain range. There is free parking outside the walls at the Porta Palatina.

Detour: Due south of Nórcia, a dead straight road passes through the town's industrial zone and leads to the hamlet of Sant Scolastica, named after the twin sister of St Benedict, about whom we know nothing. Take the left turn in the hamlet, signposted to Castellúccio. This is a wide and relatively straight road that climbs rapidly to a height of over 1 500m. Where the road divides at the summit of the pass, take another left turn. After a long haul of mountaineering with your car, you pass over the rim of Monte Ventosola and see the vast **Piano Grande** ❼ spread out before you. The landscape has changed completely: there are no more trees and nothing but bare, round hills and rocks. The empty plain, 8km in length, is as flat as a football pitch, and virtually empty except for the odd haystack and field hut. Much of Zefferelli's film about the life of St Francis, *Brother Sun, Sister Moon,* was shot here. The lone hilltop hamlet just visible in the distance, **Castellúccio** ❽, is a scruffy working village that has few facilities for visiting tourists, hikers and skiers. It still lives by agriculture – Castelluccians crop hay from the plain to feed their cows and grow tiny sweet lentils for which the area is famous all over Italy.

Getting out of the car: Castellúccio is a perfect base for walking, surrounded as it is by a landscape of great natural beauty. Immediately to the east, Monte Vettore rises (2 476m), once believed to be the home of the prophetic Sibyl. The climb is not especially difficult in good weather if you are fit and well equipped, and will reward anyone interested in alpine flora. The trails are not always clearly marked so it is important to have a good map. However, in clear weather, the visibility is almost perfect since it is all grassland.

Take the road that follows the pretty River Sordo to the junction of N320 and N396 at Serravalle.

Detour: Roccaporena ❾ is a pretty hamlet in a magnificent setting beneath limestone crags with extensive views. St Rita was born here and married (much to her disgust) in the 13th-century church of San Montano.

Getting out of the car: Nearby **Capanne di Collegiacone** is a good place to set out for mountain walks, following the footpaths through the pastures surrounding the village. More ambitious is the climb from Roccaporena to the narrow summit that overlooks it – named the Scoglio di Santa Rita.

There is never a lack of parking in **CÁSCIA** ❿. The town has huge car parks to accommodate the flow of visitors to the Sanctuary of the Saint of the Impossible. Beyond Cáscia, the valley of the Corno river unfolds many kilometres of rocky and wooded scenery with the peak of Monte Coscerno on one side and Monte Birbone on the other. It is a majestic, rugged contrast to the civilised rural scenery in other parts of Umbria. **MONTELEONE DI SPOLETO** ⓫ is an isolated mountain village in a broad valley surrounded by pastures. The road is particularly idyllic for the next few kilometres and you might well have to brake for flocks of sheep and shaggy mountain dogs. Occasionally, too, you may see small herds of Umbria's famed white cattle, still bred here as draught animals since the hillside fields are often too steep for tractors.

This spectacular mountain road descends steeply, twisting through stands of black pines and beech trees and swinging around dizzying bends. Rising out of the rock on the right (north), are the sheer flanks of Monte Coscerno and, opposite, the limestone mass of Monte di Civitella. **Gavelli** ⓬ is the second highest village in Umbria (after Castellúccio) at 1153m. The church of San Michele is the heart of the village; the frescos in the apse were painted by Lo Spagna in 1518 (*if it is locked, the guardian in the house across from it has the key; donations are always appreciated*). As you leave the village, there is an ideal picnic spot – a meadow with a small lake fed by natural springs.

The only other village on the way down is Caso, equally spectacular for its location. After countless bends in the road, you will be on level ground again in the Valnerina. Somnolent **Sant'Anatólia di Narco** ⓭ is not a bad place to chill out after hours behind the wheel. Nothing ever happens here but it has a good *trattoria* and a good story, too. It has been continuously inhabited since the 8th century BC, making it one of the oldest villages in Umbria. In 1883, the necropolis of Naharci was discovered and the findings packed off to the archaeological museum of Florence. Alternatively, return through the tunnel to Spoleto.

Also worth exploring

During the Middle Ages, **Cerreto di Spoleto** and its castle guarded the Vigi valley on one side and the Nera on the other. Behind the town is an arduous, scenic road that eventually arrives in Spoleto. The town has lots of elegant old *palazzi* to prove its former importance – one of them belonged to Umbria's famous medieval humanist, Giovanni Pontano. Cerreto fought with single-minded determination to avoid being swallowed by more powerful neighbours. Spoleto even kidnapped some of its families and forced them to live in a street that is still named Via dei Cerretani.

When troops from Nórcia sacked it in the 15th century, the displaced Cerretani set off around Italy and Europe, selling herbs, spices and medicinal compounds. The exaggerated claims that they made for their products ensured that their name – corrupted to *ciarlatani* – became 'charlatan' in English.

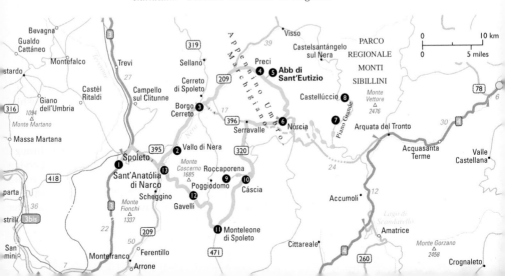

Middle Tiber and Nera Valley

Ratings

Architecture	●●●●○
Art	●●●●○
History	●●●●○
Scenery	●●●●○
Children	●●●○○
Museums	●●●○○
Nature	●●●○○
Shopping	●○○○○

Curving around the base of Todi, an ancient Umbrian border town, the Tiber river flows towards Orvieto acquiring the nickname 'dead' in places and 'furious' in others before it enters Lago di Corbara. Swinging south, it dies again in the wide Alviano marsh before reviving and continuing towards Rome. The Nera river flows into it a few kilometres west of Narni. Even by Umbrian standards, this is varied landscape: sheer gorges interrupt gentle hills and misty hilltops drop into flat valleys. History, nature and industry all claim different pieces of it. The spectrum of architecture is broad – giant polygonal stones laid by mysterious Umbrians in Amélia, feats of Roman engineering along the ancient *Via Flaminia* from Narni to *Cársulae*, and an exquisite Lombard church that graces the hill-town of Lugnano in Teverina.

AMÉLIA*

ⓘ APT office *Via Orvieto 1; tel: 0744 981453, fax: 0744 981566; e-mail: info@iat.amelia.tr.it.*

The Roman historian Pliny made a point of claiming, improbably, that Amélia was founded in 1134 BC. The town's massive walls seem to belong to a world of myth rather than history. At the base, they are composed of oversize polygonal blocks, 2m or more across, interlocked with such skill that you can't slip a sheet of paper between them. They have survived Totila the Goth and countless earthquakes. Tiny gateways piercing the walls lead to a maze of steep cobbled streets and stone staircases.

The fire and earthquake-damaged churches do not, at first, look appealing, but the church of Santi Filippo e Giacomo, in Piazza Augusto Vera, has an elegant 15th-century cloister and a series of tombs (belonging to the local Geraldini family), dating to the same century, carved with bas-reliefs by Agostino di Duccio. The ugliness of the cathedral is mitigated by another tomb to Bishop Geraldini, also by Duccio, carved with a delicate Virgin and Child. The Turkish flags in the right-hand chapel were taken at the battle of Lepanto.

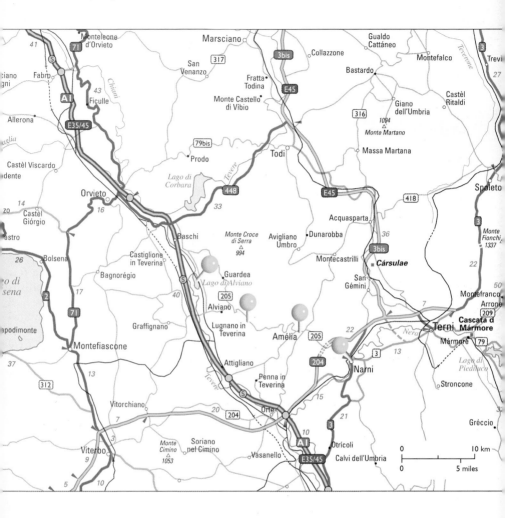

Lago di Alviano❖

<table>
<tr><td>

🛈 **Lago di Alviano**
Reserve information office, Madonna del Porto, Guardea; tel: 0744 903715; www.comunedialviano.it. Open Sep–Apr Sat–Sun until sunset, Tue–Sun rest of year.

</td><td>

This is one of the most beautiful nature reserves in Umbria, although in summer the birds are conspicuous by their absence. Winter is really the time to appreciate its importance to migratory birds. The northern end has the best viewpoints.

</td></tr>
</table>

LUGNANO IN TEVERINA*

Come for the views: to the west are Monte Cimino (1053m) in the province of Lazio and Monte Amiato (1738m) in Tuscany. Looking east, you can see the castle of Alviano.

Opposite
View over the Tiber Valley

On a clear day, you can see much of central Italy from here, on top of one of the highest hills in the region. From this distance the Tiber valley looks idyllic as its railway and *autostrada* drift in and out of the haze. The hilltop location saved the town from the bloodthirsty Goths and the dreaded Saracens but not from Cesare Borgia, who sacked it in 1503.

At its core stands one of Umbria's finest Romanesque churches, **Santa Maria Assunta**** (Our Lady of the Assumption). Its 13th-century loggia displays a wealth of mysterious sculpture carved along the capitals and eaves: symbols of the evangelists, beasts, birds and human heads. The bearded, three-faced figure – one face-on and two in profile – carved on the left-hand wall represents the Trinity. The interior has a nearly complete set of 12th-century furnishings. The inlaid marble floor represents the three theological virtues: white for Faith, green for Hope and red for Charity. The column capitals are wonderfully carved – look for the man with a serpent dangling from his lips. Reliefs in the choir show Archangel Michael and the usual Dragon as well as two men who seem to be kissing. In an atmospheric crypt, among the slender columns and walls built of chunky travertine blocks, is an early 14th-century Crucifixion fresco and a triptych by Nicolò Alunno, representing the Assumption of the Virgin.

NARNI*

ℹ Pro Loco *Piazza dei Priori 3; tel: 0744 715362.*

☾ In May, on the feast of St Juvenalis, the town celebrates the *Festa dell'Anello*, the 'Festival of the Ring'. Horsemen in knightly costume thrust lances through metal hoops, recalling the bravery of Narni's soldiers, notably the mercenary Erasmo di Narni (nicknamed *Gattamelata* – the 'honey cat'), whose equestrian statue by Donatello can be seen in Padua.

Perhaps no Umbrian town has a more medieval atmosphere than Narni with so few tourists to appreciate it. Narni likes to call itself the 'centre of Italy' and it is, geographically. The southernmost of the Umbrian hill-towns, Narni stands high above the Nera river at a place where it has cut a gorge. Its cathedral stands broadside on to the wide Piazza Garibaldi and is dedicated to the town's first bishop and patron saint, Juvenalis. A 15th-century Renaissance portico fronts the church, but inside, most of it is Romanesque.

Narni's ancient heart, the Piazza dei Priori, lies to the left of the cathedral as you emerge. It is just wide enough to be a piazza. The 20-sided fountain (recently restored) in the centre bears a vague resemblance to Perugia's famous Fontana Maggiore. The Palazzo dei Podestà is clearly made up of three separate structures, including the stump of a 13th-century defensive tower. However, the six 15th-century mullioned windows give it a semblance of unity.

The narrow Via del Monte leads off the Piazza Garibaldi and climbs up through the medieval quarter. The **Rocca Albornoz*** stands at the top of the hill – a papal castle built in the 1370s with astonishing views north and south. The adjacent park is a good spot for a picnic.

Accommodation and food

Fattoria Titignano € *Titignano, off the N79 between Orvieto and Todi; tel: 0763 308000; fax: 0763 308002; restaurant tel: 0763 308022; e-mail: info@titignano.it; www.titignano.it.* Off-the-beaten-track *agriturismo*, with guest rooms for a two-night minimum stay. Stunning location in a natural park between Orvieto and Todi and overlooking Lake Corbara.

Bramante €€ *Via Orvietana 48, Todi; tel: 075 8948381; fax: 075 8948074; www.hotelbramante.it.* A former convent with its own park and garden, swimming pool, and panoramic views from the terrace.

Hotel dei Priori €€ *Vicolo del Comune 4, Narni; tel: 0744 726843; fax: 0744 726644; restaurant tel: 0744 722744.* Intimate medieval *palazzo* with stylish rooms on a quiet lane. Its **La Loggia** (€€) is the old town's best restaurant (*closed Mon and last two weeks of Jul*).

Pomurlo Vecchio € *Located in Baschi, off the N448 between Orvieto and Todi (follow sign for Pomurlo); tel: 0744 950190 or 950475; fax: 0744 950500. Agriturismo* in a rambling fortress/inn complex surrounded by a hilltop farm that supplies the *trattoria*. There are rooms for overnight guests, including a couple with views of Lake Corbara.

La Pasticceria Evangelisti € *Piazza Garibaldi 25, Narni.* Near the Duomo di San Giovenale. Umbrian-style pastries and sweets of every description. Get in line with half of Narni.

Suggested tour

Total distance: 134km; detour add 2km (return).

Time: One day.

Links: Todi is the destination of the route on page 244. It intersects with the Nera Valley and Spoleto route at *Cársulae* (*see page 256*).

Route: Leaving **Orvieto ❶**, take the N79 bis (follow the signs for Arezzo, do not take the N448). The old road to Todi is one of the most scenic in Umbria. In places, you could be in Ireland thanks to the many overgrown hedges along the road. But olive groves and vineyards will remind you that this is Italy. It climbs through a varied landscape of isolated farms, forest and bare hills, cut by deep ravines. There are ever-changing vistas and most of the journey you will be alone with nature. When you stop to take in the views the only sound you will hear is the hum of insects among the herbs and wildflowers. At **Prodo ❷** a castle looms out of nowhere and a jerky uphill turn reveals a wide stretch of Lake Corbara. The last view, as you approach the end of the journey, is the best. The steep tower of San Francesco rises up in the distance from **TODI ❸** in a landscape that would have

Opposite
Umbrian farmstead

looked almost the same to a medieval traveller. In Todi, the easiest thing to do with the car is to leave it near the church Santa Maria della Consolazione and walk up into town. After retrieving it, drive south and get on the N3 bis Autostrada then exit at San Gémini.

Detour: The abandoned Roman town *Cársulae* ❹, on the *Via Flaminia (see page 247)*, is just one kilometre east of the *autostrada*.

San Gémini ❺ is part modern spa, part fortified medieval village. You can, for example, play mini-golf. Its throbbing little heart is the Piazza Palazzo Vecchio where a medieval tower was recycled as an 18th-century campanile for the Palazzo Pubblico (town hall). The Chiesa di San Francesco, at the opposite end of town, has the oldest pair of wooden doors in Umbria.

Continue south through hilly vineyards to the valley of the Nera river and turn right. The first thing you see in **NARNI** ❻ is a chemical plant – but it gets better. Cross the bridge over the deep gorge of the river. Watch for the first left (just before a Co-op supermarket). Keep to the left down a dirt road that leads you directly under the only surviving arch (90m) of the astonishing **Ponte di Augusto.** The bridge was built in 27 BC. It was once 160m long and formed part of the ancient *Via Flaminia.* Even in ruins, it makes the adjacent modern bridge look like a school project. Return to the road and veer up its curves to Narni.

Slow down as you enter the impressive portal of Porta Ternana. For the adventurous driver, there is a road that threads all the way up to the **Rocca dell'Albornoz** with voyeurist peeks into the living-rooms and dining-rooms of Narni and alarming views down into the abyss where the Nera flows. The Rocca itself is a lovers' lane; don't be surprised if couples sitting in their cars occasionally disappear from view.

Upon leaving Narni, retrace the curves back down to the N3, and take the N205 (Amélia is signposted) up a road that unleashes glimpses of the Nera valley and surrounding hills at every other bend. It surmounts a series of ridges to reach **AMÉLIA** ❼, where there is free parking outside the Etruscan walls. Drive around the city and north over a narrow bridge above a nameless gorge through which flows a tributary of the Tiber. From here on, the road bores through an oak forest so dense you will see little else until **LUGNANO IN TEVERINA** ❽ comes into sight.

The drive up to the central piazza is steep. From there the church of **Santa Maria Assunta** is just a few metres further on. Get back on the road. Cruise towards another hill-town on the horizon, **Alviano** ❾, with yet another wide vista and a view of the Tiber valley from a slightly lower elevation. The road drops down abruptly into the Tiber valley and follows the railway track along the humid **LAGO DI ALVIANO/OASIS DI ALVIANO** ❿.

Carry on along the overgrown bank of the swampy Tiber until the road mounts higher and **Baschi** ⓫ comes into sight perched above the Tiber valley. Erosion is a severe threat to this peaceful town graced by an 11th-century church of San Nicolò with a glowing buff-coloured baroque façade. Turn left on the N448, which crosses the Tiber going west and return to Orvieto (*see page 276*).

Also worth exploring

Petrified tree trunks similar to sequoias were discovered in 1987 near the village of **Dunarobba**. The forest grew over a million years ago on the banks of the ancient lake *Tiberino*, which occupied the whole of the valley between Spoleto, Perugia and Todi. A mudslide caused by an earthquake submerged 40 trees with a girth of 3–4m. Group visits are possible. (*For information, contact the Centro di Paleontologia Vegetale Foresta Fossile in Avigliano Umbro, tel: 0744 940348; www.forestafossile.it. Open Apr–Oct Mon–Fri 0930–1130, 1530–1730; also Sat pm Jul–Sept. Call ahead to confirm.*)

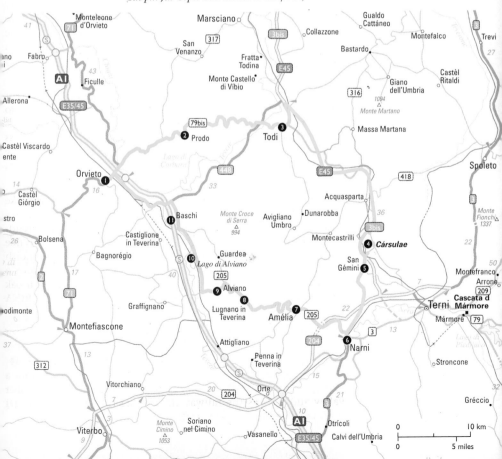

Orvieto

Ratings

Architecture	●●●●●
Art	●●●●●
History	●●●●●
Scenery	●●●●●
Children	●●●●○
Vineyards	●●●●○
Nature	●●○○○
Shopping	●○○○○

A medieval Pope predicted that Orvieto would float up to heaven on Judgement Day. It seems to already be on its way – thrust up into the Umbrian sky by a plateau of extinct volcanoes. Vineyards grow at the foot of its sheer cliffs in eroded volcanic soil that gives its famous white wine a distinct crispness. Of all the Etruscan cities that belonged to the League of 12 cities, Orvieto is the biggest puzzle. Despite overwhelming archaeological evidence of its importance, scholars still don't agree on its Etruscan name or history. The maze of tunnels beneath the city only adds to the mystery. Orvieto's cathedral is a stunning example of its unique cultural heritage. Related in style to the cathedral of Siena, it nevertheless surpasses it. Art historian Jacob Burchhardt called it 'the greatest and richest polychrome monument in the world'.

Sights

ⓘ APT office *Piazza Duomo 24; tel: 0763 341772, fax: 0763 344433; e-mail: info@iat.orvieto.tr.it; www.comune.orvieto.tr.it.* The Tourist Office sells a *Carta Orvieto Unica*, a city card that covers admission to several museums and monuments, use of the town's electric mini-buses and parking for five hours in the funicular car park.

Right
Orvieto's cathedral

Duomo✦✦✦
Orvieto's cathedral is, without a doubt, the finest of its period in Italy. From the foundations to the gables, white travertine and dove-grey tufa alternate in horizontal bands. Such refinement is not Umbrian in character. For parallels you have to look west, to Siena in Tuscany. The sumptuous mosaic of the façade is a rarity among

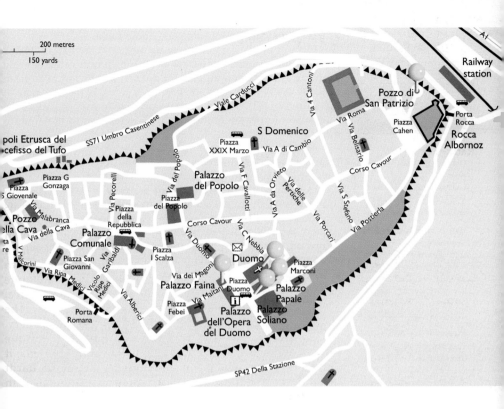

Duomo *Piazza Duomo; tel: 0763 341167. Open Nov–Feb 0730–1245, 1430–1715; Mar, Oct 0730–1245, 1430–1815; Apr–Sept 0730–1245, 1430–1915.*

Cappella di San Brizio €
Tel: 0763 342477. Open Mon–Sat Jan–Feb, Nov–Dec 1000–1245, 1430–1715; Mar, Oct 1000–1245, 1430–1815; Apr–Sept 1000–1245, 1430–1915; Sun Oct–Jun 1430–1745 and Jul–Sept 1430–1845. Only 25 people in the chapel at a time. Tickets can be purchased from the Tourist Office.

Italian churches. By contrast, the interior is calm and uncluttered, illuminated by alabaster-paned windows. Pews, monuments and baroque edifices have been swept away, leaving us with an uninterrupted view across the sun-dappled floor of ox-blood coloured marble. The sublime nave, Romanesque in conception and Gothic in details such as pointed arch windows, is remarkably unified.

There is scarcely anything else in art like the world-famous frescos (1499–1504) by Signorelli in the **Cappella di San Brizio*****, restored in 1996 to their glory after seven painstaking years. They depict the Apocalypse, the torments of hell and the Resurrection. Charon ferries the dead across the infernal waters of the Styx while metal-winged monsters and green-faced demons rush the legions of the damned into the underworld. The scene brilliantly expresses a sense of the world ending in chaos with twisted bodies flying everywhere as if, suddenly, there were no force of gravity. Skeletons then drag themselves out of the ground, acquire flesh and once again become youthful, innocent-looking men and women. Michelangelo was deeply influenced by Signorelli in his painting of the ceiling of the Sistine Chapel.

Musei Archeologici Claudio Faina €€
Piazza Duomo 29, tel: 0763 341511; fax: 0763 341250. Open Apr–Sept daily 0930–1800; Oct–Mar Mon–Sat 1000–1700.

Palazzo Papale (Museo Archeologico Nazionale) € *Piazza Duomo; tel: 0763 341039; www. archeopg.arti.beniculturali.it. Open 0830–1930 (Jun–mid-Sept Sat until 2300).*

Palazzo Soliano/Museo Greco/Museo dell'Opera del Duomo *€ Piazza Duomo; tel: 0763 344605; fax: 0763 344664; www.sistemamuseo.it. Open 1030–1300, 1400–1730 (Apr–Sept until 1800).*

Pozzo di San Patrizio € *Viale Sangallo; tel: 0763 343768, fax: 0763 344664; www.sistemamuseo.it. Open daily Apr–Sept 0930–1845; Oct–Mar 1000–1745*

Palazzo Faina (Musei Archeologici Claudio Faina)*

This is one of the most important archaeological collections in Umbria and stunning testimony to what a well-heeled private collector could get his or her hands on in the 19th century. In addition to Etruscan sculpture and pottery, there are three vases (found in the necropolis of the Crocefisso del Tufo) by Exekias, the most important Greek Attic vase painter in the 6th century BC. They were imported by Etruscans from Greece.

Palazzo Papale (Museo Archeologico Nazionale)*

Built for a bishop in the 12th century, the palace was redecorated a hundred years later by two different popes. It is easy to overlook, squeezed between the cathedral and the Palazzo Soliana. The palace contains the Museo Archeologico Nazionale. Its pride and joy is a badly damaged but fascinating tomb painting (ask to have the lights turned on) that depicts banqueting in the afterlife. There also are many other objects found in the Etruscan tombs of the burial ground at Settecamini, from a complete set of armour to polished mirrors.

Palazzo Soliano*

This palace of tufa stone was built for Pope Boniface VIII in 1297 and contains two museums. The ground-floor **Museo Greco** is filled with works by the sculptor Emilio Greco (1915–95), the artist responsible for the modern bronze doors of the Duomo. His athletic nude beauties take full control of the space, thrusting bronze legs and perky breasts in all directions. Upstairs, the **Museo dell'Opera del Duomo** has a self-portrait by Luca Signorelli and a collection of sculpture that includes work by Andrea Pisano and the early baroque genius Francesco Mochi (*closed at time of writing for restoration*).

Pozzo di San Patrizio*

Alongside the public gardens that surround the remains of the 14th-century Fortezza and the ruins of an Etruscan temple, is a highly unusual artesian well. The 63m well was dug in 1527 on the orders of Pope Clement VII, preparing for a siege that never came. It took ten years to sink.

An ingenious double helix staircase, lit by openings in the well shaft, was constructed to allow packhorses to descend to collect water and ascend via a separate set of steps, thus avoiding collisions. The design might have been influenced by Leonardo da Vinci who designed a similar staircase for a brothel and, later, for Château Chambord in France.

Half way down the shaft, you will pass an Etruscan tomb that was discovered during the excavation. The descent into the dark and chilly depths is steep, and the ascent even more so, but it is well worth it for the ever-changing vistas through the shaft openings and the strange subterranean lighting effects.

Accommodation and food

Orvieto wines: secco and Abbocato

Winemaking in Orvieto dates back to the Etruscans. Today, it produces one of the best-known Italian white wines. The *secco* ('dry') wines represent the lion's share of its production. But one of Orvieto's best wines is its opposite: Orvieto *Abbocato* is a traditionally made, naturally sweet wine. Pope Gregory XVI commanded in his will that his body be washed in it.

Hotel Maitani €€€ *Via Lorenzo Maitani 5; tel: 0763 342011; fax: 0763 342012*. The hotel terrace has a panoramic view of the Orvieto cathedral. Fortunately, it has parking, too.

Hotel Palazzo Piccolomini €€ *Piazza Ranieri 36; tel: 0763 341743; fax: 0763 391046; www.hotelpiccolomini.it*. A former nobleman's palace near the historic heart of the city. The easiest way to reach it is to drive through the Porta Maggiore.

La Badia €€€ *La Badia 8, 5km south of Orvieto; tel: 0763 301876; fax: 0763 305396; e-mail: labadia.hotel@tiscalinet.it. Closed Jan–Feb*. This medieval abbey, partly in ruins, was founded by Benedictine monks. The 13th-century church has noted frescos, cloisters, a refectory and a 12-sided bell tower. The abbey was already in use as a holiday resort by 15th-century cardinals. Today, Count Diumi di Sterpeto has converted the former abbot's palace to a many-starred hotel.

La Vulpe e L'Uva € *Via Ripa Corsica 1; tel: 0763 341612. Closed Mon and Jan; also Tue during Oct–Mar*. Probably the best traditional *trattoria* in town. Mostly locals eat here. Homemade pasta filled with duck is a speciality.

I Sette Consoli €€ *Piazza Sant'Angelo 1a; tel: 0763 343911. Closed Wed*. This tiny restaurant does daring things with Umbrian standards. It has a most rewarding *menu degustazione* (tasting menu) – five courses, with three kinds of wine. The à la carte menu includes (in season) artichoke casserole, stuffed pumpkin flowers, terrine of pheasant and truffles, and stuffed gooseneck.

Bar-Pasticceria Gastronomia Montanucci Nazzareno € *Corso Cavour 21–23; tel: 0763 341261*. The oldest café in the city and the perfect place for some homemade *baci* – chocolate 'kisses'. You are not supposed to lunch on kisses, so have a *panino* ('sandwich') first.

Suggested tour

Visitors are encouraged to park in Orvieto Scalo, the modern lower town. From there a funicular railway whisks you up to the Piazza Cahen, the western end of the city and the beginning of this route. There is another car park below the walls on the west side at Campo della Fiera (equipped with an elevator and wheelchair access). In the city itself, a large, free car park is just off Via Roma (a sharp right on entering Piazza Cahen).

Total distance: 2km.

Time: If you don't visit more than one museum, it is possible to do this route in a day trip and perhaps squeeze in a visit to the Orvieto Underground and still see the sun set over the Etruscan city of the dead, **Crocefisso del Tufo**. By then, you will wish for a second day.

Links: Orvieto is an exit on the *autostrada* to Rome and easy to reach from Tuscany. The Crete and Val d'Órcia route passes within a few kilometres (*see page 105*).

Route: Take the 19th-century funicular up to the square of **Piazza Cahen ❶** and enjoy the view of Paglia valley on the way. On the right, as you exit, is the medieval **POZZO DI SAN PATRIZIO ❷**, the extraordinary Renaissance well that was never put to use. Next to it is the stone foundation of an Etruscan temple, built almost 2000 years earlier, at the end of the 5th century BC. The **Rocca Albornoz ❸** is to the left – a fortress erected in 1364 to show that the Pope was boss in political as well spiritual matters but demolished a generation later in disgust by the people of Orvieto. Today, it makes a spectacular public garden. Looking further left (north) you also see the much older medieval gate of Postierla. Cross the Piazza and stroll down Corso Cavour. Make a left at Via Duomo, which narrows and curves past shops selling ceramics into Piazza Duomo. The stone benches on the wall opposite the cathedral are an ideal place to rest while contemplating one of the glories of Umbria, Orvieto's **DUOMO ❹**. It is bounded by the **PALAZZO FAINA ❺** to the west, the **PALAZZO PAPALE ❻** to the east and the **PALAZZO SOLIANO ❼** to the south.

Detour: Beneath Orvieto is an underground labyrinth, created over 3000 years of history as inhabitants dug an infinite number of caves in the plateau of tufa stone that the city rests on. The caves intersect and branch out in all directions beneath the modern city. It is a barely tapped reservoir of historical and archaeological information. Guided tours of the **Orvieto Underground** leave from the Tourist Office (**€€€** *Piazza Duomo; tel: 0763 344891. Start 1100 and 1600*).

Retrace your steps down the Via Duomo and make a left turn at the Corso Cavour. **Piazza della Repubblica ❽** is on the site of the Etruscan and Roman forums and remained the centre of commercial life through the Middle Ages.

Cross the Piazza and take the right-hand Via Fillippeschi, keeping to the left to find your way down the narrow Via della Cava. The street is named after the **Pozzo della Cava ❾**, a well that might have been used in Etruscan times which was expanded by Clement VII in 1527 (*open daily except Tue 0800–2000*). The street ends in the Porta Maggiore. Turn left – just before the gate – up Vicolo Malcorini and climb up to the city wall. The lane widens a bit (becoming Ripa Serancia) and leads to **Piazza San Giovanni ❿** and a dizzying view right over a cliff of gold brown rock. Carry on along the ancient rampart and duck left into the next lane, the Via Ripa Medici. It crosses the Piazza de'Ranieri and leads into Via Garibaldi, which funnels you back into Piazza della Repubblica. Return to Piazza Cahen along Corso Cavour.

Also worth exploring

The most accessible of Orvieto's cities of the dead – the **Necrópoli Etrusca del Crocefisso del Tufo** – is just below the walls to the northwest on the road that leads to Piazza Cahen. The dank tombs are empty. Their contents are in museums, in Orvieto, across Europe and in North America. This particular city reveals a remarkably egalitarian sense of town planning. Constructed of huge blocks of travertine, each tomb is almost the same with the name of the deceased scratched into the architrave above the entrance such as *Mi spuries achilenas* ('I am Spurie Achilena'). Orvieto was a multicultural city in the 6th and 5th centuries BC, with a politically correct cemetery policy. In addition to Etruscans, there are Umbrians, Oscans and Latins buried here.

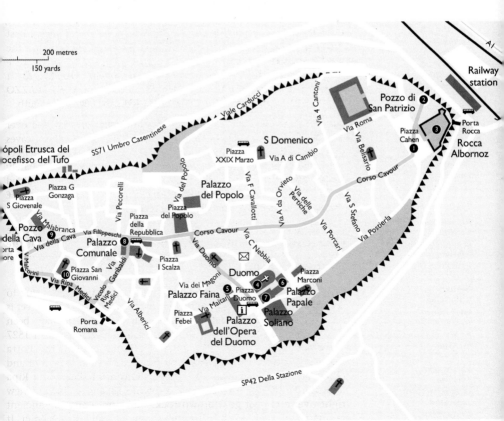

Language

'It is truly a pleasure to hear the Tuscans speak. Their expressions, full of imagination and elegance, give an idea of the pleasure one must have felt in ancient Athens when people spoke the melodious Greek that resembled a constant stream of music.' *Madame de Staël*

Basics

yes/no	si/no
thank you	grazie
please	per favore
you are welcome	prego
excuse me	scusi
I'm sorry	mi dispiace
I would like	vorrei
I don't understand	non capisco
I don't like that	non mi piace
I would prefer	preferisco
okay	va bene
big/little	grande/piccolo
hot/cold	caldo/freddo
open/closed	aperto/chiuso
right/left	destra/sinistra
good/bad	buono/cattivo
fast/slow	presto/lento
much/little	molto/poco
expensive/cheap	caro/economico

Driving

car	la macchina
petrol station	il distributore
full	pieno
petrol/diesel	la benzina/il gasolio
no-lead	senza piombo
check out	controllare
air pressure	la pressione
oil	l'olio
water	l'acqua
breakdown	il guasto
accident	l'incidente
it doesn't work	non funziona
motor	il motore
ignition	l'accensione

Signs

attenzione	watch out
deviazione	detour
divieto di accesso/senso vietato	no entry
divieto di sosta/sosta vietata	no parking
incrocio	crossroads
limite di velocità	speed limit
parcheggio	parking
pericolo	danger
pronto soccorso	first aid
rallentare	slow down
senso unico	one-way street

strada chiusa	road closed
strada senza uscita	dead-end
tenere la destra	keep right
traffico limitato	restricted access
uscita veicoli	exit
vietato fumare	no smoking
vietato il sorpasso	no overtaking
vietato il transito	no through traffic
zona rimorchio	tow away zone

Numbers

1	uno
2	due
3	tre
4	quattro
5	cinque
6	sei
7	sette
8	otto
9	nove
10	dieci
11	undici
12	dodici
13	tredici
14	quattordici
15	quindici
16	sedici
17	diciassette
18	diciotto
19	diciannove
20	venti
21	ventuno
22	ventidue
30	trenta
40	quaranta
50	cinquanta
60	sessanta
70	settanta
80	ottanta
90	novanta
100	cento
101	centuno
110	centodieci
200	duecento
500	cinquecento
1 000	mille
5 000	cinquemila
10,000	diecimila
50,000	cinquanta mila
1,000,000	un milione
2,000,000	due milione
1/2	un mezzo
1/4	un quarto
1/3	un terzo
100gm	un etto
1kg	un chilo
1 pound	mezzo chilo
1 litre	un litro

Index

Acknowledgements

Project management (first edition): Dial House Publishing Services
Project management (this edition): Caroline Ball
Series design: Fox Design
Front cover design: Pumpkin House
Cover artwork: Studio 183
Layout: PDQ Digital Media Solutions Ltd
Map work: Polly Senior Cartography
Repro and image setting: PDQ Digital Media Solutions Ltd
Printed and bound in Spain by: Grafo Industrias Gráficas, Basauri

We would like to thank John Heseltine for the photographs used in this book, to whom the copyright belongs, with the exception of the following:

Christopher Catling (pages 14, 15, 37, 76, 202B, 206, 224, 230, 231, 234, 236, 238, 242, 245, 246, 251, 254, 255, 256 and 271)

Robert Harding Picture Library (pages 52, 99, 159, 160 and 161)

Spectrum Colour Library (page 115)

Travel Ink (page 92)

Front cover: San Gimignano, Acestock

Back cover: Orvieto cathedral, John Heseltine

Feedback form

If you enjoyed using this book, or even if you didn't, please help us improve future editions by taking part in our reader survey. Every returned form will be acknowledged, and to show our appreciation we will give you £1 off your next purchase of a Thomas Cook guidebook. Just take a few minutes to complete and return this form to us.

When did you buy this book? ....
....

Where did you buy it? (Please give town/city and, if possible, name of retailer)
....
....

When did you/do you intend to travel in Tuscany and Umbria?...................................
....

For how long (approx)? ....

How many people in your party? ....

Which cities, national parks and other locations did you/do you intend mainly to visit?
....
....
....
....

Did you/will you:
❏ Make all your travel arrangements independently?
❏ Travel on a fly-drive package?
Please give brief details: ....
....

Did you/do you intend to use this book:
❏ For planning your trip?   ❏ Both?
❏ During the trip itself?

Did you/do you intend also to purchase any of the following travel publications for your trip?
Thomas Cook Travellers: Tuscany and Umbria...
A road map/atlas (please specify) ....
Other guidebooks (please specify) ....

Have you used any other Thomas Cook guidebooks in the past? If so, which?
....
....

Please rate the following features of *Signpost Tuscany and Umbria* for their value to you (circle VU for 'very useful', U for 'useful', NU for 'little or no use'):

The *Travel facts* section on pages 14–23	VU	U	NU
The *Driver's guide* section on pages 24–9	VU	U	NU
The *Highlights* on pages 40–1	VU	U	NU
The recommended driving routes throughout the book	VU	U	NU
Information on towns and cities, National Parks, etc	VU	U	NU
The maps of towns and cities, parks, etc	VU	U	NU

Please use this space to tell us about any features that in your opinion could be changed, improved, or added in future editions of the book, or any other comments you would like to make concerning the book:

....
....
....
....
....
....
....
....

Your age category: ❏ 21–30   ❏ 31–40   ❏ 41–50   ❏ over 50

Your name: Mr/Mrs/Miss/Ms ....
(First name or initials) ....
(Last name) ....

Your full address (please include postal or zip code):

....
....
....
....
....

Your daytime telephone number: ....

Please detach this page and send it to: The Project Editor, Signpost Guides, Thomas Cook Publishing, PO Box 227, Units 19–21, The Thomas Cook Business Park, Coningsby Road, Peterborough PE3 8XX, United Kingdom.

Alternatively, you can e-mail us at: *books@thomascook.com,* **or** *editorial@globe-pequot.com* **for the US.**

We will be pleased to send you details of how to claim your discount upon receipt of this questionnaire.